INTERNATIONAL COMPARISONS IN IMPLEMENTING POLLUTION LAWS

INTERNATIONAL COMPARISONS IN IMPLEMENTING POLLUTION LAWS

Edited by

Paul B. Downing
and
Kenneth Hanf

Springer-Science+Business Media, B.V.

Library of Congress Cataloging in Publication Data
Main entry under title:

International comparisons in implementing pollution laws.

1. Pollution—Law and legislation. 2. Pollution—Government policy. I. Downing, Paul B. II. Hanf, Kenneth.
K3585.4.I55 1983 344′.046 82-23433
ISBN 978-94-017-1929-2 ISBN 978-94-017-1927-8 (eBook)
DOI 10.1007/978-94-017-1927-8

Originally published by Kluwer • Nijhoff Publishing in 1983
Softcover reprint of the hardcover 1st edition 1983

CONTENTS

LIST OF FIGURES AND TABLES

Figures

Tables

PREFACE

This book is the culmination of a process that started in the summer of 1979. One of the editors was invited to work with several members of the International Institute for Environment and Society. These researchers were in the early stages of a rather ambitious project designed to study differences in the implementation of pollution control laws among European countries. Our discussions soon revealed that there was much to be learned by the sharing of our research findings in the United States and Europe. Discussions among the researchers at IIES suggested that we expected there to be wide cultural and institutional differences among countries and, therefore, significant differences in the operation and effectiveness of control efforts in different countries. It has been argued almost universally that differences in institutional form will lead to differences in pollution control outcomes. By comparing implementation in various countries, we could observe the effects of institutional differences. The IIES project was only one study of the implementation process. Perhaps by analyzing the results of various studies by various authors and for a wide variety of countries and situations, more could be learned. The conference idea was born.

The idea culminated in two conferences. The first conference was sponsored by the Policy Sciences Program at Florida State University and was held in Tallahassee, Florida, March 6–7, 1981. The second conference was sponsored by the IIES and was held in Berlin, Germany, October 1–3, 1981. As these conferences proceeded it became obvious that others were interested in our findings. This led us to seek publication of the papers. A source of relatively quick publication was a special symposium in the *Policy Studies Journal*, which was published in September, 1982. Due to space limitations the *PSJ* publication does not contain all of the arguments developed in these two conferences. The published papers had to be shortened. This was done at the loss of discussion of some issues. In addition, some valuable contributions had to be excluded. The book redresses these deficiencies by allowing authors more space and by including five chapters that were not in the symposium.

While this book is more complete than the *PSJ* symposium, it represents only a portion of the existing studies of implementation of pollution laws and only a sample of the possible countries from which we might learn. We are not representing this book as the end of the study. Rather, it is the first progress report on what we hope will be a continuing and growing effort to understand implementation issues through cross-jurisdictional comparisons.

The editors wish to thank the International Institute for Environment and Society, a part of the Science Center, Berlin, and the Policy Sciences Program, Florida State University, and their staffs for all their help in organizing and funding the conferences, the *PSJ* issue, and this book. We also wish to thank Thomas Dye and the Policy Studies Organization for allowing us to produce this expanded version. Special thanks are due to Mary Schneider who produced the intermediate and final versions of this book.

Paul B. Downing
November, 1982 *Kenneth Hanf*

1

INTRODUCTION: A PERSPECTIVE FOR THE STUDY OF REGULATORY ENFORCEMENT

Kenneth Hanf and Paul B. Downing

FROM GOOD INTENTIONS TO PERFORMANCE: THE BOTTOM LINE OF IMPLEMENTATION

In both Europe and the United States the late sixties and early seventies witnessed numerous far-reaching and important developments in the area of environmental protection. In country after country comprehensive programs of pollution control were passed and older programs of more modest scope expanded as national governments took on more responsibility for improving or maintaining the quality of the natural environment. After this initial flurry of legislative activity and the tooling up of the administrative apparatus to implement these programs, attention shifted to a critical examination of the results achieved.

As in other policy areas, so too here there has developed a growing realization that the results of the efforts to regulate industrial activity to prevent or reduce environmental pollution have time and again turned out to fall short of the original intentions of policy makers. To some this failure of the traditional regulatory approach to produce the desired results is not at all surprising. In those cases where this situation is not decried as one more instance of the general failure of regulation and grist for the deregulation mill, the call goes out for replacing the existing system of regulations and standards with some set of market-like economic incentives. Others, whose optimistic faith in the ability of such control programs, in principle, to achieve their stated objectives remains unbroken, offer structural or procedural prescriptions for improving the effectiveness of the implementation of environmental policy.

What is striking amidst all this critical clamor is how frequently the diagnosis and prescription of one or the other for improving or replacing inadequate regulatory instruments and practices are based on an inadequate understanding of how such programs are or might be implemented and of the factors that account for the behaviors observed and the results actually achieved in enforcing such programs.

This volume of essays is intended to be a contribution to closing this information-analysis gap with regard to the implementation of pollution control programs. It focuses quite explicitly and self-consciously on the empirical description and analysis of a number of aspects of the implementation and enforcement of current regulatory programs in a number of countries in Europe and in the United States. The purpose of this chapter is to introduce some of the themes discussed in the individual chapters, as well as to outline a perspective from which to examine the behavior of actors involved in the implementation of environmental regulatory programs.

In the following chapters this common theme of focus is defined in different ways, with attention being drawn to different (varying) aspects of the implementation process. There are, first of all, those studies of the implementation of a control program that look at the overall results of a period of implementation activity without, however, examining the institutions and procedures through which these programs were executed. Here the emphasis is on a discussion of the extent to which the legislative intent was in fact translated into the desired results and, to the extent this was not the case, the problems encountered along the way are considered in terms of the appropriateness of the objectives set and the instruments chosen to pursue them.

While such studies begin with a program already in place, others focus on that phase of the implementation process that begins with the translation of general policy statements and authorizations into more concrete specification of emission quality standards to be applied to the different branches of industry. Here the focus is on the decision-making process, and the strategies employed by the various actors involved, at the level of program formulation.

And still other authors descend even further down the levels of the policy process to examine the enforcement process for environmental regulations, the implementation of environmental control programs in terms of the enforcement process in the sense of the granting of permits (or issuing of order), the monitoring of compliance and the taking of measures to ensure compliance in cases where infractions are detected. Along with those studies that focus still more narrowly upon regulatory enforcement as monitoring and sanctioning activities, such studies tend to draw upon material from specific regulatory decisions to examine the behavior of enforcement officials and other actors in the making of concrete decisions.

We find, therefore, roughly two groups of studies — with some combining elements of both approaches. On the one hand, there are those that concentrate on a discussion of the results and problems of implementation, with more or less attention to the organizational arrangements and procedures through which these activities are carried out. What is missing in these studies is a link between the overall implementation structure and the behavior of those actors taking and shaping enforcement decisions. On the other hand, there are those studies that tend to focus on a narrower aspect of the implementaion process — standard setting or one of the other elements of the enforcement of these regulations — in order to examine the behavior of the various actors involved and the factors that shape that behavior.

Whatever it may mean, implementation draws our attention to the fact that after the dust has settled over statements of overall purpose, decisions on the range of acceptable control instruments, and the authorization of more detailed programmatic specification of how all these good intentions are to be carried out, there comes a time when the general control program must be applied to concrete cases or instances of behavior or activity. Although a complete description (and understanding) of the regulatory process must consider the interrelationships among these different stages (phases), the appropriate point of departure for an analysis of enforcement behavior and the factors that shape the interactions of agency officials, specific sources, and other interested parties is this interface between control instruments and individual activities to be regulated.

At present firms find themselves confronted by an increasing number of governmental regulations of both the more traditional economic and the newer so-called social regulatory types. How these regulations are enforced and what, in fact, is required of firms in complying with them are obviously important factors with which decisions regarding investments and plant operations must reckon. Indeed, these factors are important enough to bring firms to invest a certain amount of their resources in attempting to influence the way in which these regulatory programs are enforced and/or to modify the programs themselves. In short, for the firm the costs of government regulation will be determined by the extent to which the particular regulatory structure, representing a set of external constraints upon decision making by the firm, are subject to manipulation; i.e., actions by the firm can influence the manner in which enforcement officials will apply constraints in a given case.

Likewise, the extent to which the enforcement agency responsible for the implementation of a given control program for environmental quality is able to realize the objectives contained in the program will depend on its success in bringing the firm in question to comply with the conditions imposed on its behavior by the regulations. What may seem like a quite straightforward matter of enforcing formal legal requirements turns out to be something more complicated as the enforcement officials find themselves in a position where the formal authority and regulatory instruments turn out to be inadequate for achieving the purposes of the law.

As many students of the enforcement process have pointed out, it can be assumed that any concrete instance of enforcement is, at a minimum, potentially conflictive insofar as the structurally determined positions and material interests of the actors involved led them to have different interests and opinions regarding the measures required in connection with pollution control programs. It is at the enforcement level, however, that these conflicts must be confronted in concrete implementation episodes; i.e., the buck of conflict displacement cannot be easily be passed on since here some sort of action (or inaction) must be taken. This does not necessarily mean that the conflict involved will be resolved. It can be avoided by refusing to take action, or it can be reduced — without being removed — to a level where some kind of action (mutually acceptable) can be taken, albeit an enforcement action likely to fall short of what formally was required or expected. Thus, an enforcement agency, when confronted by concrete cases, may choose not to search agressively for and penalize those failing to comply with the regulations or the conditions of permits.

In any case, the importance of the enforcement stage for determining what, in fact, a given control program will mean to the firms being regulated as well as the public represented by the enforcement agency makes it interesting — both for enlarging our knowledge and understanding of the dynamics of this phase of policy making, and for establishing a basis on which to consider both the need and direction of possible reforms — to examine how environmental regulatory programs are actually implemented and what strategies are used by the different actors involved in pursuing their respective interests and dealing with the conflicts confronted in regulatory situations.

ENFORCEMENT DEFICIT OR THE REALITIES OF PROGRAM IMPLEMENTATION

In its annual report for 1974, the Federal German Council on Environmental Quality expressed its agreement with the opinion of various legal scholars that "environmental law suffered from a considerable enforcement deficit."[1] However, after asserting that such a deficit existed, the Council hastened to admit that little was known about either the extent of this problem or its nature and causes. The suggestions it advanced for coming to terms with the "inadequate enforcement of laws and regulations by state and local agencies" were familiar pleas for better training of personnel — including providing them with better information regarding the laws and regulations, the nature of the problem, and the need for a broader perspective — and for a tighter integration and coordination of the insititutionally fragmented administrative jurisdictions and powers.

As an example of classical regulatory policy, air and water pollution controls in the Federal Republic of Germany operate with the legal instruments of orders, prohibitions and conditional permits. The logic of such policies is that they seek to effect desired behavior on the part of members of the designated target groups by applying and enforcing norms and standards. It is here that traditional law enforcement in the narrower sense is at home. In a study commissioned by the Council, Mayntz et al. (1978) observe that in such regulatory situations the legal norms embodying the policy objectives are not likely to be complied with by the target groups without the threat that appropriate sanctions will be applied in cases of noncompliance or violation of the standards.[2] This means that considerable effort and resources must be invested in control and monitoring activities, as well as in the prosecution and sanctioning of violators, if regulations are to be effectively enforced. However, according to the authors, regulatory enforcement problems arise from the fact that the practical limit to any further extension of inspections and more strict sanctions is often reached before the number of violations has been reduced to a minimum and the risk associated with noncompliance has therefore been maximized. That is, the costs to control agencies of increasing the probability of detection rise more rapidly than do the corresponding costs to the firms for noncompliance.

The study goes on to note that the failure to achieve or maintain the desired level of environmental quality can be attributed to two interrelated factors. Assuming that the instruments selected, if effectively applied, would be appropriate for reducing emissions to a point commensurate with the quality objectives, the immediate cause of deficiencies in policy enforcement is the failure of the target groups to behave in conformance with the intentions of the policy. This, in turn, is the consequence of shortcomings in the enforcement activities of control agencies that are not able to motivate the appropriate behavior on the part of the firms or other polluting sources.

A recent article on the situation in Switzerland also begins with the observation that the history of water pollution control and of environmental protection in general has been a history of problems of enforcement (Bussmann, 1980). These problems are seen as a consequence of Swiss executive federalism, which places responsibility for water quality control (both organizationally and with regard to the legal norms) jointly in the hands of federal, cantonal, and local actors. Consequently, the pursuit of water quality objectives requires the close cooperation of organizational units on both the same and different hierarchical/jurisdictional levels.

In the German and Swiss cases the fact of bargaining was discovered as a phenomenon that caused enforcement outputs to diverge from policy goals. While some analysts have come to accept this state of affairs as a structurally determined feature of regulatory enforcement, others have sought ways of effectively reducing, if not eliminating, the opportunities for bargaining, and thereby achieving a higher coincidence between what control agencies do and what they were intended to do. There are, of course, other countries in which cooperation and bargaining between control agencies and firms is expected and actively sought and supported.[3]

In England and Wales, decisions on the acceptable quantity and quality of aqueous discharges have traditionally been left to the local enforcement authority, which is responsible for "conducting a dialogue with dischargers so as to find a mutually satisfactory solution" (Storey, 1979). The terms with regard to the concentration, volume, and nature of the effluent discharged, as incorporated in the formal consent document, are the outcome of discussions between the dischargers and the responsible water (river) authority. In his analysis of the economics of environmental law enforcement, Storey stresses the importance of this feature of the control system by noting that "although the Authority may have applied fixed standards for minor dischargers, consent conditions for the more significant effluents will be the product of protracted bargaining and discussion."

Once the conditions of consent have been agreed to, the enforcement procedures for ensuring that they are complied with are characterized by what Sorey describes as "a general reluctance to prosecute dischargers found breaching consent conditions." Again it will often be the minor rather than the major polluters who are likely to be prosecuted and brought to court. This approach to enforcement is justified by a line of reasoning that argues that it is preferable to ensure compliance through arm-twisting (defined as all forms of nonovert pressure that the authority can exert) rather than to enforce the law through the courts. In particular, it is felt that such prosecution is likely to be counterproductive since it would destroy the cooperation between the responsible authorities and the dischargers, which is seen as a major factor in improvement in the quality of water ways in England and Wales.

These, and other studies, document that, contrary to the model of regulatory policy, one finds unequal treatment of the regulated subjects as a result of the fact that policy enforcement occurs through bargaining instead of according to the consistent, even-handed application of general decision rules. Under existing conditions, the real content of a regulation is, in effect, determined through interactions between the control agency and the target group in question that fix the conditions of conduct to be held as constituting compliance with the regulations.

REGULATORY ENFORCEMENT AS AN INTERACTIVE PROCESS: THE APPROPRIATE UNIT OF ANALYSIS

The bottom line of studies — both in Europe and the United States — is that what actually gets done with regard to pollution control policy is often (usually?) considerbly less than what was promised. Not surprisingly the recognition of this fact has led to an interest in finding out why, when viewed from the perspective of national policy makers, policies fail to have the desired or intended impact; i.e., why they are not put into effect. In search of an answer to these questions, analysts have come to ask, "What's wrong with the implementation process and with the organizations responsible for carrying out these policies?" (Hall, 1979). Viewed from the top, enforcement is seen as a process of subdividing a comprehensive mission into ever more specific tasks, into ever more operational objectives. From this perspective, the enforcement problem is one of "structuring and controlling the exercise of choice" (Diver, 1980). Such a "top-down enforcement policy" would consist of "a set of rules, increasingly specific as one descends the hierarchical ladder, for allocating resources among, and specifying the content of various surveillance and prosecutorial tasks."

Looking up from the bottom, the process of enforcement has a quite different appearance. According to Diver, from this perspective the enforcement of regulations can be viewed as ". . . a production process . . . a series of sequential screening operations" by means of which "a universe of regulated acts (is distilled) into a handful of legal consequences. . ." In this sense, the problem is not so much to carry out a policy as it is to meet a production demand.

While Diver tends to focus on behavior of agency officials as they go about making the various choices through which enforcement policy at the bottom becomes manifest, he also suggests a broader persepctive for the analysis of this process. He observes that the participants in this production process are locked in interdependent relationships. Thus the strategies and choices of the inspectors and prosecutors, which form the core of what Diver refers to as enforcement, depend on the actions of others, either in the form of inputs or support for their own actions or in the form of predictions about the subsequent behavior of others shaping the immediate decisions of the actor in question.

Various studies of the enforcement process have noted that the implementation of environmental protection laws occurs through an "inter-organizational interaction system consisting of a variety of actors; e.g., enforcement agencies and industrial associations, other agencies, hierarchical superiors and those at the same levels, citizen groups and courts" (Hucke and Ullmann, 1980). Thus, for example, Mayntz and friends remind us that, despite the focus imposed on their study by various research-practical considerations, it is clearly not enough to examine the implementing authorities in isolation. Implementation is, they stress, an interaction process and, consequently, the "factors that determine this process, and its result, cannot be sought alone in the features of the implementing authorities, taken by themselves, but also in the characteristics of the other relevant actors and in the interactions taking place among the members of this actor system" (Mayntz et al., 1978).

Not surprisingly, we can find a similar situation with regard to the factors shaping the behavior of the agency. It too, in choosing its course of action, is confronted by the constraint under which any actor must operate: the existence of other actors — either those already engaged in a given interaction or those which could be mobilized should they perceive their interests to be affected.

From an economic perspective regulatory enforcement agencies employ a set of policy parameters to which a cost minimizing firm will react by producing different levels of emissions. In principle the agency can adjust or change these parameters by deciding how violations are to be defined, how much effort to invest in detecting violations, and what kinds of penalties to apply to provide incentives to comply. Downing and Watson have maintained that a firm's response to different enforcement actions will depend on what actions the control agency takes insofar as these actions will affect key variables in the cost calculation of the firm on the basis of with which actions it decides to comply. This means that the expense the firm is willing to incur to meet a standard will vary with the parameters of the problem. As the probability of inspection or being fined increases, the expected penalty is raised so that it is more likely that the cost of compliance will be lower than the expected cost of noncompliance (Downing and Watson, 1974).

Thus, in order to understand how the efficient level of control for the firm is determined we must consider the effects of several policy parameters that the control agency can manipulate. As Downing and Kimball remind us, it is "the combined effects of these policy parameters that produces the effective penalty and, consequently, generates the least cost emissions level for the firm" (Downing and Kimball, cahp. 13, this book). Choices by the agency will determine the conditions attached to the permit specifying the impact of the standard in a concrete case, the likelihood of inspections, and the severity of penalties imposed. Since each of these policy choices employs real resources, there would be some combination of policy that would generate a desired level of control of the firm's emissions at lowest cost to the agency (Downing and Kimball, chap. 13). Higher levels of control would require greater effort by the agency and would, therefore, be more costly.

However, it is important to note that these parameters are not exogenous factors to which the firm responds by adjusting its cost calculations. The firm itself may be a significant active factor in influencing the regulatory activities of the control agencies. The parameters are not givens to which the firms react or respond; they can themselves be shaped by the interactions between the firms and the agency, since what the agency is likely to do is in part determined by what other actors, especially the target firm, do. Part of these increased costs (for the agency) may be imposed by the firm itself, which now, in face of potentially higher costs for greater control, has a greater incentive to resist or to try to modify the parameters. A given firm may be in a position to influence the enforcement process directly in its interaction with the control agency or indirectly through lobbying and political influence.

For its part, the control agency can be expected to trade off the costs of bargaining with the individual firms in a given locality sothat the result will be a set of controls of individual sources that reflects their relative costs, the relative costs to the agency of controlling them, and their relative political power (Downing and Kimball, chap. 13).

The typical enforcement situation is then characterized by various kinds of dependencies or interdependencies that join the different actors in the sense that they depend on others for resources, that what they do depends on what others do but also calls forth responses from others which, in turn, affect their own position and, finally, that the final output desired depends on others insofar as no one actor is in a position to produce it directly (Downing and Watson, 1974).

What we are trying to stress with this point is that we are not dealing with a product (be it a permit or a sanction) of a single actor to which then another actor in some way responds. Rather the product of enforcement activity itself is a joint product of the different actors involved. What is difficult to convey is the jointness or coproduction quality of enforcement actions, the fact that they emerge from the interactions among (or at least between) different actors, and that the product must be explained in terms of the characteristics of the interaction (process) itself and not of the individual actors alone.

It is this rather straightforward and obvious fact of interaction among actors involved in a given enforcement output that should be taken as the unit of analysis for the study of behavior in the enforcement phase of environmental regulation. There is, however, something more at issue here than merely restating that no actor in the policy process can be understood without also considering its relations with its environment. We are also arguing that the outcome/product of a given enforcement action is the result of the interactions of the parties involved, and that to understand how it came about and why it is as it is, we must examine not the individual actors but rather the nature of their dynamic interrelationships. We are obviously also saying that the behavior of the individual actors will be a function of the interaction processes in which they are involved. To be sure, the dynamics of this pattern of interactions will be the function of characteristics of the actors as well as the nature of the interrelationships among them. But viewed from this perspective, the features of the control agency and of the firm become factors accounting for the nature of the interaction. Thus, the pattern of interaction is, in an important sense, not an additive phenomenon that can be constructed out of or reduced completely to its separate parts alone. Consequently, irrespective of the formal decision making by a public agency, the enforcement output is a product of the interaction and not of a given individual actor.[4] It is the structure and dynamics of these interactions among interested actors that will determine both the amount of regulatory activity and the quality of the outputs produced; i.e, strictness or leniency, interests favored, etc.

CONSTRAINED SELF-INTEREST REVISITED: SHARPENING A NONDISCRIMINATING TOOL

A number of the authors of these chapters make reference to the fact that self-interest and economically rational behavior are characteristics of the actions of the actors involved in enforcement. The simplistic explanation of the behavior of the actors involved assumes that a control agency, representing sovereign governmental power and acting in the public interest, confronts dutifully complying firms. In place of this simplistic view, Ullmann (1981) takes the following assumptions of implementation studies as his point of departure:

> The actors involved act purposefully and in an economically rational manner. This means that within a given budget, known costs, available information, and particular time horizons, they will seek to maximize their discounted, net utilities — a fact that affects their choice of strategies and the point at which they attempt to intervene in the decision process.
>
> The behavior of decision-makers in organizations is not completely determined by the rules of the organization; on the contrary, a certain amount of discretionary leeway remains that can, in concrete situations, be filled by considerations that include the personal goals of the officials involved.

Consequently, each actor can be expected, in line with its goal function, to try to influence the bargaining process through which enforcement decisions are made by using appropriate strategies applied in anticipation of the utility expectations of the other parties (Hucke and Ullmann, 1980)

On the whole, the figure of constrained self-interest can provide a useful bridge from the analysis of structures to the behavior of individual actors. Often structural analysis leaves out the individuals through which organizations act; just as freqeuntly, a focus on the manifest behavior of individuals fails to take sufficient account of the structural determinants of individual actions. The most important contribution of the notion of constrained self-interest to the analysis of enforcement behavior lies in the reminder it gives of the importance of constraints and costs in the decisions of the actors involved in the policy process. Likewise, it draws our attentin to the general question of motivations and incentives in connection with the behavior of these actors. The central point here is the fact that resources available to actors are limited and that control strategies are shaped by considerations of alternative uses of these resources as well as of the costs of acquiring new resources. The fact that these actors try to calculate the consequences of a set of action alternatives in terms of some utility function underscores the realization that decision making involves some element of costing the courses of action contemplated. By focusing on the rational calculations of actors in such situations this perspective suggests how constraints can become premises of the actors' behavior.

So far so good; things become more problematic when we turn to the content given to self-interest as the substantive point of reference in terms of which the above calculations are performed. It may well be that everything can, in the last analysis, be reduced to self-interest or, alternatively, that self-interest can be extended to encompass everything else. However, to the extent this is true, the concept loses a good deal of its discriminatory power, which was, after all, the alleged strength of individual self-interest in the model of economic man. If indeed every action is ultimately self-interest motivated, then we need subcategories to define the distinctions we intuitively perceive with regard to the behavior of the actors under examination.

Another way of getting at the same point is to note that it is correct that the various objectives and interests reflected in actions attributed to organizations are ultimately, in some way, mediated through the behavior of individuals, as are the reasoning or calculation processes on which this behavior is based. This is, however, not the same as saying that everything can be reduced to terms of individual psychology and motivation, thereby neglecting the structural determinants of the behavior of individual members of groups or organizations.

We can go further and argue that we do not really need to stress the **self** aspect of interest motivated behavior — once we have made the observation that the points of reference or orientation (the interests) by which individual behavior is guided are multiple. One of these interests may indeed be a concern for one's own skin — however defined. Of course individuals are concerned with their own fate when making choices — but this fate may be defined by, or at least closely interrelated with, the fate of other persons or of the organization of which one is a part. For this reason, in order to know what is likely to motivate an actor or to what he is likely to orient himself, it is important to know to what organizations he belongs, his functions within the organizations, his training and socialization experiences, etc. ("Tell me where a person sits and I'll tell you where he stands.") These kinds of factors, useful for understanding the behavior of organizational members, have traditionally been concerns of the sociology of organizations; they may indeed be more helpful for understanding or predicting individual behavior than a rather amorphous notion of self-interest.

Again the important message of the notion of constrained self-interest is that a good deal of behavior relevant for enforcement action is intendedly rational in the face of the need to make choices under constraints and under considerations of the costs of alternative courses of action, measured in terms of the limited resources available. As far as the substantive interest toward which this behavior is directed is concerned, this is likely to be a highly complex interweaving of individual, organizational and larger programmatic concerns. The law or the regulations will depend on the results of the calculation process that weighs a number of considerations viewed as important in a given situation. In addition to the realization of policy objectives, decision makers will consider whether, and to what extent, the contemplated action will affect powerful interests, the size of the budget, or the balance of support for and opposition to the agency.

Consequently, it would seem sufficient at least to note that most agencies, for example, in going about their official business will try to protect their resource base (conceived of very widely to include the domain as well as the different kinds of resources to which they have access for achieving the various instrumental and systems goals of the different parts of the organization) and will make some attempt to consider the consequences of actions to be taken both in terms of immediate costs (in resources expended, other opportunities forgone) and likely repercussions on the future position of the organization, unit, or individual involved. No doubt, there is an important element of looking out for old number one in such prudent behavior. Future work with assumptions of self-interest behavior would profit from trying to integrate the above considerations into the more structurally oriented analysis of incentive structures and motivations underlying the actions of human beings assumed to have bounded rationality and a concern for their own fate.

Another crucial aspect of interest analysis in connection with the behavior of actors involved with the enforcement of environmental regulations should also be noted. If we want to know why certain actor-interests get their way during implementation (enforcement), it is not enough to follow the visible (manifest) interest-behavior that takes place during this phase of the policy process. It is also necessary to analyze the system specific social structures and their function in limiting the articulation of needs and interests (even shaping the interests expressed), the potential for conflict regulation, and opportunities for influencing the relevant actions constituting government performance. An approach that restricts itself to the analysis of manifest behavior and decision- making activities, with a focus on visible group conflict, will risk missing important constraints on behavior that are mediated by selective mechanisms inherent in the broader social structure.

In this connection there are at least two levels involved. One is the deeper lying, basic, structural features of a given socio-economic constellation; e.g., industrial capitalism in its particular national manifestations. At least in the short-run this structure is given. A second level at which interests are shaped by the interests and power relations determined by these more basic structures and operating within the overall constraints set by these structures are the institutions — procedures and organizations — of the politico-administrative system itself. These institutional arrangements reflect more fundamental interest and power structures and, in turn, prestructure the environmental quality game with regard to the relative advantages and disadvantages of the different parties interested in participating so as to promote their own objectives/interests.

To be sure, the constrained self-interest perspective, with the notion of institutions as differential cost structures for the various actors concerned, provides a point of departure for a more systematic treatment of this point. As often used, however, the notion of counting resources, calculating costs, and then deciding whether or not to enter the game at a given point is too volitional, as though choosing to act is nothing more than a matter of some sort of rational-economic equation. Such a view tends to neglect the important fact that some actors are systematically excluded from effective participation to the point of not being aware of opportunities to act; of having no resources to speak of to begin with; or of not having, in effect, any real choice regarding what they might or should undertake in pursuit of their respective interests. Part of the analysis must be an examination of the factors that determine why certain actors enter the game at one point and not another, why some are not able to enter at all; and how the unequal distribution of resources (and other structural barriers) affect the way the game is played once a group has entered. As we have noted, these circumstances do not just happen. They are themselves the results of both the more fundamental socio-economic structures and the politico-administrative institutions reflecting these basic relationships.

It is to be assumed that certain interests have already been accommodated during the program formulation phase (whereby we conceive of program broadly to include the core quality objectives as well as the various standards, monitoring procedures, administrative procedures, and organization, along with the allocation of the different financial, personnel, and material resources). Since decisions with regard to these different program elements tend to prestrucure the subsequent implementation process, it is important to examine the program structure to see to what extent and in what way it tends to provide unequal opportunities for access and influence to the different interests involved as well as to determine which configuration of interests has effectively shaped the program itself.

In order to capture both dimensions of the policy process it is necessary to combine a behavioral approach (with its primary focus on the empirically reconstructed behavior and decisions of the actors involved) and a structural approach (which stresses the extent to which these interactions themselves are decisively shaped and structurally biased — with regard to their characteristic pattern of interest and selectivity). With this dual approach it should be possible systematically to examine the reciprocal relations between socio-economic structural variables and the institutional arrangements of the policy process as they shape the interactions among interested actors involved in the formulation and implementation of pollution control programs.

PROGRAM STRUCTURE AND IMPLEMENTATION: DO INSTITUTIONS MATTER?

Implementation of pollution control programs involves, then, situations in which different actors find it necessary to act within a given set of unavoidable cost constraints. These consist of, on the one hand, the limited resource budget of any given actor and, on the other, the situation in which all relevant decisions or actions in connection with individual outputs are not under the control of any one actor; i.e., each finds itself in a relation of mutual dependence with regard to others.

The constraints upon the pursuit of an actor's interests as a result of these dependencies (and the limited resources at its disposal) means that different kinds of exchange relations in the broadest sense (voluntary and nonvoluntary; symmetrical and asymmetrical) will develop, some of which involve bargaining between actors. An examination of bargaining and other forms of strategic behavior of the different actors brings us inside the interaction patterns discussed above. Here we find the dynamics of the structures described. Although some bargaining will be found in the interactions concerning individual outputs, the nature of the bargaining process will vary depending on the kind of output, the type of emitter, and the locality involved. For example, while the core bargaining relation will, at a minimum, involve the responsible control agency and the source being regulated, it can at any given time include a range of other actors concerned with outputs for that locality or emitter in particular.

Since the basic structural factor that makes some form and amount of bargaining inevitable is this pattern of mutual dependence that results from what Hucke has called the particular "partitioning of resources" among the different actors involved, both the program and other more general institutional factors must be examined in a given case to see in what way they shape the opportunities for bargaining, the issues over which it occurs, the actors involved (including their relative position and weight), and the strategies they employ.

Looking at pollution control programs in different countries, we find that they contain decisions regarding not only the substantive objectives to be pursued (e.g., some kind of statement on air or water quality to be achieved) but also the organization and procedures (as well as resources available) to be used in seeking these objectives. Knoepfel and Weidner argue in chapter 10 of this book that it is useful for understanding the impact of programs on the interaction processes through which the different regulatory outputs are produced to view control programs not in terms of their substantive goal statements alone, but also in terms of the statements they contain regarding the manner in which these performance standards are to be applied in practice when implementing these programs.

For them, therefore, the structure of a given program will result from the fact that some decisions on individual program elements will be made at the national level, some will be left to regional authorities to make on the basis of nationally set parameters, while still others will be left to local enforcement officials to make on a case-by-case basis in connection with the regulation of individual emitters. The decisions of the different elements of the control program give a particular structure to the implementation process. The program fixes the implementation game, if you will, by determining the arenas in which the different outputs are to be produced, by specifying the rules to be followed in making decisions regarding these outputs, and by distributing differential bargaining positions among the players seeking to influence these decisions. The program can, for example, have the following consequences for the pattern of interaction through which the outputs are produced:

- It will define the opportunities for and the issues over which bargaining will occur.
- It will define the initial set of actors to be involved in decisions regarding regulatory outputs as well as the general relations among them.
- It will define the rules under which these interactions, surrounding formal administrative activities, will take place, and in doing so will determine the relative position of the different actor groups attempting to influence decisions on the outputs.

As we have seen, what a given set of rules and regulations will mean in specific situations — in terms of the limits they place upon a firm's behavior and, therefore, the costs incurred — will depend on the manner in which they are enforced in concrete situations. At the same time, it must be kept in mind that these constraints themselves can become the targets of political action as the various actors affected invest scarce resources in attempts to modify the rules or the general conditions under which they are to be applied. Indeed, the present program itself is the result of earlier attempts to shape the rules under which the regulatory game was to be played. As such, the program will reflect the relative balance of power (and pattern of interest consideration) that pertained at the time of program formulation. At the same time, a given program structure is an important factor shaping the differential chances of the various interests effectively to enter the regulatory process (enforcement).

While these program decisions will to varying degrees and in different ways tend to prestructure the implementation process, experiences at the direct enforcement stage can in turn lead to efforts to influence either the general conditions under which the existing program is implemented or to changes in the rules of the game as such — a redefining of the program and its implementaion. Such initiatives can come from any of the actors involved or interested in the program and its enforcement. It is in this sense that an initial focus on the implementation of pollution control programs at the interface of general instruments and specific instances of regulated activity must reach back (or up) to consider the process (and associated patterns of interaction) through which the general control strategy was selected and the different program elements specified in order to determine in what ways self-interested behavior has led various actors to invest resources in efforts to influence the definition of the rules of the game under which individual enforcement activities occur. Thus if we would understand the way in which the game is presently played, i.e., who is able to affect the outcomes of the regulatory enforcement process, as well as anticipate the future moves, we must consider how these rules originally were selected as well as the possibility that some actors may choose to modify them. It can be assumed, therefore, that interested parties will attempt to move the constraints under which they act in one or all of the following ways: by seeking to influence the enforcement decisons in a given case; by seeking to affect the conditions under which enforcement in such specific cases takes place, or by trying to modify the game itself by revising the law or otherwise amending the control program.

The preceding discussion of the impact of program structure seems either to ignore or to answer affirmatively a recurring question of political analysis: to what extent — if any - and in what way do institutional arrangements make a difference for the way in which people behave and the kinds of policy outcomes that are achieved? (Downing, 1979). It would appear that the actors involved must assume that institutions matter — otherwise they would be wasting a good deal of time and energy in their attempts to influence the conditions under which an existing program is carried out or in trying to effect fundamental changes in the rules of the game as such. Although even those directly affected by or involved in applying regulatory programs may be mistaken with regard to the importance of particular structural or procedural factors, it is likely that their immediate experiences do indicate that they are better able to influence the outcome of the enforcement process under certain conditions than under others.

The "what difference" question can, of course, be posed another way: to what extent do differences in program structure (and thus institutional arrangements) account for variations across localities and regions within a given country or for the differences in enforcement behavior and results observed in different countries? On the national level the formal answer to the question is quite simple: insofar as we find the same program applying to all areas under study within a given country (leaving aside those special zones that may be governed by differnt regulations), program structure cannot, logically, be an explanatory factor accounting for observed variations since it does not itself vary. Thus, while Dente and Lewanski (chap. 6, this book) point out that the structural differentiation of the administrative arrangements under which the Italian air pollution control program for SO_2 was implemented in different regions had important consequences for the behavior and, ultimately, the performance of the enforcement system, there were, at the same time, different responses and accommodations to the same set of formal institutions and programmatic guidelines. Variations within a country must be accounted for by factors other than program structure.

Cross-nationally it would seem more likely that the institutional hypothesis could be saved in explaining observed variations. What we do find, however, is a wide range of important similarities or common features of the behavior of enforcement officials in different countries, irrespective of institutional or programmatic differences. It is, of course, possible that the similarities discovered across national boundaries are at such a general level that equally important differences between these countries are obscured. As is so often the case, more research is needed. In designing such research and in formulating the hypotheses to be tested, the material presented in the following chapters can be quite useful, precisely because it does stress the general commonalities between countries and thereby clears the way for zeroing in on remaining differences. In particular the concepts of program structure and implementation incentive system (Bower, chap. 11) should prove helpful in developing a more differentiated and sensitive typology of institutional arrangements based on variation in program structure and mixes of regulatory instruments characterizing different implementation incentive systems. At the same time, such investigations would need to link these programmatic-structural factors to observed variations in some kind of outcome measures, i.e., changes in observed environmental quality.

There remains still a further question regarding the extent to which public policy measures in the area of environmental protection make any difference for the behavior of the emitters on which environmental quality ultimately depends. Various authors in this book touch on this point when they ask whether or not emitter behavior is determined by factors either in other policy areas, i.e., energy or economic policy, or by developments outside the sphere of public policy such as improvements or declines of economic activity (see White, chap. 3; Knoepfel and Weidner, chap. 10; Dente and Lewanski, chap. 6).

Finally, the implementation process — as well as the formulation of the control programs themselves — is influenced by more fundamental structural factors characterizing the particular socio-economic formation in which the political, and consequently the more narrow regulatory, process is embedded. These factors, such as the imperatives of the economic order, the balance of power among different actor groups, and the resulting relative strength of the different social interests, affect both the kinds of institutional arrangements that will be possible at a given time and the way in which they will, in fact, function. Thus, it is certainly true that within the system parameters set by these factors, changes in formal institutions alone will not significantly affect the substantive outcomes of the regulatory game. However, within these broader structural constraints — that in the short and intermediate run cannot be changed — there are other factors (including the formal structures and procedures) that shape behavior of the actors involved in the enforcement of pollution control programs.

Of particular importance in this connection are the situational factors characterizing the more general context within which regulation occurs as well as their more specific manifestation within the immediate implementation process. The following aspects of this process would seem to be particularly important in shaping the pattern of interactions through which specific enforcement outputs are produced.

The political definition of local need or demand for regulation. In the course of producing concrete regulatory outputs, the national objectives are adjusted to the conditions of the local area in which they are implemented. Whatever the reason, the need to come up with courses of action in concrete cases on which agreement can be achieved among locally relevant actors means that an important feature of the implementation field will be the process by which this need for regulation of a given population of emitters is determined. The results of this will be a function of the objective environmental conditions as these are filtered through the interests and priorities of the relevant actor groups involved in both the larger local political decision process and the interaction process with regard to specific instances of regulation. An important job of analysis is the description of this politically relevant demand for regulation in a given locality as the context within which bargaining over concrete outputs occurs.

The balance of power among the actor groups operating within the locality. Clearly, the outcome of decision processes through which the demand for regulation, both in general and in concrete cases, is determined will depend on which groups are influential. On the basis of data gathered on the pool of actors, some conclusions can be drawn regarding the relative weight of the different groups involved in the interaction processes.

The pattern of conflict and consensus characteristic of the relations among the different actors involved. In addition to describing the present pattern of agreement and disagreement characteristic of the field — and the pattern of coalitions or other cooperative efforts - attention must be paid to these relations as they exist and develop over time. That is, it is important to know to what extent such interactions are one-shot affairs or, conversely, something persisting over time, where the actors involved learn about each other and come to understand each other's problems. Equally important is the extent to which the interactions reflect an attempt to pursue long-term interests over a series of interactions. For example, behavior may reflect concern with the consequences on future resources of overly aggressive action at the present.

The political pressures and counterclaims on the local political system. It is to be expected that the pattern of outputs produced with regard to the emitters in a given locality will be shaped by the fact that the actors interacting at the local level will be more exposed to and sensitive to various cross-pressures and competing claims for attention and priority. In particular, local government will be confronted with such conflicts of policy objectives. Thus pressures for stricter environmental control will be challenged by the growing concern with economic growth and the employment situation in the area. These cross-pressures will shape the general problem definition as well as the pattern of support/opposition with regard to concrete outputs.

EVALUATING PERFORMANCE IN THE FACE OF BARGAINING AND INCOMPLETE ENFORCEMENT

From the top-down perspective of the traditional approach to the implementation of regulatory programs, the enforcement problem has been seen as one of structuring and controlling the choices of actors at lower organizational or jurisdictional levels. This is the perspective of the enforcement deficits discussed above, as well as of the more general implementation shortfalls described and lamented in much of the implementation literature. From this point of view, any deviation from what are presumed to be the clearly stated goals articulated in the program in question are seen as performance gaps to be corrected by manipulating those features of the implementation system held to be crucial for "maximizing congruence between policy objectives, decisions of the implementing agencies, and the actual impacts of these decisions" (Sabatier, chap 12). Not surprisingly, when viewed in this context the bargaining characteristic of the enforcement process is problematic and must, in some way, be eliminated completely or reduced to a minimum — or, at least, strictly controlled to ensure the uniform and equitable application of national regulations.

In one sense it is, of course, not new to point out the slippage between the (assumed) intentions of policy makers and the actual degree of compliance achieved (sought) in enforcement practice. The experiences in the different countries reported on in the following chapters do, however, document how widespread both bargaining behavior and incomplete enforcement are as well as indicate some of the factors that shape the strategic behavior observed. At the same time, however, viewing bargaining as inevitable draws attention to both the structural factors shaping these enforcement processes and the positive functions that such bargaining can have in the management of environmental quality.

Whereas social policy programs are intended to be implemented selectively in response to the differential need for the services offered and are therefore intended to be tailored (within the general limits set by the program) to the characteristics of the particular target group, the assumptions underlying effective implementation of regulatory programs tend to be exactly the opposite. Here general standards are to be applied uniformly and equitably on all members of the relevant category wherever they are located. However,even here arguments can be advanced to justify a differentially enforced policy. Be that as it may, however, in practice such regulatory programs are in fact implemented selectively — even though that may be the involuntary result of the conditions under which agency officials are forced to go about their business in dealing with the firms to which the regulations are to be applied.

When considering the functions that bargained adjustments of general standards to concrete cases may have, it is interesting to recall the continuing argument — pursued primarily by economists interested in socially efficient programs for environmental quality — concerning the relative advantages and disadvantages of taxes/effluent charges versus regulatory standards. It is usually argued that the uniform standards approach to the regulation of industrial activity is inefficient in that it is insensitive to the differential costs of individual emitters in responding to these regulations. Since the uniform standards approach does not allow adjustment to the cost situation of the specific firm, we do not get a lowest cost solution to our regulatory problem. Thus, a policy based on such a regulatory instrument is assumed to be unable to take the heterogeneity of individual firms into account and to recognize or respond to the fact that different firms have different compliance costs, that the distribution of quality varies by product and industry, and that consumers and workers may have different trade-offs between quality and money.

In fact, however, it could be argued that bargaining inherent in the practice of enforcing regulator standards does indeed introduce a necessary element of flexibility and differentiation into control program implementation and thus makes such programs responsive to the varying costs of different firms. Furthermore, the bargaining between firms and control agency officials as well as the set of political pressures and direct group interventions within which these interactions take place are important elements in the determination of the effective demand for environmental quality in a given locality.

When we consider the effective demand for regulation, which is assumed to stand in some relation to what is actually supplied by enforcement agencies, it is clear, given the conditions under which program implementation occurs, that these agencies are unlikely to run about offering or imposing controls where the costs for them are too high in the face of the unwillingness of a number of firms to comply and in the absence of the kind of political support that would either reduce these costs or make more resources available with which to confront or reduce this resistance.

The determination of this demand occurs at two levels. First of all, there is a definition of general political demand for environmental regulation — in the pursuit of certain quality goals as laid out in the overall policy and program statements that mark out the action space within which concrete enforcement actions can be taken. At the second level, enforcement officials will be guided in translating general regulations into concrete demands in individual situations under given local conditions by both their own perceptions and the representations by other actors of the demand for environmental quality as determined by locally relevant political decision makers and other actors. This means that in addition to the direct interactions between the firm and control officials in specific cases, another important factor determining the way in which actors approach the bargaining situation and in terms of which they will define an acceptable outcome of the enforcement activity will be their respective judgements of what the traffic will bear with regard to the level of regulation.

Given the biases that are built into the bargaining process as it presently operates, it is clear that all this does not by any means approach something that could be called a socially optimal solution to the regulatory problem. Indeed, it is more likely that the enforcement actions taken will represent an efficient solution for the individual firms involved rather than for society however we may define it. Of course it is a question for empirical investigation to determine which types of industrial activities (and under which conditions) are more able to achieve an acceptable solution when viewed from their perspective. It cannot be assumed a priori that the regulating authority always comes out second best in its relations with the emitters within its jurisdiction.

The discovery (once again!) that enforcement decisions with regard to the regulation of individual emission sources often involve a heavy element of bargaining between (at least) the emitter and the control agency is certainly no longer very newsworthy. The value of reconfirming this piece of conventional wisdom lies in the chance it offers for moving beyond the nature of this bargaining, the structural conditions under (and the context within) which it occurs, its consequences for the products (outputs) of policy enforcement, and its meaning for the evalution of the performance of the implementation processes for environmental policy.

The following chapters offer a variety of empirical material on the structures, processes, and results of program implementation in a number of different countries that illuminates further the themes touched upon in this introductory chapter. On the basis of the discussions of the various national experiences, the concluding chapter will draw out a number of common elements and advance an approach with which to integrate the different aspects of the enforcement process that we have noted and on the basis of which we can proceed to more systematic analysis of the cross-national analysis of experiences with the enforcement of regulatory programs for environmental quality.

NOTES

1. Sachverstandiger Rat Fur Umweltfragen, Umwelt-Gutachten, Bonn, 1974).
2. Mayntz has also published a number of articles and essays that have been influential in stimulating discussion of implementation problems in the Federal Republic of Germany. See for example, "Die Implementation politischer Programme: Uberlegungen zu einem neuen Forschungsgebiet," Die Verwaltung (1977): 51-66 and the volume edited by her, Implementation politischer Programme Konigstein/Ts, 1980.
3. Even a quick examination of the approach to environmental regulation taken in Sweden and Denmark, for example, makes clear the extent to which it is asumed that the necessary trade-offs between different social values and the adjustment of general regulations to local conditions in concrete cases will involve bargaining between the interests involved. For a discussion of some of the general features of the Swedish case see Lundqvist, 1974 and 1979, and Richardson, 1979.
4. Regarding the general problem of selecting the appropriate unit of analysis for policy studies and the arguments favoring a focus on the pattern of interorganizational relations, see Gregg, 1974, and Hjern and Porter, 1981.

REFERENCES

Bussmann, W. 1980. "Wasserqualitat in der Schweiz: Implementationstheoretische Aspecten," MS, p. 1.

Downing, P. 1979. "Implementing Pollution Laws: Observations from the American Experience," Zeitschrift fur Umweltpolitik 4: 357.

Downing, P.B., and W.D. Watson, Jr. 1974. "The Economics of Enforcing Air Pollution Control," Journal of Environmental Economics and Management 1: 219-236 (November).

Gregg, Phillip. 1974. "Units and Levels of Analysis: A Problem of Policy Analysis in Federal Systems," Publius (Fall): 59-86.

Hall, Michael. 1979. "Implementation and the Central-Local Relationship," MS: 4.

Hjern, B., and D. Porter. 1981. "Implementation Structures: A New Unit of Administrative Analysis," Organizational Studies 2: 211-227.

Hucke, J., and A. Ullmann. 1980. "Kontliktregelung zwischen Industriebetreib und Vollzugsbehorde bei der Durchsetzung Regulativer Politik," in R. Mayntz (ed.) Implementation Politscher Programme (Konigsstein/Ts: Anton Hain).

Lundqvist, L. 1979. "WHo is Winning the Race for Clean Air: An Evaluation of the Impacts of the U.S. and Swedish Approaches to Air Quality Control," Ambio: 144-151.

Lundqvist, L. 1974. Environmental Policies in Canada, Sweden and the U.S.: A Comparative Overview (Beverly Hills: Sage).

Mayntz, R. et al. 1978. Vollzugsprobleme der Umweltpolitik, Stuttgart.

Richardson, J.J. 1979. "Agency Behavior: The Case of Pollution Control in Sweden," Public Administration (Winter): 471-490.

Ullmann, Arieh. 1981. Unternehmensverhalten im Umweltschutz. Die Implementation von Umweltschutzgesetzen in der deutschen Industrie. (Wissenschaftszentrum Berlin: IIUG): 9.

I
DETAILED STUDIES OF THE UNITED STATES

EFFECTIVENESS OF THE U.S. REGULATORY APPROACH TO AIR QUALITY MANAGEMENT: STATIONARY SOURCES 2

Gordon L. Brady and Blair T. Bower

INTRODUCTION

The focus of the discussion herein is the effectiveness of regulatory implementation incentives in air quality management with respect to stationary sources. However, before it is possible to evaluate effectiveness, some terms must be defined and the setting of the implementation problem must be delineated.

Definitions

An **activity** is a decision unit that consists of a set of one or more unit processes and unit operations. An industrial plant, a farm, a mining operation, a restaurant, an office building, a household, a management unit of a national forest, a motor vehicle — each is an activity, and each generates residuals according to some time pattern. Often the activity involves several interprocess transport operations, such as by flume, pipeline, or conveyor belt, as in manufacturing activities. These in turn may involve valves, junctions, or flow dividers. Residuals generation and/or residuals discharge may occur in relation to the unit process or in relation to the transport operation. Leaks of gases from valves and solid material blown from a conveyor belt are examples of the latter.

Traditionally, particularly in the economic and business literature, **firm** was used to refer to an activity in the classical sense of the individual entrepreneur who owned a single plant. This has long since ceased to be the reality, with the multi-plant firm or company becoming common in both production and service sectors. Thus, there are single-plant firms and multi-plant firms. If an individual activity is one plant of a multi-plant firm/company, then decisions on how to respond to incentives are taken within the context of the entire company.

A **residual** is a nonutilizable output of material or energy from an activity that has zero value or a value less than the cost of its recovery and transport for use in the same or another activity. Traditionally such residuals have been termed pollutants, with the implicit assumption that their discharge would have adverse effects on ambient environmental quality and hence on users of the environment. Because not all discharges of residuals result in adverse effects — in some cases the effects are positive — the neutral term "residuals" is used.

An **implementation incentive** refers to a behavior-modifying factor that induces an activity to reduce discharges of residuals. It may be economic, regulatory, administrative, informational, judicial, or combinations of these (see Bower, et al., 1977).

An **implementation incentive system** consists of one or more implementation incentives plus the related monitoring, sampling, inspection, reporting, and sanction-imposing procedures and requirements.

Setting of the Implementation Incentive Problem

At a minimum, the following five facts of life characterize the setting of the implementation incentive problem.

1. In virtually all cases there are multiple sources of residuals discharges from an activity. Thus, the term "point source" — often termed concentrated and/or stationary source — is misleading. An integrated steel mill, an integrated pulp and paper mill, a petroleum refinery, and a metallurgical plant all represent a set of unit processes and unit operations occupying a given site, which may comprise several hundred hectares. Each of these plants will have dozens of stacks through which gaseous residuals are discharged. There will be hundreds of thousands of nonstack sources, such as valves, pumps, flanges, and storage tanks. Thus, there are multiple origins of residuals generation in an activity and multiple locations of residuals discharges from an activity.

2. There is large variability from day to day — and even from hour to hour — in the generation and discharge of gaseous (and liquid) residuals from individual activities, even under normal operating conditions. The variation is a function of changing output demands and level of production, changing quality of raw materials, changing weather conditions, upsets and breakdowns, and startups and shutdowns. This inherent variability in residuals generation and discharge, combined with the natural variability in the assimilative capacities of air and water environments, makes it difficult to design and execute implementation incentive systems that will achieve ambient quality standards continuously.

3. No pure regulatory implementation incentive system to reduce residuals discharges exists in relation to air quality management. All existing systems have some mix of regulatory and economic incentives. For example, they may combine two or more of the following: input standards, product standards, discharge standards, specifications with respect to technology of production, residuals modification equipment specifications by type and/or level of performance, grants for some portion of the construction cost of

"pollution control facilities," grants for some portion of the operation and maintenance costs of pollution control facilities, tax credits for investment in pollution control facilities, grants to cover some portion of investment in "less polluting" production technology, and low interest rate loans to cover some portion of investment in pollution control facilities and/or less polluting production technology. It is the mix of incentives to which the activity responds, thereby presenting the problem of how to isolate the effects of regulatory incentives from the effects of other incentives and from the effects of other factors, such as increased energy and other raw material costs.

4. A discharge (effluent) standard for an activity that permits a discharge greater than zero is in fact a permit for the free use of some of the assimilative capacity of the common property resource of the atmosphere. Some amount of an essential factor input is being obtained daily by the activity at zero cost.

5. Regulations on the discharge of gaseous residials have impacts on water quality management and solid residuals management. For example, requiring the installation of a wet scrubber to reduce discharges of SO_2 and particulates from a power plant stack or requiring the use of a water curtain in a spray operation to reduce hydrocarbon discharges to the atmosphere both result in the generation of liquid residuals that can have adverse impacts on ambient water quality if discharged directly to water bodies. Requiring an electrostatic precipitator on a power plant stack to reduce the discharge of particulates to the atmosphere results in a solid residual requiring disposal.

NATURE OF THE REGULATORY APPROACH TO AIR QUALITY MANAGMENT IN THE UNITED STATES

Attempts to regulate discharges of gaseous residuals to the atmosphere have evolved from early regulations on the location and performance of the "offensive trades" of the Industrial Revolution during the 19th century to the major legislative acts of the post-World War II period. Although public, political, and professional perceptions of what constitutes the air pollution problem have probably changed over this extended period, the principal approach to achieving desired levels of ambient air quality has remained basically unchanged. That approach involves: (a) direct regulation through a permit mechanism, where the permit includes conditions such as the specification of discharge limits, the specification of production processes (technology), the specification of the quality of input materials to production, the specification of performance in reducing discharges, e.g., 95% collection efficiency; (b) a monitoring and enforcement program to ensure that the sources are complying with the conditions specified in the permit; and (c) various types of economic incentives from among those listed above.

More specifically, a regulatory system in air quality management can be defined operationally as consisting of the following elements:

1. development and promulgation of ambient air quality standards to be achieved — in the United States, the National Ambient Air Quality Standards (NAAQS);
2. development of guidelines defining (a) "appropriate" levels of discharges of gaseous residuals for various types of activities; and (b) the various physical measures, e.g., input raw materials, production processes, residuals modification equipment, that would enable achieving those discharge levels;
3. grant of a permit in which the conditions the discharger is to meet are specified, e.g., in terms of raw material input specifications, discharge limits, process specifications, air pollution control equipment performance standards, and product standards;
4. development and promulgation of operational definitions of compliance and noncompliance, with respect to the conditions specified in the permit, e.g., procedural deficiencies, permit compliance schedule violations, and violations of standards, such as discharge, input quality, process, pollution control equipment performance, and product;
5. establishment of conditions for obtaining variances;
6. specification of the self-monitoring and reporting requirements imposed on the activity;
7. design and execution of the monitoring, inspection, sampling, and data analysis procedures of the regulatory agency; and
8. the availability, types, and modes of imposition of sanctions against noncomplying dischargers.

Conceptually, regulations are imposed on the dischargers with the objective of achieving the desired ambient air quality standards.

Figure 2-1 illustrates the regulatory approach to air quality management in the United States as it existed in 1980. Note that all three of the basic levels of government — national, state, and local — are involved. In some cases a fourth level is involved, in the form of a regional agency with jurisdiction larger than a municipality but

Figure 2-1

Major Elements in Air Quality Management in the U.S.

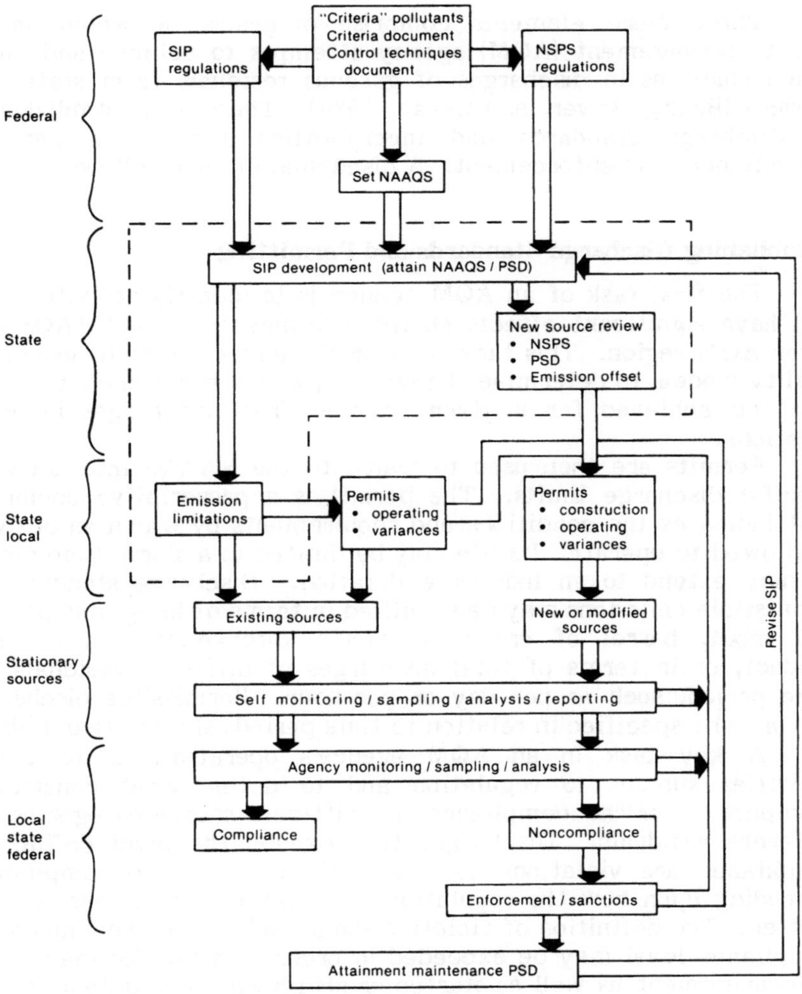

SOURCE: Brady and Bower, Benefit-Cost Analysis in Air Quality Management, 15 *Environmental Science and Technology* 256 (1981)

smaller than a state. Such regional agencies may be created by, and be part of, agencies of a state government, or they may be formed by agreement among several local jurisdictions.

PROGRAMS OF AIR QUALITY MANAGEMENT AGENCIES

Three basic elements comprise programs by which an air quality management (AQM) agency attempts to achieve and maintain reductions in discharges of gaseous residuals from stationary sources (Brady, Bower, and Zayac, 1980). These are: establishment of discharge standards and incorporation thereof in permits, surveillance, and enforcement. A discussion of each follows.

Establishing Discharge Standards and Permitting

The first task of an AQM agency is to identify activities that will have significant effects on the attainment of the NAAQS in a given AQM region. This task is generally accomplished by use of air quality models to determine the quantity of discharge reduction that must be achieved for a given residual from discharges in given locations.

Permits are then used to translate the NAAQS into activity-specific discharge limits. The permit is a prescriptive document that indicates the conditions and requirements by which an activity is allowed to operate. Its life may be limited to a single time period or may extend to an indefinite duration. Discharge standards or permissible emissions may be specified in terms of kilograms per 10^6 Btu input, barrel of crude petroleum throughput, ton of final product, or in terms of total discharges of different residuals per time period, such as per day or per hour. Permissible discharges may also be specified in relation to time periods shorter than a day.

A key task in an AQM agency's operations is to define activities subject to regulation and to define what constitutes "compliance" or "noncompliance" for different source categories and different residuals. Discharges that exceed the level defined as compliance are violations but may not constitute noncompliance, depending upon how the regulations are stated and the permits are written. The definition of violation should indicate by how much the compliance level may be exceeded in order to allow for inaccuracy in measurement as well as startup or shutdown for maintenance. It should also indicate how often the compliance level may be exceeded because of breakdowns before a violation occurs.

Permitting serves three functions in the attainment of the goals of an AQM agency. First, it provides a means to identify new, modified, and existing sources and to set specific requirements for allowed discharges from those sources. Such requirements may include any combination of discharge levels, record keeping, equipment design, operation and maintenance procedures, and self-monitoring and reporting procedures. Second, a permit provides a legally enforceable commitment on the part of the activity to meet the requirements specified in the permit. Third, permits provide the AQM agency with discharge estimates and information with respect to the equipment and operating procedures — to reduce discharges — that are in place or under contract for delivery by each permitted activity, thereby serving as a compliance tracking tool to ensure continual adherence to requirements.

Most states and cities require activities discharging more than 100 tons per year, or various categories of sources with lesser discharges, to apply for a permit to construct and/or apply for a permit to operate. Typically certain activities are exempted from having permits, e.g., state or local governmental facilities such as boilers for schools, jails, and municipal buildings. Federal installations may also be exempt.

A permit to construct enables the agency to review the physical measures to be installed by a source to achieve specified levels of emissions before construction begins. Typically the following types of information are requested in the permit application:

1. a list of emission sources including flow rates, stack heights, and temperature and velocities of flow;
2. complete descriptions of unit processes and operations, including internal transport;
3. types and quantities of raw material inputs;
4. total weights and kinds of discharges per ton, per day; and
5. designs of physical measures to achieve the indicated discharge quantities.

An engineering evaluation of the permit to construct by the AQM agency should reduce the likelihood of unplanned and costly redesign, repair, or replacement of equipment to reduce discharges. In addition, the evaluation specifies detailed design and/or operating conditions that become part of the permit.

An existing source not under a permit but which qualifies as requiring a permit is brought into initial compliance with a so-called variance procedure. A source may obtain a variance from an agency that allows it to continue to operate even though it is in violation of applicable standards. Generally, the variance includes a compliance schedule that specifies the dates when the source will contract, build, and complete the installation of equipment which, when operated, will presumably bring the source into compliance with the specified standards.

The permit to operate provides a critical juncture to determine whether the source can demonstrate compliance with permit conditions before operation is initiated. The permit-to-operate process involves field inspection and possibly a source test. Or the agency may require that a source test be performed by consulting engineers before the permit-to-operate application is reviewed. Most AQM agencies charge a fee based on the cost to the agency of processing, evaluating, and administering the permitting program. Fees are based on the type and complexity of activity.

Surveillance/Monitoring/Inspection

The second element of an AQM program involves methods for insuring that a source maintain continuous compliance after initial compliance has been achieved; i.e., the meeting of discharge limitations has been demonstrated and a permit to operate has been issued. Surveillance/monitoring/inspection programs provide a means of tracking source response in order to:

1. determine whether or not a source is in compliance with permit conditions.
2. monitor a source's progress in correcting violations;
3. provide additional evidence of a violation for enforcement actions; and
4. verify that a source is not constructing a new or modified production facility without the required construction or operating permits.

The results of such efforts constitute the basis for administrative and enforcement actions.

A general surveillance strategy involves a number of activities, including routine field inspections pursuant to annual state implementation plan inspections and permit renewals; unannounced inspections; visible emission evaluations; and responses to citizen complaints. Field inspections may entail one or more of the following:

1. stack tests;
2. opacity readings;
3. ambient property line measurements;
4. material balance calculations;

5. evaluation of work practice procedures;
6. sampling and analysis of quality of inputs, e.g., fuel and solvent;
7. review of monitoring records, both of operations and of discharges; and
8. checking to see if emission reduction equipment is operating.

Field inspections are the key to the effectiveness of the surveillance/monitoring/inspection programs. The two basic categories of field inspections are announced, planned inspections, and unannounced, spot-check inspections. All sources are inspected periodically, the frequency depending upon the complexity and performance record of each source. Spot checks are randomly performed and unannounced so that the discharger is always — theoretically — subject to meeting the performance standards. Depending upon their frequency, spot checks can help to ensure that the discharger will have the incentive to maintain performance in accord with his permit at all times. A major disadvantage of announced inspections is the disincentive for the discharger to maintain constant compliance. For example, annual inspection at approximately the same time each year may encourage the discharger to be able to demonstrate compliance for at most two months of the year, i.e., one month before and one month after the anticipated date of inspection.

Because of the complexity of the procedure, stack tests must be planned, and therefore the discharger must be notified in advance. Stack tests are an important tool in surveillance and monitoring activities. However, it is the most expensive evaluation technique, requiring on the order of $5,000 (1980) of AQM agency and/or activity resources per test. Agency resources may be stretched by requiring the source to have a stack test performed in the presence of an agency representative. Other less expensive tests are available to an AQM agency. Opacity and visible discharge evaluations are generally part of spot-check inspections. Although these techniques are effective in detecting visible discharges, they fail to detect the more hazardous nonopacity violations. Ambient property line measurements have proved successful in dealing with the problem of fugitive particulate matter and sulfur dioxide. Measurements are taken downwind of the discharger and are subtracted from the upwind ambient concentrations measured at the property line. This figure is compared with permitted standards. Property line ambient sampling equipment is easier to use and more economical than stack testing. However, there are other problems that must be considered. One problem is that the discharger may be bordered by roadways, making it difficult to trace discharges conclusively. Wind variations may cause inaccurate readings. In addition, tall stacks, which increase the dispersion of residuals beyond the property line, make some discharges undetectable at ground level.

Enforcement

The third element of an AQM program is enforcement. An extensive and thorough permit and surveillance program cannot be effective without a thorough enforcement system. The function of enforcement is to penalize current violators and to deter future violations by maintaining the threat of enforcement. The incentive to the source to maintain compliance with permit conditions depends upon the level of expected costs or penalty, the probability that it will be imposed, and the probability of a violation being detected and a civil sanction imposed. The level of penalty/sanction imposed varies among agencies and among sources. For some sources, bad publicity alone may be a sufficient deterrent.

Examples of violations include:

1. failure to apply for a permit or permit renewal;
2. misrepresentations in permit applications or other documents;
3. failure to adhere to a compliance schedule;
4. noncompliance with discharge standards or permit requirements; and
5. violations of input standards.

An AQM agency has a number of tools to deal with violations. These include: (a) administrative conference; (b) notice of violations; (c) abatement order; (d) special order by consent; and (e) civil and criminal sanctions. The approaches taken by AQM agencies vary because of differences in administrative procedures, the courts with which the agencies must deal, and the political support for enforcement activities. In general, some type of administrative action is the first step taken by an agency. This may be an informal conference by phone or in agency headquarters.

The notice of violation normally requests the source in violation to submit a compliance schedule. If the agency does not accept the compliance schedule or the source fails to submit one, the source will be requested to appear for an administrative conference or hearing. During this meeting the agency negotiates with the surce to obtain a compliance schedule for the installation or modification of equipment to reduce discharges. If the agency's inspection indicates that violations are not corrected, the agency may take legal enforcement action as a last resort to obtain compliance. The effectiveness of agency enforcement is determined by its ability expeditiously to impose sanctions for violations.

SOURCE RESPONSE

Given the existence of simultaneous regulatory and economic incentives, evaluation of effectiveness can really only be done in terms of the response to both types of incentives. Separation of the effects of the two types of incentives is difficult. (A crude estimate for a profit maximizing or cost minimizing activity might be made by: (a) estimating response to regulatory incentives in the absence of any economic incentives; plus (b) estimating response to economic incentives in the absence of regulatory incentives; plus (c) estimating response to the simultaneous imposition of regulatory and economic incentives.)

Effectiveness should be evaluated in relation to at least two criteria. The first criterion is the time required to bring the discharger into **original compliance** with his permit conditions. That is, an activity is considered to have achieved original compliance with the conditions specified in a permit to discharge when the physical measures — including types of inputs — have been installed and are operating to achieve the discharge levels and/or other conditions specified in the permit. Economic incentives that currently exist, such as tax credits, rapid depreciation on pollution control equipment installed, and low interest rate loans, can affect responses in relation to original compliance.

The second criterion is the extent to which the discharger is in **continuing compliance**. That is, an activity is considered to be in continuing compliance if, on a day-to-day basis, the behavior of the activity is within the limits/conditions specified in the permit; e.g., discharges of gaseous residuals are within the limits specified, and quality of raw material input is within the limit specified. It is this second criterion of effectiveness that is the focus of this section.

Three additional points should be mentioned before presenting some empirical evidence on effectiveness. First, the effectiveness of an implementation incentive system, in terms of inducing response on the part of a discharger, is a function of costs as the discharger sees those costs and perception by the discharger of the probability of **significant** sanctions being imposed for noncompliance. Costs as the discharger sees them reflect the discharger's opportunity costs in terms of alternative internal and/or external uses of available resources. These costs may well vary among single-plant firms, multi-plant firms, regulated companies, and conglomerates. The tax position of the firm is a critical variable. Payout periods reflecting rates of return used by large corporations range from two to three years. (Somewhat longer payout periods may be used by some medium-size and smaller firms.) Costs as the discharger sees them are a function of various factors, including direct and indirect subsidies, federal and state. Direct subsidies include investment tax credit, rapid depreciation on pollution control equipment, and less than market interest rate loans for installation of pollution control equipment. Indirect subsidies include depletion allowances and expensing provisions on raw materials such as oil and gas, iron ore, other metallic ores, and limestone, and capital gains provisions on virgin timber. All of these reduce the costs of these materials in relation to the costs of secondary materials. Thus, to the extent that the costs of virgin materials are artificially decreased, less materials recovery and less energy recovery are economically feasible, thereby **increasing** residuals generation.

Second, if sanctions for non-compliance with regulations are minimal or are not likely to be imposed, there is little incentive to respond continuously to regulations. This is true even where certain types of economic incentives accompany the regulations. Thus, making a grant for 50% of the capital cost of installing wet scrubbers on a stack — often not the least cost physical measure for reducing discharges — may well provide incentive for the capital investment. But no incentive is provided by such a grant to operate the equipment at design level after construction. It is reasonable to assume that enterprises — public as well as private — evaluate the costs of noncompliance and of compliance and generally choose their least cost option in responding to regulations. (Costs may well include the perceived costs of unfavorable public image.) Even high-priced lawyers are likely to be less expensive to a private — or public — activity than constructing and operating end-of-pipe discharge reduction facilities.

Third, the organizational form of the activity — corporate, nonprofit, government, single-plant firm, or multi-plant firm — will affect the choice of the physical measures to reduce discharges. Also, the size of the activity will affect the manager's response to any one set of regulations or conditions. For example, the set of physical and financial options available to an activity will differ for small and medium activities using boilers for process heat. Managers of industrial, commercial, and institutional activities are subject to many other constraints that limit their choices, e.g., input prices, capital availability, and constraints imposed on the activity in terms of dealing with solid, semi-solid, and liquid residuals.

How effective then, have regulatory implementation incentives been in air quality management, i.e., in actually inducing dischargers to reduce discharges and maintain those reductions over time.

Empirical Evidence of Performance in Relation to Continuing Compliance

Assuming that original compliance has been achieved by any given activity, the relevant problem becomes that of determining performance of the activity with respect to continuing compliance. Ideally one would like to have a **continuous** record of the **actual** discharges from each major source in the activity in order to compare those discharges with the specified discharge and/or input standards. Such records rarely exist, even for a single residual discharged from a single source by an activity. This is because of multiple sources of a given residual within an activity, nonexistence of continuous monitoring equipment, the expense of continuous monitoring, and the existence of many "nonstack" sources within the activity. Consequently, only relatively little empirical evidence relating to continuing compliance is available. A few samples follow.

Table 2-1 shows the results of source tests on two 800 megawatt units of a coal-fired power plant. Two points should be emphasized. First, source tests are prearranged. Therefore, they generally represent the optimal operating conditions that can be achieved. If the discharge standards are not met during source tests, it is highly unlikely that they are being met during other operating days. Combining the results shown in Table 2-1 for both units, in only half the years was the mean discharge less than the standard. Second, the source tests do not consider the fact that no discharge standards have to be met during startup periods. Startups are relatively frequent, averaging nineteen per year during the period 1972-1976 for each of the units listed in Table 2-1 (see Harrington, 1981: ch. 6). As a result, the quantity of particulates discharged during the total of all startup periods during a year represents a significant portion of the total annual particulate discharge. Also, no economic incentives are imposed in relation to startup periods.

Table 2-2 summarizes estimated performances of activities analyzed in the five jurisdictions of Chicago, Houston, New Jersey, North Carolina, and San Diego (Brady, Bower, and Zayac, 1980). Estimating performance on the basis of interviews and few recorded data required basic understanding of technology, plus creativity and a significant amount of deduction. From 50% to 70% of the

Table 2-1

Results of Source Tests on Units 4 and 5,
Four Corners, New Mexico, Coal-Fired Power Plant

Year	Number of Tests	Mean Emission[a]	Emission Standard[a]	Number of Violations	Violations as Percent of Tests
UNIT 4[b]					
1974	10	0.56	0.5	4	40
1975	7[c]	0.35	0.5	0	0
1976	18	0.52	0.5	4	22
1977	10	0.51	0.5	4	40
1978	4	0.32	0.5	1	25
TOTALS	49			13	27
UNIT 5					
1974	10	0.44	0.5	2	20
1975	10	0.73	0.5	5	50
1976	8	0.62	0.5	4	50
1977	20	0.42	0.5	6	30
1978	2	0.36	0.5	0	0
TOTALS	50			17	34

[a]Pounds particulates per 10^6 Btu input

[b]Units 4 and 5 are base load units, each of 800 megawatts capacity.

[c]Results of tests in the first half of 1975 are missing.

Source: Harrington, 1981.

Table 2-2

Percentage of Activities in Five Jurisdictions Meeting Gaseous Residuals Discharge Standards, by Percentage of Time

	In Compliance 67-100% of Measurement Period	In Compliance 34-66% of Measurement Period	In Compliance 0-33% Measurement Period	Impossible to Estimate[a]	Sample Size
Chicago	53 %	11 %	36 %	0 %	19
Houston	70	10	5	15	20
New Jersey	61	35	0	4	23
North Carolina	50	20	20	10	20
San Diego	59	3	7	31	21

[a]Discharge profile construction was impossible due to data limitations.

Source: Brady, Bower, and Zayac, 1980.

activities were in compliance 2/3 to 100% of the time. This compliance category allows for occasional breakdowns while production continues; normal maintenance, and startup periods, during all of which emissions are in excess of standards. From 3% to 35% of the activities were in compliance from 1/3 to 2/3 of the time. This category covers design deficiencies and selective operation of physical measures. Zero percent to 36% of the activities were in compliance from 0% to 1/3 of the time. This category contains both activities that have not undertaken discharge reduction measures and those that have frequent excess emissions.

Reasons for Failure to Achieve Continuous Compliance

In the analyses of individual activities, a number of reasons were found for failure to achieve continuing compliance, i.e., reasons resulting in excess discharges. Some of these reflect deficiencies in the programs of the air quality management agencies; others may be attributed to technical problems encountered by activities. Examples of the former include inadequate permit review, infrequent and cursory inspections, announced inspections, poorly trained inspectors, high turnover of inspection staff, and inadequate monitoring techniques or equipment. These deficiencies severely undercut the effectiveness of air quality management agency programs; they may encourage sources not to take the air quality management agency seriously.

There are other aspects of agency behavior that can contribute to noncompliance. For example, poor guidance of an activity in the selection of vendors and equipment may impose substantial costs on sources trying to comply with the agency's regulations. In cases where penalties are sought through the courts, it is necessary that evidential standards be met. Sources may not have had proper record-keeping procedures specified by the agency, which records would allow the air quality management agency staff to determine the extent of continuing compliance. Or, the inadequacies of staff inspection and monitoring efforts may lead to the failure to obtain adequate sanctions and penalties for those out of compliance. Finally, there may be regular agency procedures that allow excess discharges in the short term, as when an upset or breakdown occurs.

The primary reasons on the part of activities for failure to be in continuing compliance include: design deficiencies of equipment to reduce discharges, inadequate operation and maintenance of equipment, unanticipated changes in unit production process variables, changes in raw material inputs for reasons other than air pollution control, changes in energy costs, and the unavailability of specified fuels or other material inputs.

CONCLUDING COMMENT

Maintaining ambient air quality standards in any region requires that individual activities continuously meet whatever discharge conditions or limits are imposed on them. Achieving original compliance is not necessarily an indication that continuing compliance will be achieved. The incentives inducing the former often have little impact in terms of achieving the latter. The empirical evidence presented on continuing compliance, albeit meager, suggests that many activities are probably not in compliance a substantial portion of the time. This conclusion in turn suggests that the quest for that mix of economic and regulatory incentives that would result in achievement of continuing compliance at least 90% or 95% of the time must continue.

REFERENCES

Bower, B.T., et al. 1977. "Incentives for Managing the Environment," Environmental Science and Technology, 11, 3: 250-254.

Brady, G.L., B.T. Bower, and J.M. Zayac. 1980. "Source Response to Regulatory Implementation Incentives in Air Quality Management," report to the Council on Environmental Quality.

Harrington, W. 1981. The Regulatory Approach to Air Quality Management: A Case Study of New Mexico, Research Paper R-25 (Washington, D.C.: Resources for the Future).

3 U.S. MOBILE SOURCE EMISSIONS REGULATION: THE PROBLEMS OF IMPLEMENTATION

Lawrence J. White

INTRODUCTION

The U. S. federal government's efforts to control emissions from mobile sources (cars, trucks, and buses) have now encompassed a fourteen-year period. Much of the discussion of the program has focused on the appropriate levels of the standards and on broad strategies, e.g., direct regulatory requirements versus effluent fees (e.g., Jacoby et al., 1973; Dewees, 1974, 1978; NAS-NAE, 1974; Grad, et al, 1975; Mills and White, 1978; White, 1982; for a review of the reviews, see White, 1980). This chapter instead will focus on implementation questions. But implementation will be interpreted broadly and so, perforce, we will also touch on the questions of appropriate levels and of broad strategies.

THE CLEAN AIR ACT AND THE MOBILE SOURCE STANDARDS

National Ambient Air Quality Standards

At the heart of the Clean Air Act is a system of National Ambient Air Quality Standards (NAAQS). These are nationwide standards for the cleanliness of the ambient air with respect to a number of air pollutants. The Environmental Protection Agency is required by the Act to set primary standards and secondary standards. The primary standards are supposed to "protect the public health . . . allowing an adequate margin of safety" (Clean Air Act, 1977). The secondary standards are supposed to "protect the public welfare from any known or anticipated adverse effects associated with the presence of such air pollutant in the ambient air" (Clean Air Act, 1977). EPA has thus far set NAAQS for photochemical smog (ozone), carbon monoxide (CO), nitrogen oxide (NO_x), sulfur dioxide (SO_2), particulates, and airborne lead.

The NAAQS are, in effect, goals or targets for the cleanliness of the ambient air. (The primary standards have been the operative ones; the secondary standards have been considered to be long-range hopes rather than short-run targets.) The remainder of the Clean Air Act is largely devoted to the programs for reducing emissions of pollutants from various sources so that these ambient goals can be met. There are three major programs: (1) reductions in emissions from existing stationary sources of pollutants; these reductions are guided by implementation plans drawn up by the individual state governments (but approved by EPA); (2) standards for emissions from new stationary sources that will be built in the future (e.g., new power plants, new refineries); and (3) standards for emissions from mobile sources (motor vehicles). It is to this last set of standards that we now turn.

The Mobile Source Standards

The Clean Air Act pays special attention to motor vehicles. An entire title (Title II) of the Act is devoted to motor vehicles. Unlike other sections of the Act that provide general guidelines for EPA's regulatory actions, Title II provides specific numerical targets for EPA's actions. Exhaust emissions of HC and CO from automobiles are to be reduced by 95% from uncontrolled levels.[1] Emissions of NO_x from automobiles are to be reduced by 75% from uncontrolled levels. HC and CO emissions from trucks are to be reduced by 90% from uncontrolled levels, and NO_x emissions are to be reduced by 75%.[2] Table 3-1 provides the specific schedule for automobiles.

The emissions control requirements apply only to the sale of new vehicles. Vehicles are supposed to meet the standards for the first five years or 50,000 miles, whichever comes first. Preproduction vehicles are given extensive tests to determine if those models meet the standards. Models that fail to meet the standards but that are nevertheless sold are subject to fines of up to $10,000 per vehicle; the fines are meant to be punitive and prohibitive rather than to serve as effluent fees. Since 1976 EPA has been conducting spot checks of assembly line automobiles in addition to conducting the preproduction tests.

THE PROBLEMS OF IMPLEMENTATION

The attitude of the Clean Air Act and of EPA's administration of the Act has been relatively "hard-nosed" toward the motor vehicle industry. The Act and the agency have tried to force the development of new technology; they have insisted on a strategy of "every vehicle must meet the standard"; and they have placed virtually all of the burden of control on the manufacturers rather than on motorists. As we shall argue, this attitude has generated substantial implementation problems in two areas: enforcing the announced schedules and preventing the deterioration of control systems in actual use.

Table 3-1

Federal Exhaust Emissions Standards for Automobiles

	HC^a	CO	NO_x	Particulates
Typical Uncontrolled	8.7	87.0	4.0	1.0[b]
1968	5.9	50.9	c	c
1970	3.9	33.3	c	c
1972	3.0	28.0	c	c
1973	3.0	28.0	3.1	c
1975	1.5	15.0	3.1	c
1977	1.5	15.0	2.0	c
1980	0.4	7.0	2.0	c
1981	0.4	3.4[d]	1.0[e]	c
1982	0.4	3.4[d]	1.0[e]	0.6
1985	0.4	3.4[d]	1.0[e]	0.2

[a] Emissions are in grams per mile; crank-case blow-by and evaporative emissions are not included.

[b] Applies to diesel automobiles using exhaust gas recirculation to control NO_x.

[c] No federal requirement.

[d] Exemptions possible, up to 7.0 g/mi for 1981 and 1982.

[e] Exemptions possible for diesel automobiles, up to 1.5 g/mi for 1981-1984.

Enforcing the Announced Schedule

The actual historical process of establishing the emissions schedules has been a tortuous one of setting, delaying, revising, and amending the standards. The currently applicable HC and CO standards for automobiles were originally scheduled (by the 1970 Amendments to the Clean Air Act) for 1975; the NO_x requirement was originally much more stringent and was scheduled for 1976. These original standards were delayed for a year (to 1976 and 1977 respectively) by EPA in 1973. They were delayed another year (to 1977 and 1978) by Congress in 1974. The HC and CO standards were delayed yet another year (to 1978) by EPA in 1975. Finally, in the late summer of 1977, as the U.S. automobile industry prepared to introduce to the market its 1978 model vehicles which did not meet the tight standards for that model year, Congress passed the 1977 Amendments to the Act, which established the currently applicable automobile schedule of a 95% reduction in HC for 1980, a 95% reduction in CO for 1981, and a 75% reduction in NO_x for 1981.[3]

This tortuous process is traceable to the basic regulatory orientation of the Act: it is designed to be "technology forcing." The architects of the Act recognized that pollution was a negative externality and that emissions control would not occur in the absence of government action; further, they recognized that the companies had no market incentives to develop control technologies that would achieve increasingly greater degrees of emissions control. Hence, they established emissions requirements, to be effective at future dates, that were beyond the current state of the manufacturing art. This was designed to force the companies to conduct the necessary research and development so as to achieve the necessary technology to meet the standards.

The designers of the Act ignored, however, one important problem: what would happen if the industry **failed** to develop the technology that would allow the standards to be met. It is true that EPA was given the authority by the 1970 and 1974 Amendments to delay the standards for one year (which it did in 1973 and 1975). The 1977 Amendments gave EPA the authority to grant exemptions to the CO standard (for 1981 and 1982 only) and to grant (for diesel autos only) exemptions to the NO_x standard (for 1981-1984 only). And Congress was always free to revise or delay the standards (which it did in 1974 and 1977). But these revisions, delays, and exemptions have always been last-minute actions. Because the regulations are supposed to be technology forcing; providing revisions, delays, and exemptions too early in the process would defeat the whole purpose of the strategy. But taking these actions late in the process has been costly for the companies; it has created a great deal of uncertainty and substantial planning problems for them. Further, it may well have encouraged bluffing and less than "whole-hearted" efforts by them (Mills and White, 1978).

These problems of technology forcing have been compounded by a second strategy of the Act and of EPA: the insistence that every vehicle meet the appropriate standards for its class or incur prohibitive penalties. This has added an extra element of inflexibility to the emissions control process. The companies have not had the alternative of paying modest (but nontrivial) penalties as an alternative to meeting the standards; they have not had the opportunity for trading-off low cost ways of meeting the standards (in some vehicles) against high cost ways (in other vehicles). They have not been able to trade-off a vehicle's beyond-standard performance for one pollutant against its below-standard performance for another pollutant. Any tendencies toward bluffing or the absence of whole-hearted efforts have surely been reinforced by the inflexibility that this strategy has created.

There are, of course, alternatives to the strategy of "every car must meet the standard". Modest, nondraconian penalties, which would allow a manufacturer to sell vehicles even if they did not meet the standards, would be one. A system of offsets would be another. Fleet averaging of emissions (comparable to the fleet averaging that is the basis for the Department of Transportation's fuel economy standards) would be a third.

In sum, the "technology forcing" orientation of the Clean Air Act, combined with the inflexibility introduced by the strategy of "every vehicle must meet the standard," has led to problems in implementing the schedule that EPA and the architects of the Act had desired. Congress and EPA have been moving slowly toward allowing greater flexibility in the program. And EPA has been more sensitive (at least in this author's opinion) to the wisdom of trying to avoid confrontations with the motor vehicle industry over technologies that may not be available within short time periods (White, 1981, chs. 5, 7, 16). Still, progress has been slow. This author has argued on a number of occasions that a system of effluent fees, by offering the industry a clearer set of incentives and greater flexibility to develop new and better control technologies, would have led to faster and less costly emissions control (Mills and White, 1978; White, 1980, 1982). I still believe this to be the case.

Emissions from Vehicles in Actual Use

Implementation of an effective emissions reduction program requires more than just the establishing of a schedule of standards (and trying to stick to that schedule). It should also involve a method for ensuring that vehicles in use are actually meeting the standards. Here, again, the program has had problems.

As noted above, the emissions standards are supposed to apply to the first five years or 50,000 miles of a vehicle's life, whichever comes first. It should immediately be noted that this is only half of the typical automobile's life and even less than half of the typical heavy-duty vehicle's life.

Further, even with respect to the part of the vehicle's life that is covered by the standards, EPA's primary method of determining compliance with the standards has been the testing of preproduction vehicles. Only in 1976, nine years into the program, did EPA begin spot checks of assembly line automobiles. Most importantly, there are no federal requirements with respect to vehicles in use; vehicle owners bear no responsibility for ensuring that their vehicles meet the Federal standards in actual use. (A few states and localities have emissions requirements and periodic inspections, but these are only loosely tied to the the federal standards.)

It should come as no surprise, then, that many vehicles in actual use do not meet the standards. Over the past decade EPA has annually collected samples of the emissions from automobiles in actual use. The patterns found in these surveys are quite clear: on average, cars with medium amounts of accumulated mileage (e.g., 25,000 miles or more) tend to exceed the HC and CO standards; even significant numbers of low mileage cars exceed the standards (for a summary of these surveys, see White, 1982). The performance record is better with respect to the NO_x standards, but a significant number of in-use cars exceed those standards also. (Recall that the standards are, in principle, supposed to apply to each individual car and not just to the average of vehicles.) A similar pattern has also been occurring for light-duty trucks.

Thus, vehicles in use are emitting considerably more pollutants than the standards appear to allow. Implementation in this area has definitely had problems. These problems have been the logical consequence of the attitude of the Clean Air Act toward the motor vehicle industry. In effect, the Act has said to the industry, "Emissions are **your** problem; **you** clean it up." This attitude has ignored the fact that emissions are the joint product of the technology and hardware that the industry provides on its vehicles, the choices that vehicle buyers make among models, the maintenance that owners give to their vehicles, and the amount of driving they do.

It is worth noting the contrast between the Clean Air Act's posture with respect to motor vehicles and its posture with respect to other sources of air pollution. In other parts of the Act, the

emitters are held responsible for their emissions, but for motor vehicles, the manufacturers of the vehicles are held responsible. Thus, the owner of a petrochemical factory is responsible for the HC emissions that emerge from his production processes; but he is not responsible for the HC emissions from his delivery trucks; the truck manufacturer is responsible for the latter.

This lopsided emphasis on the vehicle manufacturers and not on the vehicle users has yielded an excessively costly and inefficient emissions control program. Again, a properly structured effluent fee system would have provided the proper incentives for proper vehicle users.

In the past, one barrier to the adoption of programs that would have put more emphasis on maintenance by vehicle owners, besides the reluctance of motorists politically to support these programs, has been EPA's apparent difficulty in finding a quick test (that could be performed on an already warmed-up engine) that would correlate highly enough with the lengthy and elaborate test (e.g., an overnight "soak" at 60 to 86°F. is required) that serves as the basis for preproduction certification. The certification test is a reasonable approximation of in-use driving patterns, and one would not want to base a control program solely on a quick test that might have little relationship to actual driving patterns. (Control systems might be designed so as to meet only that quick test, while emissions during normal driving might be only slightly reduced or might even be increased.) But compromises could have been found. This seems to have been a case of the pursuit of the best (the certification test that closely replicates actual driving patterns) interfering with achievement of the good (a quick hot test that could be used to enforce maintenance).

In the 1980s EPA may push hard to have a number of states and localities adopt inspection and maintenance (I&M) programs, so as to reduce the deterioration of emission control systems in use. But, on top of the very stringent requirements already imposed on the manufacturers, the I&M programs may well be excessively costly (White, 1982). A more sensible approach would be to combine the I&M programs with a slackening of the federal requirements to, say, the 1979 standards. This approach would avoid costly efforts to achieve the last 15-20% of reductions in emissions (which, in automobiles, may cost as much as $700 per vehicle in extra hardware, maintenance, and fuel consumption), while it would improve the cost-effectiveness of the I&M programs.

TESTING THE MACAVOY HYPOTHESIS

Recently, Paul MacAvoy (1979, ch. 3) has advanced the hypothesis that regulatory actions may have had little or no effect on environmental quality, health, or safety. He argues that macroeconomic events may be more responsible for any air or water quality changes. Referring specifically to mobile source emissions, he argues, "Automobile emissions of the major pollutants were being reduced by improvements in fuel-burning performance in new models each year, for example. Regulation of auto emissions may have done little beyond taking credit for the improvements that would have been saleable in any event." In effect, he is arguing that "implementation" of emissions reductions did not occur through regulation; it occurred through consumers' purchases of smaller, more fuel-efficient vehicles.

MacAvoy does offer tests of his hypothesis for a number of industries, using gross annual emission rates. For automotive usage, he finds that regulation did have a significant negative effect on emissions, contrary to the statement quoted above. Still, MacAvoy's test is a relatively crude one, and more refined tests of the hypothesis are possible. Even if the hypothesis is overstated, it is nevertheless interesting to try to determine how much of actual emissions reductions has occurred because of down-sizing and the switch of consumers to more fuel-efficient cars and how much has occurred because of emission regulation. This section will provide some empirical results that shed further light on these propositions.

A test of the MacAvoy hypothesis requires a model of pollutant emissions "production" by automobiles. It also requires data on the characteristics and emissions from cars in actual use. We can then use the model to estimate the emissions from an "average" car during the precontrol period (pre-1968) and during the subsequent years of control. By using the baseline (precontrol) model and the average specifications (other than emissions) of cars for subsequent years, we can estimate the levels of emissions that were likely to have occurred in the absence of emissions controls. The difference between the emissions estimated to be actually occurring and the estimate of emissions that would have occurred in the absence of controls constitutes our measure of the effectiveness of the emissions control program.

Our model is a fairly simple one. For each year, we hypothesize that a vehicle's emission of each pollutant is related to the accumulated mileage of the vehicle at the time the emissions are measured, the engine characteristics of the vehicle, the vehicle's manufacturer, and the location of the test. Mileage is an important variable because pollution control systems tend to deteriorate with use. Engine characteristics are important because emissions tend to increase with the size of the engine and possibly with other engine characteristics as well. The manufacturer has been included as an explanatory variable because some manufacturers' vehicles were notorious for their excessive emissions in some model years. The location is included because HC and CO emissions tend to be greater at higher altitudes.

Specifically, our model takes the form

$$E = f\ (MILES, CID, CARB, FI, MT, FORD, CHRY, AMC, IMP, DEN)$$

where

E = the emissions of HC, CO, or NO_x in grams/mile;
MILES = the accumulated mileage on the vehicle at the time of testing ($x10^{-4}$);
CID = cubic inches of displacement of the engine;
CARB = the number of carburetor barrels;
FI = a dummy variable taking the value 1 if fuel injection is present, 0 otherwise;
MT = a dummy variable taking the value 1 if the car has manual transmission, 0 otherwise;
FORD = a dummy variable taking the value 1 if the car was manufactured by Ford Motor Company, 0 otherwise (similarly, CHRY = Chrysler, AMC = American Motors, IMP = imported make);
DEN = a dummy variable taking the value 1 if the car was tested in Denver, 0 otherwise.

The data for this empirical work come from the EPA tests of vehicles in actual use, mentioned above. The model years of the vehicles tested extend from 1957 to 1979. The testing dates range from 1971 to 1980.

The model was estimated using ordinary least squares regressions. Both a linear and a logarithmic formulation were tried. The above equation was estimated for each pollutant and for each model year separately. The results from the two procedures were similar. In addition, we pooled all observations and added dummy variables (0, 1) for each model year.[4] For reasons of economy of presentation, Table 3-2 presents only the pooled results (for more complete results, see White, 1982).

Let us first comment on the overall results. Our pooled model can explain significant percentages of the variances, with the model year dummy variables accounting for much of the explanatory power. Emissions of HC and CO increase significantly with mileage; i.e., the pollution control systems for these pollutants deteriorate with use. But NO_x emissions appear to decline or rise insignificantly with mileage, so the systems relevant to NO_x do not deteriorate and may even improve slightly with use. Engine size has only a modest positive effect on HC emissions. But CO and NO_x emissions tend to increase significantly with engine size. The number of carburetor barrels (which is positively associated with engine size) increases HC and CO emissions but decreases NO_x emissions. A manual transmission increases HC emissions, has little effect on CO emissions, and decreases NO_x emissions. Finally, HC and CO emissions are significantly greater at high altitudes, while NO_x emissions are significantly lower.

The pooled results show significantly lower emissions for 1968 and after, as compared with the precontrol models. In the years in which the emission standards were tightened, the coefficients become increasingly negative. The NO_x results for 1968-1972 are not an exception to these statements, since NO_x controls were first required on 1973 models (and it was well known that the control systems for reducing CO and HC emissions during 1968-1972 tended to increase NO_x emissions). Thus, if we hold vehicle characteristics constant, the pooled results indicate that there have been significant reductions in emissions that, presumably, have been caused by the emission control regulations.

This last statement, though, does not fully address the MacAvoy hypothesis. It might be the case that changes in vehicle characteristics caused yet greater reductions. To address this proposition, we have estimated the emissions from a car with average characteristics for the pre-1968 model years. We then use the coefficients derived from the pre-1968 models, along with the average characteristics for cars during the model years covered by the regulations, to predict the emissions that would have occurred in the absence of regulation. Finally, we estimate the emissions that actually occurred from a car with average characteristics during the years covered by the regulations. The emissions are calculated at 10,000, 50,000, and 100,000 miles. The first measurement point corresponds to a time interval of six to eight months after the typical new car owner buys his vehicle. (Measurement at zero miles is not feasible for the logarithmic specifications.) The second point represents the statutory requirements for cars. The third point is close to the median lifetime of cars.

The results are presented in Table 3-3. For reasons of economy of presentation, we have limited the presentation of results to pre-1968, 1968, 1973, 1975, and 1979. (Again, similar calculations based on the equations for single years yield similar results.)

As can be seen, the results of these calculations indicate that the changed specifications alone do not account for much of the

Table 3-2

Regression Results: All Years Pooled

	HC		CO		NO_x	
	Linear	Logarithms[a]	Linear	Logarithms[a]	Linear	Logarithms[a]
Constant	6.40	1.18	62.51	3.21	3.34	0.28
MILES ($x10^{-4}$)	0.21 (10.36)	0.18 (24.19)	2.35 (13.35)	0.18 (18.14)	-0.05 (6.24)	0.002 (0.37)
CID	0.0011 (1.66)	0.06 (2.55)	0.04 (6.63)	0.15 (4.60)	0.0014 (5.80)	0.15 (7.34)
CARB	0.18 (3.35)	0.06 (3.39)	1.95 (4.05)	0.03 (11.74)	-0.08 (4.03)	-0.09 (6.63)
FI	0.61 (1.92)	0.24 (6.26)	6.39 (2.29)	0.11 (1.75)	0.06 (0.53)	0.005 (0.14)
MT	0.76 (5.40)	0.18 (8.66)	0.26 (0.21)	0.001 (0.04)	-0.64 (12.35)	-0.21 (12.62)
FORD	-0.19 (1.91)	0.001 (0.01)	-3.79 (4.28)	-0.17 (8.98)	0.38 (10.38)	0.10 (8.21)
CHRY	0.38 (3.11)	0.20 (10.99)	12.37 (11.51)	0.29 (12.62)	0.42 (9.30)	0.11 (7.72)
AMC	-0.51 (2.81)	-0.12 (3.49)	-4.08 (1.96)	-0.16 (3.58)	0.25 (2.85)	0.06 (2.33)
IMP	-0.55 (2.94)	-0.08 (2.62)	-3.07 (1.87)	-0.03 (0.67)	0.29 (4.27)	0.12 (5.04)
DEN	1.12 (5.16)	0.35 (21.12)	29.98 (30.21)	0.63 (29.36)	-1.04 (25.21)	-0.39 (29.85)
D68	-2.14 (9.87)	-0.30 (9.36)	-20.37 (10.58)	-0.28 (6.83)	0.65 (8.11)	0.22 (8.61)

D69	-2.81 (9.84)	-0.36 (11.77)	-25.58 (14.20)	-0.33 (8.09)	1.24 (16.00)	0.39 (15.77)
D70	-3.15 (15.35)	-0.43 (14.63)	-29.72 (16.33)	-0.40 (10.28)	0.66 (8.67)	0.28 (11.89)
D71	-3.62 (17.90)	-0.52 (18.13)	-36.19 (20.22)	-0.50 (13.49)	0.70 (9.41)	0.31 (13.44)
D72	-3.88 (21.06)	-0.60 (22.58)	-37.74 (23.15)	-0.56 (16.49)	0.52 (7.68)	0.26 (12.67)
D73	-4.05 (21.24)	-0.63 (23.31)	-37.35 (22.10)	-0.55 (15.66)	-0.42 (6.00)	-0.02 (9.95)
D74	-4.06 (19.93)	-0.59 (20.92)	-38.72 (21.47)	-0.55 (14.77)	-0.68 (9.02)	-0.11 (4.68)
D75	-6.00 (31.58)	-1.42 (53.47)	-58.91 (34.97)	-1.24 (35.76)	-1.02 (14.62)	-0.20 (9.60)
D76	-5.94 (30.93)	-1.42 (53.58)	-62.26 (36.63)	-1.51 (43.54)	-1.05 (14.93)	-0.19 (8.99)
D77	-6.11 (29.37)	-1.50 (52.28)	-62.67 (34.01)	-1.40 (38.38)	-1.49 (19.41)	-0.43 (18.48)
D78	-6.10 (21.13	-1.50 (36.19)	-63.19 (24.70)	-1.37 (25.41)	-1.67 (15.71)	-0.56 (16.75)
D79	-6.33 (24.54)	-1.71 (45.62)	-63.20 (27.66)	-1.52 (30.97)	-1.79 (18.81)	-0.56 (18.46)
R^2	0.29	0.62	0.42	0.50	0.34	0.37
F	176.76	692.35	316.63	434.86	223.92	255.92
Number of Observations	9458	9458	9458	9458	9458	9458

[a] Dependent and independent variables are in natural logarithms.

Note: All numbers in parentheses are t-statistics.

Table 3-3

Hypothetical and Estimated Actual Emissions
from Cars with Average Characteristics at Various Mileages (g/mi)

			Linear			Logarithmic		
		EPA Standard	10K miles	50K miles	100K miles	10K miles	50K miles	100K miles
HC								
Pre-1968	Estimated actual	—	7.44	8.28	9.33	5.07	6.78	7.68
	Hypothetical[a]		7.44	8.28	9.33	5.06	6.76	7.66
1968		5.9						
	Estimated actual		5.30	6.14	7.19	3.89	5.20	5.89
	Hypothetical		7.39	8.23	9.28	5.04	6.73	7.62
1973		3.0						
	Estimated actual		3.37	4.21	5.26	2.62	3.50	3.96
	Hypothetical		7.39	8.23	9.28	5.05	6.75	7.64
1975		1.5						
	Estimated actual		1.38	2.22	3.27	1.22	1.63	1.85
	Hypothetical		7.36	8.20	9.25	5.02	6.70	7.60
1979		1.5						
	Estimated actual		1.03	1.87	2.92	0.91	1.21	1.37
CO								
Pre-1968	Estimated actual	—	81.46	90.86	102.61	58.90	78.69	89.15
	Hypothetical		83.15	92.55	104.30	60.26	80.50	91.20
1968		50.8						
	Estimated actual		62.78	72.18	83.93	45.54	60.84	68.93
	Hypothetical		81.33	90.73	102.48	59.13	79.00	86.45

1973		28.0						
	Estimated actual		43.98	53.38	65.13	32.95	44.03	49.88
	Hypothetical		80.99	90.39	102.14	58.86	78.64	89.09
1975		15.0						
	Estimated actual		22.08	31.48	43.23	17.03	22.76	25.78
	Hypothetical		78.72	88.12	98.87	56.85	75.95	86.04
1979		15.0						
	Estimated actual		15.52	27.27	39.02	12.43	16.61	18.82
NO_x								
Pre-1968	Estimated actual	—	3.63	3.43	3.18	2.91	2.92	2.93
	Hypothetical		3.72	3.52	3.27	3.00	3.01	3.01
1968		—						
	Estimated actual		4.37	4.17	3.92	3.74	3.75	3.75
	Hypothetical		3.65	3.45	3.20	2.94	2.95	2.96
1973		3.1						
	Estimated actual		3.23	3.03	3.78	2.88	2.89	2.90
	Hypothetical		3.65	3.45	3.20	2.94	2.95	2.95
1975		3.1						
	Estimated actual		2.63	2.43	2.18	2.41	2.41	2.42
	Hypothetical		3.53	3.33	3.08	2.81	2.82	2.83
1979		2.0						
	Estimated actual		1.74	1.54	1.29	1.61	1.61	1.62

[a]Using the regression coefficients from Table 1 and actual model years average characteristics.

emissions reductions.[5] Even if we use the 1968 characteristics (the 1968 models have the highest average CID) as the base against which the effects of subsequent changes in characteristics should be compared, those effects are still comparatively minor. Thus, it appears that almost all of the actual reductions in emissions should be credited to the regulations themselves.[6]

There are two caveats that should be added to this last statement. First, some of the changes in specifications, particularly the down-sizing of the late 1970s, may have partly occurred as a consequence of the emissions control requirements themselves. It was generally recognized that smaller cars with smaller engines could meet the standards more easily. This author's personal judgment is that very little down-sizing occurred because of the regulations; the American manufacturers appeared to be quite determined to meet the requirements through changes in technology rather than changes in size. But, to the extent that the requirements may have caused some of the down-sizing, our results **understate** the net effects of the regulations. Second, to the extent that fuel economy improvements involved increases in the pure efficiency of combustion, this would have decreased HC and CO emissions (but increased NO_x emissions), and our results would **overstate** the effects of the regulations. Again, though, this author's judgment is that this second influence is also a minor one. (Also, the two influences would tend to offset each other). Thus, the results that we have found are probably fairly robust.

CONCLUSION

The history of the mobile source emissions control program is an instructive one. Both Congress and EPA are learning, albeit slowly, that there is more to achieving an effective emissions control program than just establishing an ambitious emissions reduction schedule. As we have seen, emissions have in fact been reduced by the regulatory program — the MacAvoy hypothesis does not appear to be valid for automotive emissions regulation — but the program has proceeded more slowly and less effectively than would otherwise have been the case. Greater attention should be given to the enforcement of standards on in-use vehicles. Greater flexibility in enforcement tools can lead to a less costly, yet more effective, program. In this area, as in most others, incentives matter. The proper use of incentives could have reduced the costs and increased the effectiveness of the program in the past and could still promise to do so in the future. One can only hope that Congress and EPA will continue to absorb and build on this lesson.

NOTES

1. The Act calls for 90% reductions from 1970 levels, which in turn involved 50% reductions from uncontrolled levels. Also, standards for evaporative emissions of HC from carburetors are required.
2. The Act specifically refers to heavy-duty trucks, which it classifies as vehicles with a gross vehicle weight of 6,000 lbs. or more. It is silent on the category of light-duty trucks. EPA has adopted a policy of aiming for the same percentage reductions in light-duty trucks as in heavy-duty trucks.
3. As this is written, EPA appears to be involved in a similar delay and revise process for heavy-duty trucks and is likely to do so for particulate emissions from diesel vehicles.
4. Slope-shift dummy variables on the mileage term were also tried, but they provided no additional explanatory power.
5. The major exceptions are the NO_x results for the years 1968-1972. As mentioned above, the controls on HC and CO during those years increased NO_x emissions (to which no regulations applied).
6. Also, reductions of 3 to 6 grams/mile in HC emissions from blow-by and evaporations emissions should probably be credited to the regulations.

REFERENCES

Clean Air Act. 1977. Section 109(b)(1), as amended August 1977.

Dewees, D.W. 1974. Economics and Public Policy: The Automobile Pollution Case (MIT Press).

Dewees, D.W. 1978. "The Costs and Technology of Pollution Abatement" in Friedlaender.

Friedlaender, A.F. (ed.). 1978. Approaches to Controlling Air Pollution (MIT Press).

Ginsburg, D.H., and W.J. Abernathy (ed.). 1980. Government Technology, and the Future of the Automobile (McGraw-Hill).

Grad, F.P., A.J. Rosenthal, et al. 1975. The Automobile and the Regulation of Its Impact on the Environment (Oklahoma University Press).

Jacoby, H.D., J.D. Steinburner, et al. 1973. Clearing the Air: Federal Policy on Automotive Emissions Control (Ballinger).

MacAvoy, P.W. 1979. The Regulated Industries and the Economy (Norton).

Mills, E.S., and L.J. White. 1978. "Government Policies Toward Automotive Emissions Control" in Friedlaender.

National Academy of Sciences and National Academy of Engineering. 1974. Air Quality and Automotive Emission Control, prepared for the U.S. Senate, Committe on Public Works.

White, L.J. 1980. "Automobile Emissions Control Policy: Success Story or Wrongheaded Regulation" in Ginsburg and Abernathy.

White, L.J. 1981. Reforming Regulation: Processes and Problems (Prentice-Hall).

White, L.J. 1982. The Regulation of Air Pollutant Emissions from Motor Vehicles (American Enterprise Institute).

REVEALED RULES FOR REGULATORY DECISIONS: AN EMPIRICAL ANALYSIS OF EPA RULEMAKING BEHAVIOR

4

Alan J. Krupnick, Wesley A. Magat, and Winston Harrington

INTRODUCTION

Despite a growing literature in economics and political science on explanations for the existence of regulation, little work has focused on how regulatory agencies translate broad legislative mandates into specific rules. Administrative law provides most of the literature on this subject, but as these studies rely upon case studies of one, or at most a few agency decisions, it is difficult and potentially misleading to draw general conclusions about rulemaking behavior from them. Both to explain agency behavior and to devise more credible reforms of the porcess, we need a unified theory of agency rulemaking behavior.

Unfortunately, such a theory does not yet exist. On the more abstract side, Stigler (1971) and Peltzman (1976) suggest general hypotheses about the balance of interest group power and offer a framework for modeling individual regulatory decisions, but their work is not intended to explain all the factors that influence a specific decision, such as an Occupational Safety and Health Administration standard for benzene exposure or a Food and Drug Administration new drug approval. On the behavioral side, organizational theorists, such as Simon (1957) and Cyert and March (1963) have carefully studied decision-making rules used by firms in the private sector, but their approach has not been applied to regulatory agency decisions, where it must be integrated into a model that also explains the influences of external factors, such as pressures from regulated firms and from Congress. On the methodological side, McFadden (1975, 1976) has developed a useful statistical approach to understanding agency decision-making rules, but he concentrates primarily upon the development of a technique and applies it to explain administrative rather than regulatory decisions. Joskow (1972) uses a similar approach to study specific agency decisions. All this literature lacks a more general analysis of the dynamics of the rulemaking process, the different types of variables that may influence agency decisions, and the form that this influence actually takes.

Given the lack of unified theory, we can instead follow the Joskow and McFadden approach and let the analyses of decisions reveal the underlying decision-making rules. To do this, we examine how an important and fairly typical social regulatory agency, the

Environmental Protection Agency (EPA), promulgated a large and representative set of industrial water pollution standards, the "best practicable technology" (BPT) effluent guidelines. The goal is for our methodological approach and our empirical results to provide a better understanding of EPA rulemaking behavior, as well as to stimulate further research on the regulatory process that leads to more refined general models.

To develop testable hypotheses we draw on the literature discussed above, as well as on existing case studies and our own interviews with key participants in the effluent guidelines rulemaking process, both inside and outside EPA. These hypotheses are tested econometricly using our federal regulations data base containing values of the effluent guideline standards and the relevant variables hypothesized to affect EPA's standard-setting decisions. The chapter concludes with a brief discussion of the results of the hypotheses tests and their implications for both regulatory reform and further research. For a more detailed description of this work plus other quantitative and qualitative tests of rulemaking theories, see Krupnick et al. (1982).[1]

THEORIES OF RULEMAKING BEHAVIOR

Theories of regulatory agency decisionmaking can be broadly divided into two categories, external and internal, depending upon whether the theory explains rulemaking decisions as made by balancing external forces seeking to influence the agency or as shaped by the internal organization and motivations of the bureaucracy.

One way of representing the external influences on agency decisions is through what Noll (1976) calls the external signals theory (see Peltzman, 1976). This model treats the agency as a monolithic bureaucracy striving to maximize the value of success indicators given to it by industry, the public, and interested third parties, subject to constraints on agency resources. For the case of BPT rulemaking, industry objections to shouldering heavy compliance costs took many forms. The two comment periods before the initial proposal and final promulgation of a regulation provided formal access to the rulemaking process, while Congress, the Office of Management and Budget (OMB), and other agencies sometimes interceded on an industry's behalf on a less formal basis. Also, during the data gathering stage of determining the feasible control technologies, industry officials communicated frequently with EPA and its technical contractors.

Industry pressure cannot be treated as homogeneous, for firms within the same industry often differed because their plants came from varying vintages, possessed different control technologies, used many distinct production processes, and the like. Since some firms would have been more affected by a set of regulations than others, regulatory agencies often received mixed signals as these firms engaged in efforts to lessen or shift their compliance burdens.

Although environmental groups chose not to participate in the details of BPT rulemaking for each industry, EPA analysts were keenly sensitive to the environmental interests, both because of professional training as sanitary engineers and because of the strong public support for environmental protection in the early 1970s.[1] The enabling legislation, the 1972 Federal Water Pollution Control Act Amendments, also stressed the goals of creating "fishable and swimmable" water by 1983.

A number of internal, or bureaucratic, theories can also be applied to help explain BPT rulemaking. They differ from the external signals theory because they make the bureaucracy itself the key factor in determining regulatory decisions. Examples of elements of these theories that we draw upon for hypotheses about BPT rulemaking include Cyert and March's (1963) organizational learning, Down's (1967) categorization of bureaucratic types, Mitnick's (1980) views on organizational conflicts, and theories of information applied to private firms.

MODEL STRUCTURE

Our econometric work focuses on explaining one major decision made for each industry subcategory — the level, or stringency, of the BPT standards. We analyze the initial levels of the standards suggested by the contractors, the changes in those standards over the rulemaking process, and the levels of the standards finally promulgated.[2] Although BPT regulations apply to many pollutants, we address only the standards for the two most common pollutants regulated, biological oxygen demand (BOD) and total suspended solids (TSS).[3] Following standard engineering practice, BOD standards are measured in percent removal (denoted PER) and TSS standards are measured as a concentration in units of milligrams of TSS per liter of water (MGL).

Some additional notation needs to be introduced at this point. EPA usually issued three standards for each pollutant in each subcategory, one at the contractor stage (denoted C), one at the stage of initial proposal in the Federal Register (denoted P), and one at the stage of final promulgation in the Federal Register (denoted R). These three stages divide the process into two periods, one from the contractor's suggested standards to the proposal stage (denoted C-P) and another from the proposal to promulgation states (denoted P-R). During both of these periods, EPA received industry comments and gathered new information on which to base changes in its regulations. When referring to the entire period from the contractor stage to the promulgation stage, we use the notation C-R.

Our empirical work estimated separate equations for both pollutants for: (1) the level of the contractor's standard (denoted PERC for BOD and MGLC for TSS); (2) the level of the promulgated standard (labelled PERR for BOD and MGLR for TSS); (3) the percentage change in the standard in the period between the contractor and proposal stages (called CPB for BOD and CPT for TSS); (4) the percentage change in the standard in the period from the proposal to promulgation stages (denoted PRB for BOD and PRT for TSS); and (5) the percentage change in the standard over the entire period from the contractor to promulgation stages (called CRB for BOD and CRT for TSS).[4] For each pollutant, these five dependent variables were hypothesized to be affected by a set of explanatory variables, some differing from one equation to another (see section titled Specific Hypotheses).

DATA BASE

Forty-six industry categories called the Group One industries were regulated by EPA in two phases during the BPT rulemaking process. We have constructed a data base containing all the BPT regulations set for each of the forty-six Group One industries at all three stages of the rulemaking process. These data provide measures of the five dependent variables for both BOD and TSS. For the regression analysis, a sample of twenty-three Group One industries was selected for which data were collected on the explanatory variables, including industry characteristics, expected economic impacts, and a host of other variables suggested by the hypotheses as influencing the standards.

These industries were selected to eliminate those with regulatory decisions easily explained by political intervention. We preferred to focus on the more subtle decision-making rules characterizing the rulemaking process for the majority of industries.

Our unit of observation is the subcategory, rather than the industry category, because our interviews with EPA project officers convinced us that once the subcategory decision was made, standards were independently set for each subcategory. However, some aggregation of our subcategory observations was necessary because of data limitations. After making this adjustment, our data base contains observations on 102 subcategories in 23 industries for 10 dependent variables and 22 explanatory variables.

SPECIFIC HYPOTHESES

Our choice of the explanatory variables was guided by hypotheses about the determinants of regulatory decisionmaking derived from the two broad categories of theories, external and internal, discussed in Krupnick, Magat, and Harrington (forthcoming). The specific hypotheses to be tested follow.

External Theories

Investment Costs (IC) and Annual Costs (AC)

For each subcategory EPA published the projected investment costs and annual costs of compliance with the proposed standards in the Economic Analysis reports. From these reports and the technical reports known as Development Documents, we were also able to estimate the value of sales by plants subject to the BPT regulations. IC and AC were constructed by normalizing total investment costs and annual costs by the value of sales, providing two measures of the relative costs of the BPT regulations imposed upon different subcategories. The external signals theory suggests that the higher the values of normalized investment costs (or annual costs), the greater the opposition, or negative signals, given to EPA, with this greater opposition causing the promulgated standards to be weaker for the subcategory and causing the standards to be weakened more in the P-R period of the rulemaking process.

Unemployment (UP) and Plant Closures (PC)

The Economic Analysis reports project the number of plant closures and the unemployment likely to result from the proposed rules. Two measures of economic impact, UP and PC, were created by dividing total unemployment and plant closures by the number of plants in the subcategory affected by the BPT regulation, providing measures of the relative impacts of the BPT standards across subcategories. High projected values of UP and PC associated with EPA's proposed regulations are hypothesized to create strong pressure to weaken them from both the Congressional representatives of the affected communities and from firms that used these projections to bolster their case for less stringent standards. The external signals model predicts that the adverse pressure caused by high values of UP and PC caused EPA to weaken the BPT standards in the period between the proposal and promulgation stages.

Percentage Price Increase (PPI)

The Economic Analysis reports also projected the inflationary effects of the proposed standards by measuring the average percent increase in price for the products produced by plants in each subcategory. High price increases associated with a proposed standard meant more negative pressure, or signals, from consumers and their agents within the government (e.g., Congress and OMB), as well as from firms that used these projections to their advantage, resulting in a weakening of the standard from the proposed to promulgated stages.

Number of Small Plants (NSP) and Percentage of Small Plants (PSP)

Small plants were usually defined by EPA to be those employing twenty or fewer employees (the Bureau of the Census definition). The idea that small plants were particularly subject to closure and other lesser economic difficulties caused by their compliance burden permeates the Economic Analysis reports. Small plants were routinely characterized as being old and therefore having more primitive waste management practices and relatively high abatement costs. They were also thought to operate with low profit margins and to be vulnerable to changing business conditions. Thus, for both equity and efficiency reasons the external signals model predicts that subcategories with many small plants or with a high percentage of small plants would have been given weaker standards to provide them with special relief.[6,7]

Percentage of Plants Affected by BPT Regulations (PPA)

Within any subcategory some plants were not affected by the BPT regulations, either because they discharged into municipal treatment plants or they already complied with the standards before promulgation. Given that these plants competed with BPT-regulated plants in their product markets, the former group gained a competitive advantage through stricter standards imposed upon the latter group. The latter group benefited from weaker standards two ways, through lower compliance costs and through a more favorable competitive position vis-a-vis firms in the subcategory that were not affected by BPT standards. Thus, the larger the proportion of plants in a subcategory that were subject to BPT standards, the greater was the industry pressure for weaker standards and the more likely EPA was to have set weaker rules.

Number of Comments (NC)

EPA invited comments on their rules from all interested parties during both periods of the rulemaking process, one after the release of the contractor's standards and their accompanying report (i.e., C-P) and the other after the proposed rule was published (i.e., P-R). As these comments were received primarily from industry, we used the number of significant comments summarized in the Federal Register (and aimed at weakening the standards) as a proxy for the signal strength of industry opposition. The external signals model argues that more comments in favor of weaker standars influenced EPA to weaken its regulations.

Testing this hypothesis required using six variants of the NC comment variable, since we divided the comments into those applying to BOD standards and those applying to the TSS standards, and since for each pollutant standard we estimated equations explaining its percentage change over three periods (C-P, P-R, and C-R). The six comment variables are NCBCP, NCBPR, NCBCR, NCTCP, NCTPR, and NCTCR, where the third letter corresponds to the pollutant and the fourth and fifth letters connote the period during which the comments were received.

Trade Association Budget (TAB)

Trade associations exist, in part, to provide lobbying expertise to help member firms influence the regulatory process. They also serve as conduits of information among firms and between firms and government. In addition, the existence of a trade association may increase the likelihood of opposition because the trade association keeps industry informed of EPA activities and helps its members organize. Thus, a trade association with a Washington office, a large budget, a large staff, a special regulatory task force, established government ties, and membership of firms with homogeneous interests should be effective in obtaining weak regulations and in weakening the standards during the rulemaking process. For lack of better data we used the relevant industry's trade association budget (TAB) as a proxy for all of these characteristics of trade associations that make them effective in weakening regulations.

Concentration Ratio (CR4)

Firms with substantial market power are more able to pass on the costs of regulation to their customers than firms with less market power. Thus, if the industry four-firm concentration ratio correlates closely with market power, more concentrated industry subcategories should have offered less opposition to stringent BPT regulations than less concentrated subcategories and therefore received tighter standards.

Rate of Return (ROR)

We used rates of return on equity as a proxy for the profitability of firms in a subcategory facing compliance with BPT regulations. Profitability can affect the strength of industry opposition in two contrary ways. On one hand, higher profitability gives a firm more internal resources to use in fighting regulations, for example, through hiring technical consultants, collecting more data, undertaking more refined analysis, and boosting lobbying efforts.[8] On the other hand if a more profitable firm can better afford the costs of compliance it may be less likely to resist stringent standards, even if only because for this firm compliance does not require borrowing to cover negative cash flows. Because these two factors cause profitability to influence the degree of industry resistance (and thus the stringency of standards) in opposite directions, the external signals model provides no hypothesis about the direction of the effect of rate of return (ROR) on the stringency of BPT standards.

Raw Waste Load (RWLB, RWLT) and Wastewater Flow (WF)

Investment costs (IC) and annual costs (AC) both measure the projected costs of complying with the proposed BPT standards. Values of the two costs can vary across subcategories either because the stringencies of the standards vary (with costs being measured at different points on the curves), or because some curves lie everywhere above others (due to their inherently higher costs of pollution control). An ideal measure of compliance costs would indicate the relative heights of the cost **curves.** Using this measure, the external signals theory would predict that subcategories with inherently higher costs of control would oppose regulations more strongly than those with lower control costs and so receive weaker standards.

BOD raw waste load (RWLB), TSS raw waste load (RWLT) and

wastewater flow (WF), all normalizd by the value of subcategory sales, each serve to some extent as proxies for this ideal measure of costs. All else being equal, higher TSS raw waste load values raise the cost of meeting any given TSS concentration standard (although the RWLB value should not affect the cost of meeting BOD percentage removal standards). A higher wastewater flow increases the cost of meeting any given BOD percentage removal standard (but does not affect the cost of meeting TSS concentration standards as much). Thus, the external signals theory predicts that subcategories with higher RWLT levels should be associated with weaker TSS standards, and subcategories with higher wastewater flows should be associated with weaker BOD standards, ceteris paribus.

We must caution that RWLB, RWLT, and WF could serve as proxies for other factors besides costs that affect the stringency of EPA's standards. Therefore, these hypotheses about RWLB, RWLT, and WF provide only a weak test of the external signals theory.

Internal Theories

Development Document Quality (DDQ) and Economic Analysis Quality (EAQ)

The decisions made through the social regulatory process are often driven by the quality of the supporting data possessed by the regulatory agency. EPA's effluent guidelines provide an excellent example of this point. As one project officer said, "Data ruled the system."

The Effluent Guidelines Division (EGD) at EPA lead the rulemaking effort and generally sought to promulgate protective (i.e., strict) BPT standards. Success at this goal required developing sufficient data to justify both the technical feasibility and economic viability of the standards issued. Without good data the agency would have been forced to accept industry data that usually supported weaker standards, or else use its own poorer quality data and risk a court remand. Thus, we hypothesize that the better the quality of the technical and economic data that supported a BPT standard, the more stringent was that standard.

We used two dummy variables (DDQ and EAQ) to measure the document quality, with a one representing a high quality document and a zero representing a low quality document. DDQ measures the quality of the technical analysis in the Development Documents, as evidenced by our difficulty in extracting basic technical information from them, such as raw waste loads, water flows, and treatment in place. EAQ grades the quality of the economic impact analysis in the Economic Analysis reports, as revealed by whether the major estimates in the report could be derived from the stated methodology and assumptions.

Personnel Turnover (PT)

Turnover of key personnel within the agency resulted in the loss of knowledge about the technical and economic characteristics of an industry, which in turn widened the information gap between EPA and the industry. We expect this led to the promulgation of weaker standards. To test this hypothesis we constructed a dummy variable (PT) taking the value of one if only one project officer supervised the entire process and zero if more than one project officer was involved.[9]

Order of Promulgation (ORDER)

For three reasons we expect that, ceteris paribus, industries regulated later in the process were given weaker standards than those regulated earlier. First, faced with tight deadlines, heavy workloads, and resistance to tight standards from the Economic Analysis Division (EAD), the EGD staff may have been forced to compromise more in rulemakings for later industries.[10] In Downs' (1967) terms, the environmental "zealots" at EPA (primarily within EGD) should have become more like "conservers" as the process wore on (i.e., convenience and necessity became more important than their environmental goals). Second, industries regulated later in the rulemaking process should have learned from earlier rulemakings how most effectively to argue their views (for weaker standards) within the context of EPA's informal rulemaking process. It is possible that EPA may have also learned how to resist more effectively industry pressures for weaker rules, but this would have required generating more supporting data of higher quality. Highly limited staff, funding, and time made this defense difficult to implement. Finally, the industries judged by EPA to have more complex wastewater problems or to need more detailed analyses were left for later in the process when it was felt that earlier rulemaking experiences would make the process move more smoothly. More complex industries present EPA with a greater problem in assembling and analyzing information, which increases the advantage to industry in arguing and proving its points.

Number of Regulated Pollutants (NRP)

For each industry subcategory EPA regulated the discharge levels of several pollutants, usually including BOD and TSS, plus several others. Since pollution control technology produced a joint product and one pollutant was often more difficult to control than the others, control of this pollutant imposed the primary regulatory constraint. This fact may have led EPA, as well as industrial and other rulemaking participants, to adopt the standard operating procedure of focusing the debate and analysis upon the "controlling pollutant" during the two comment periods, while leaving the other pollutants' standards unchanged or only slightly altered. Assuming that industries with many regulated pollutants were more likely to have a pollutant other than BOD (or TSS) as the controlling one than were industries with few pollutants, the BOD and TSS standards were less likely to be modified during the two comment periods the greater the number of regulated pollutants.[11]

Changes in Standards (CPB, CPT) and Standard Levels (PERC, PERP, MGLC, MGLP)

The theory of organizational learning (Cyert and March, 1963) suggests that EPA's decisions about how much to change standards over the rulemaking process depended upon the extent to which the organization had reached a consensus on the original standards. If the consensus were reached before the proposed regulations were issued, then little additional change in the standards was necessary at the promulgation stage. However, if the internal debate had not been well resolved before issuance of the proposed standards, then the continued debate often lead to significant revisions at the promulgation stage. Since the technical contractors generally suggested strict standards that were weakened over the rulemaking process, significant changes usually meant significant relaxation of the standards. This argument implies that the larger the weakening of the standard during the C-P period (CPB and CPT), the smaller the weakening in the P-R period (PRB and PRT).

We have already explained that EAD's influence tended to cause relaxation of standards. Since EGD, with its environmentalist goal, supervised the construction of the contractor standards without EAD involvement, it is to be expected that EAD's impact and industry's impact at the proposal level would have been stronger the tighter the contractor standards. We test this proposition through the hypothesis that the extent to which standards were weakened in the C-P period (CPB and CPT) is directly proportional to the stringency of the contractor standards (PERC and MGLC).

Similarly, the weakening of standards in the P-R period (PRB and PRT) should have been directly related to the stringency of the proposed standard (PERP and MGLP).

ECONOMETRIC RESULTS

The regressions specified contain variables that cut across different theories and their respective hypotheses. Thus, the overall results of these regressions indicate how well the outcomes are predicted by the combination of theories used to specify the regressions (see Tables 4-1 and 4-2).

In general, the BOD regressions out-perform the TSS regressions, as judged by their R^2 and F values. The regressions on TSS concentration standards (MGLC and MGLR) show little explanatory power. The variations across subcategories of the percentage changes in both the BOD and TSS standards over the entire rulemaking process (CRB and CRT) are better explained than the changes during either the C-P or P-R periods. For BOD, the regressions for changes in standards over the latter period yield better results than those for the former period. For TSS, the reverse holds.[12]

Chow tests run on each regression revealed that, at the 1% level of significance, the hypothesis that subsamples of our observations yield different results than the full sample can be rejected. For a weaker 5% test, several regressions are on the borderline. We conclude that the regression results reported here are not likely to be much different if a different sample of industries were drawn.

We find evidence of some collinearity, but it mainly results from the relationship between the intercept and PERC and PERP. In addition, the relationship between CP and UP is quite close and may mask their individual effects. Heteroscedasticity did not appear to be a problem for our data set.

RESULTS OF HYPOTHESES TESTS

To evaluate the extent of support provided each of the hypotheses stated above requires a judgment that must combine: (a) the coefficient values of the relevant variables and their associated standard errors for all five BOD and all five TSS regression equations; (b) the robustness of these results (i.e., Chow test outcomes); and (c) the appreciation for why the greater heterogeneity of TSS abatement technologies versus those for BOD would be expected to add more noise to the TSS results. This section summarizes our judgments about results of the hypotheses tests.

External Signals

We found some support for the hypothesis that the higher the investment costs per dollar of sales (IC) required by a proposed regulation, the greater the weakening that results in the promulgated standard. The BOD coefficient is significant at the 95% level, but the TSS coefficient is insignificant, although taking the expected sign. Since IC and annual cost per dollar of sales (AC) are colinear, we could only test the AC hypotheses by excluding IC from the regression equations. The results of this procedure (not reported here) show no significant support for the hypothesis that higher values of estimated average cost cause weaker standards.

In contrast to the above results about the influence of economic costs (IC, AC), we found fairly strong support for the influence of projected unemployment (UP), a short-term economic impact, in weakening the standards.[13] Despite the claims of several EPA officials who were interviewed, projected plant closures (PC) did not show up as a determinant of the stringency of the BPT regulations; however, UP and PC are colinear (r = 0.7), so we urge caution in interpreting this result. Similarly, a third economic impact, that of price increases (PPI), did not appear to affect the standard levels.

The BOD results confirm the more generous treatment that industry subcategories with a high percentage of small plants (PSP) are given. However, the percentage of small plants did not appear to influence the TSS standards. In other regressions (not reported here), the number of small plants (NSP) showed the same pattern of infuence, although with less statistical significance. Taken together, we believe these results provide modest support for the hypothesis that EPA regulates small plants less stringently than larger plants, but the unsupportive TSS results forbid drawing any strong conclusions, even though they are probably due to the greater noise in the TSS data.

None of the BOD results and only portions of the TSS results support the hypothesis that the higher the percentage of plants in a subcategory affected by a BPT regulation the weaker the standard. Either our measure of the proportion of plants affected is inaccurate or the hypothesis is false, i.e., rivalry among firms in an industry does not affect the stringency of regulations.

Our industry comments (NC) hypothesis also showed little support from the regression analyses, despite using several different

Table 4-1
Regression Results for BOD

Explanatory Variables	Dependent Variables				
	PERC	PERR	CPB	PRB	CRB
IC				110.449* (55.578)	-91.582* (44.076)r
UP				-.0474 (.6609)	1.6859* (.9735)
PC				-2.4701 (26.333)	-36.211 (45.264)
PPI				-3.196 (2.385)	-5.687 (4.111)
PSP	-.0103+ (.0066)r	-.0114+ (.0074)r	.1589 (.1822)	.4255* (.1474)r	.2852 (.2755)
NP	.0044* (.0023)r	-.0050+ (.0033)r	-.0057 (.0820)	.0198 (.0608)	-.0217 (.1123)
PPA	-.0743 (.6705)	-.0869 (.7759)	-23.765+ (17.739)r	-5.445 (15.715)	-39.082+ (27.048)r
NC		.0988 (.0531)	.8337 (2.8085)	-1.543 (1.195)	.7112 (1.9824)
TAB	-.00025* (.00015)	.0004 (.0002)	-.0129* (.0057)	-.0145* (.0050)	0.0048 (.0077)
CR4	-.0490* (.0106)r	-.0593* (.0164)r	.6209+ (.4138)	.3036 (.5281)	.3302 (.7229)
ROR	-.2886* (.1032)r	-.0545 (.1233)	.6600 (3.421)	5.277+ (2.652)	.4459 (4.1832)
RWLB	.00168 (.00153)	.0028* (.0017)			
WF	-.0020* (.0010)r	-.0023* (.0010)			
DDQ		(.9420* (.5413)	-53.051* (15.048)r	-20.936* (12.131)r	-54.022* (17.415)r

Table 4-1
Regression Results for BOD
(continued)

Explanatory Variables	Dependent Variables				
	PERC	PERR	CPB	PRB	CRB
EAQ		1.2570* (.7380)r	21.783 (20.214)	-29.752* (17.35)r	6.6522 (27.725)
PT		-2.2885* (.8413)r	33.208* (13.357)r	43.359* (20.331)r	58.896* (31.900)
ORDER	-.1297* (.0739)r	.0253 (.0934)	-2.787 (2.954)	.5361 (2.1738)	-5.4943* (3.121)r
NRP		.5899* (.2349)r	-5.262 (5.881)	-13.277* (4.986)	-5.0895 (7.625)
CPB				-.2019* (.0944)	
PERC/PERP			1.048* (.3477)	1.323* (.488)	.7556+ (.5138)
CONSTANT	7.7299 (.9495)	1.1378 (1.9018)	-57.1743 (63.2249)	-49.1007 (54.6426)	-3.8804 (87.2825)
r^2	.50	.54	.49	.73	.76
Adj r^2	.41	.37	.32	.55	.63
F	5.24	3.13	2.87	4.25	6.17
DF	47	37	39	29	54
CHOW	.64	1.84	1.28	2.39	2.20
CI[a]		41	47	39.88	32.61

Note: Values in parentheses are standard errors. An R by the standard error means that the variable is robust as measured with a Chow test.

a CI refers to the condition index; only 30 are reported. See Belsley, Kuh, and Welsh (1980)

* Significant at 95% level for a one-tailed test. For ROR we made a two-tailed test to be consistent with the associated hypothesis.

+ Significant at the 90% level for a one-tailed test. For ROR we made a two-tailed test to be consistent with the associated hypothesis.

Table 4-2
Regression Results for TSS
(continued)

Explanatory Variables	Dependent Variables				
	MGLC	MGLR	CPT	PRT	CRT
EAQ		-18.5895 (39.7832)	-14.6461+ (10.3367)r	-15.456+ (11.084)r	-20.5506+ (13.9003)
PT		75.2271+ (46.6243)r	68.252* (9.269)r	40.869* (13.291)r	85.2899* (16.5363)r
ORDER	4.458+ (3.165)r	6.3567 (6.6441)	-1.5141 (2.0846)	2.972 (2.460)	-1.6237 (2.3935)
NRP		6.3481 (10.7256)	.9771 (2.1298)	.4477 (2.1013)	.7864 (2.9526)
CPB				-.0011 (.1019)	
MGLC/MGLP			.2413* (.0548)r	.0261 (.0543)	-.3037* (.0724)r
CONSTANT	-8.4288 (42.0453)	-12.9341 (114.139)	-19.9415 (29.7528)	17.6584 (29.1551)	22.9829 (39.8156)
r^2	.11	.15	.64	.43	.66
Adj r^2	.01	-.00	.59	.29	.59
F	1.11	.97	11.227	3.00	8.74
DF	85	75	81	71	76
CHOW			.59	1.52	.76
CI				32	31

Note: See notes to Table 4-1.

Table 4-2
Regression Results for TSS

Explanatory Variables	Dependent Variables				
	MGLC	MGLR	CPT	PRT	CRT
IC				22.227	-25.2410
				(18.864)	(23.3408)
UP				1.510*	2.4731*
				(.871)r	(.8141)r
PC				-24.744	10.8424
				(31.964)	(35.7043)
PPI				.3378	-.1692
				(2.1336)	(2.7718)
PSP	-.3118	-.2848	.0127	.0521	-.1464
	(.286)	(.5609)	(.1448)	(.1556)	(.2184)
NP	-.0526	-.0435	-.0196	.0391	.0360
	(.0716)	(.1471)	(.0371)	(.0361)	(.0507)
PPA	41.050*	44.0804	-27.294	29.177*	-12.5499
	(22.22)r	(43.6673)	(11.854)	(14.017)	(15.8549)
NC		-1.4362	6.4347*	-2.155*	-.9239
		(2.9718)	(2.2856)r	(.8103)r	(1.0299)
TAB	.0018	.0034	.0019	-.0031	.0026
	(.0041)	(.0102)	(.0025)	(.0026)	(.0035)
CR4	-.4769	-1.0710	-.1235	-.6202	-.7750
	(.3930)	(.9501)	(.2229)	(.2444)r	(.3442)
ROR	7.522+	11.1140	5.6210*	2.683	8.7322*
	(4.432)	(9.5081)	(2.3398)r	(2.593)	(3.4051)r
RWLT	-.0008	.0015			
	(.0019)	(.0037)			
WF	-.0092	.0015			
	(.0126)	(.0241)			
DDQ		-4.1605	-43.664*	12.375	-29.1229*
		(30.6732)	(8.313)r	(8.909)	(10.4644)r

approaches to counting the number of significant comments in the Federal Register. We cannot distinguish between two possible explanations of this result. Either our new measure (NC) is a poor proxy for the influence of industry comments on EPA rulemaking, or else the comments themselves do not affect EPA since their content was already being conveyed by groups within EPA, such as the Economic Analysis Division and the Office of Enforcement.

Like the comments results, our regressions showed industry trade association budgets (TAB) to have little relationship to the stringency of industry standards. This result may indicate that trade associations are ineffective in influencing EPA rulemaking. More likely it reflects the unsatisfactory nature of our budget variable as a proxy for the influence of trade associations on regulatory decisionmaking.

The market power hypothesis is supported by the BOD but not by the TSS data. While the BOD results only hint that more concentrated industries (CR4) are better organized to oppose stringent standards, no strong conclusions should be drawn. The hypothesis may be untrue, or the concentration ratio data may be too aggregated to provide a good measure of market power. Turning to a related hypothesis, both the BOD and TSS results weakly support the conclusion that more profitable firms (higher ROR) spend more resources to resist stringent regulations than do less profitable companies. The results show the influence of profitability to be strongest before final promulgation, but they should be interpreted cautiously due to the inaccuracy of the highly aggregated ROR data.

The final external signals hypothesis concerns the extent to which wastewater flow (WF) and raw waste load (RWLB, RWLT) affect regulatory decisions. The wastewater flow results generally support the hypothesis that WF, acting as a proxy for abatement costs, did cause EPA to set less stringent standards for higher flows (i.e., cost). The BOD and TSS raw waste load results together do not support the hypothesis that higher RWLB and RWLT reflect higher costs and therefore cause weaker standards. However, the lack of consistency with both these hypotheses comes from the less reliable TSS data, so the positive wastewater flow results should probably be accorded more credence.

Internal Theories

Both the BOD and TSS data provide strong support for the hypothesis that higher quality technical and economic information (DDQ, EAQ) leads to more stringent standards. The hypothesis about the turnover of key personnel (PT) causing loss of information was also strongly supported, thus requiring EPA to issue weaker standards. Taken together, the clear support for both hypotheses confirms the central importance of high quality information in the regulatory process.

The ORDER results are puzzling, for at the contractor level both the BOD and TSS data confirm the hypothesis that industries regulated later were given weaker standards. However, over the two periods (C-P and P-R) no systematic pattern of weakening was shown. Overall, the data does not provide convincing support for the hypothesis, except at the contractor stage.

The NRP hypothesis about BOD (or TSS) being the controlling pollutant was also not clearly confirmed. The BOD results provide weak support, with the TSS results offering no support, for the hypothesis that more pollutants cause attention to be diverted from BOD (or TSS), making them less likely to be changed.

Finally, our BOD results provide reasonably strong support for the organizational learning hypotheses that tight standards are relaxed more than weak standards and that a large percentage of weakening in the C-P period ise followed by smaller changes in the P-R period. Unfortunately, the TSS results do not confirm those for BOD, calling for caution in accepting these hypotheses.

CONCLUSIONS

This study demonstrates that a statistical evaluation of regulatory agency decisions can be a useful tool for identifying the implicit decision rules used to promulgate standards. The biggest problem with the approach appears to be the cost of data gathering for both data on the regulations and data on the factors that influence regulatory decisions. Government publications, such as the Federal Register and agency technical support documents, provide much help, but other sources are often difficult to find and they sometimes present data on firms at different levels of aggregation of firms than that used by the regulatory agencies.

Despite this caveat, we did discover several significant impacts on EPA's "best practicable technology" standards. The quality of supporting data was shown to affect strongly the agency's willingness and ability to promulgate stringent standards, a finding with important implications for rulemaking reform. Equity issues, such as the size of plant, also appeared to play a role. The enabling legislation required EPA to consider economic costs in setting standards, and our evidence supports EPA's compliance with this directive. Of more interest, transitory economic impacts (primarily unemployment) were revealed to be an important factor, suggesting that Executive Order 12291 (Federal Register, February 17, 1981) may not be easy to implement. This order directs real resource costs to be balanced against benefits, while recognizing that the agency must continue to consider transitory impacts, such as unemployment, closures, and price increases, to the extent required by the law. Given the political pressures to focus on short-term impacts and the patterns of cost analysis developed by EPA over the last decade (for which unemployment and perhaps closures are important), our study suggests some difficulty in achieving the order's emphasis on real resource costs.

Several issues need further research. We found some support for the hypotheses about organizational learning, but more study is needed to understand why this phenomenon occurs. Better data characterizing trade association power and industry comments' influence are needed to sort out the reasons for the ambiguous results concerning these hypotheses. Finally, more indirect measures of political power, such as environment group ratings of legislators, may provide some insights into the environmental side of the process.

NOTES

The authors would like to thank Henry M. Peskin for his assistance and the Sloan Foundation for its generous support of a larger research project at Resources for the Future from which the material in this chapter is taken.

1. The Natural Resources Defense Council did force EPA onto a schedule for promulgating effluent guidelines. See the settlement in NRDC v. Train (1973), 6 ERC 1033.
2. Space does not allow us to discuss the other important decision of industry subcategorization — this is how EPA divided all plants in an industry category into subcategories, each with a separate and often different set of standards.
3. BOD is a commonly used measure of the organic content of wastes discharged into water.
4. All the percentage change variables (CPB, CPT, PRB, PRT, CRB, and CRT) are defined so that positive values reflect a weakening of the standard. Note that equation (2) must necessarily be determined by equations (1), (3), and (4), while equation (5) can be derived from equations (3) and (4).
5. Standards for another eighteen industries, denoted as Group Two, were subsequently issued.
6. We note that if small plants have higher marginal costs than other plants, it is also efficient to weaken their standards while tightening those on the other plants.

7. Within any subcategory the number of plants subject to the subcategory BPT standards (NP) includes all plants discharging wastes into water bodies other than municipal treatment plants (those plants were subject to pretreatment standards instead) that were not already meeting the standards. The exernal signals model predicts that more plants would have created more negative opposition to EPA regulation, causing the standards to have been weakened (given nonparticipation by environmentalists). However, the regression results fail to confirm this hypothesis.
8. Note that less profitable firms can borrow money to finance these same activities, but the cost of funds may be higher.
9. The four cases of project officer turnover (out of twenty-three industries in our sample) included both voluntary and involuntary personnel changes with no obvious common thread linking the reasons for the personnel change, so we have no reason to suspect that PT represents the effect of some other colinear variable.
10. The Economic Analysis Division was located in the Office of Planning and Management (not in the Water Office with EGD), and was composed primarily of MBAs concerned chiefly with the economic impacts of the regulations upon industrial plant closures, employment, and price increases.
11. Modification usually meant weakening of the standards.
12. For two reasons we expected the TSS regressions to contain more noise and therefore yield less conclusive results than the BOD regressions. First, the engineering problem of controlling BOD discharges is much more similar from one industry to another than is the TSS engineering control problem. Second, unlike BOD discharges, TSS emissions sometimes served as a proxy for the level of other more difficult to measure pollutants that were controlled through the same technologies.
13. Economic **costs** reflect the use of real resources to abate pollution, while economic **impacts**, such as unemployment, plant closures, and price increases, measure only transitory costs that are of primary concern because of their distributional consequences.

REFERENCES

Belsley, David A., Edwin Kuh, and Roy E. Welsch. 1980. Regression Diagnostics: Identifying Influential Data and Sources of Colinearity (New York: John Wiley and Sons).

Cyert, Richard M., and James G. March. 1963. A Behavioral Theory of the Firm (Englewood Cliffs, N.J.: Prentice-Hall).

Downs, Anthony. 1967. Inside Bureaucracy (Boston: Little, Brown).

Joskow, Paul L. 1972. "The Determination of the Allowed Rate of Return in a Formal Regulatory Hearing," Bell Journal of Economics and Management 3, no. 2: 632-644.

Krupnick, Alan J., Winston Harrington, Wesley A. Magat, and Henry M. Peskin. 1982. "Federal Regulation: Statistical Analysis," Discussion Paper D-94, Resources for the Future, Washington, D.C.

McFadden, Daniel. 1975. "The Revealed Preferences of a Government Bureaucracy: Theory," Bell Journal of Economics and Management 6, no. 2: p. 401-416.

McFadden, Daniel. 1976. "The Revealed Preferences of a Government Bureaucracy: Empirical Evidence," Bell Journal of Economics and Management 7, no. 1: p. 55-72.

Mitnick, Barry M. 1980. The Political Economy of Regulation (New York: Columbia University Press).

Noll, Roger. 1976. "Government Administrative Behavior and Private Sector Response: A Multidisciplinary Survey." California Institute of Technology, Social Science Working Paper No. 62 (October).

Peltzman, Sam. 1976. "Toward a More General Theory of Regulation," Journal of Law and Economics 19, no. 2: 211-240.

Simon, Herbert A. 1957. Models of Man (New York: John Wiley and Sons).

Stigler, George T. 1971. "The Theory of Economic Regulation," Bell Journal of Economics and Management Science 2, no. 1: 3-21.

II
DETAILED STUDIES OF ONE COUNTRY

THE ROLE OF THE BRITISH ALKALI AND CLEAN AIR INSPECTORATE IN AIR POLLUTION CONTROL **5**

Michael Hill

INTRODUCTION

The British Alkali Inspectorate is responsible for air pollution control policy implementation with respect to most of the major industrial emitters. It operates with a statutory framework that provides very considerable administrative discretion. In short, emitters are required to use the "best practicable means" (bpm) to eliminate or, if that is not possible, render safe emissions. What bpm implies for each process is determined by the Inspectorate after a negotiation procedure involving the main interests. This is published but has no statutory force; it is likely that the courts will find for the Inspectorate in the event of any legal action, in which it claims failure to use bpm, but that has been little tested. The relationship between the Inspectorate and individual emitters is a private one in which bpm is used as a standard to be reached by new processes at the outset. When bpm is updated existing processes are given time to meet the new requirements. However, in each case, since bpm consists of an elaborate code to be applied to individual circumstances, many aspects of the determination of the right fit between its requirements and technological realities must often involve negotiation and trial and error.

A regulatory system that rests upon two related sequences of private consultations designed to protect trade secrets and maximize adaption of enforcement to individual circumstances, the first to determine bpm for collective processes and the second to relate it to an individual plant, is naturally hard to investigate. The Inspectorate is hardly likely to give a researcher access to information denied to all other outsiders. When having, therefore, to include the activities of the British Alkali Inspectorate in a comparative European study of the making and implementation of sulphur dioxide air pollution prevention policy, the author was forced to adopt an approach that inadequately fulfilled the requirements laid down by the overall directors of the study at the International Institute for Environment and Society (IIUG) in Berlin. In any case a system so complex and flexible did not allow for the quantitative study of the relationship between emission permits and actual behavior, even where such data might have been provided by regulatory agencies and emitters were the veil of secrecy to be lifted. Regulation just does not operate in such a way. The study instead consisted of the detailed examination of what the Alkali Inspectorate says in its annual reports, the scrutiny of comments from its critics, and interviews of actors involved with the system. The chief alkali inspector and one of his assistants commented in detail on a first draft of the report, and granted a very lengthy interview, but they necessarily dealt with the general description of the system and not its application to individual cases. This chapter is based upon these sources.

THE STATUTORY FRAMEWORK

The work of the Alkali Inspectorate involves the regulation of most of the more complex processes that produce chemical emissions to the air within England and Wales. There is a similar body for Scotland, the Industrial Pollution Inspectorate, with substantially the same responsibilities. The latter will not be discussed here.

The Alkali Inspectorate was formed in 1863 and reported directly to a minister (most recently the Secretary of State for the Environment) until the end of 1974. In 1975 it was brought within the Health and Safety Executive, a quasi-autonomous body responsible to the Health and Safety Commission. Despite the fact that the latter is responsible to the Secretary of State for Employment, the Inspectorate continues to report "through the Executive" to the Secretary of State for the Environment.

The legal framework for the work of the Alkali Inspectorate currently sounds rather complicated because of the incomplete transition from the statutory framework that applied before 1974. The position until 1974 was that the Inspectorate operated under the Alkali etc. Works Regulation Act 1906, as amended by the Clean Air Act 1956 and by a number of Alkali etc. Works Orders of which the most important recent ones were enacted in 1966 and 1971. In 1974, two new Acts of Parliament, the Health and Safety at Work etc. Act and the Control of Pollution Act, partly superceded the 1906 Act, while not altering its basic content. Subsequent Regulations under Section Five of the Health and Safety Act were expected to continue this process of updating the legislation, but for the time being the 1906 Act remains partly in force.

HISTORICAL BACKGROUND

The first Alkali Act was enacted in 1863 as a result of concern by landowners about the damage being done to the countryside nearby factories established in the Merseyside and Tyneside areas which emitted large quantities of hydrogen chloride in the course of the manufacture of soda. It was recognized that the preexisting Smoke Prevention Acts could not deal with this problem. The initial Act set an emission standard and allowed for the appointment of an inspector, to be supported by subinspectors, to enforce the Act by taking action for the recovery of civil damages if appropriate.

The inspector appointed was an eminent industrial chemist, Robert Angus Smith. His response to his task embodied three important features. First, he was aware that comparatively little scientific advice was available to the emitters. Therefore, he saw the Inspectorate's role as providing help to companies in meeting the statutory standards, and not to immediately have recourse to the prosecution weapon. In fact, there was available a technique for converting the waste products of this industry into commercial bleach. Hence, by a happy chance, which rarely again characterized emission control, the new regulatory agency was able to steer the regulatee into a profitable commercial venture while achieving the necessary abatement. Second, he recognized that progress would have to rest upon the development of new emission monitoring and control practices (MacLeod).

Third, and leading on from this activity, the Inspectorate became aware of other chemical emission problems. Hence it initiated a pattern of government growth similar to that noted by historians of other inspectorial activities (see MacDonagh, 1961; Roberts, 1960). An Act of 1868 continued the initial legislation indefinitely. It had originally been enacted for a trial five-year period, and an Amendment Act of 1874 extended regulation to all alkali works producing "noxious gases." The latter included sulfuric acid, nitric acid, sulfuretted hydrogen, and chlorine. In making this extension, Parliament required alkali makers to use the "best practicable means" to prevent the escape of noxious gases. The concept of best practicable means had been used in other public health legislation, notably in relation to smoke control, but in a slightly different way , i.e., as something to which a manufacturer could appeal in his own defense. Hence, as Rhodes (1981) points out:

> Smoke and river pollution operated by means of a simple prohibition which it was open to the person to challenge, whereas the alkali legislation in theory left the challenge to the enforcing agency to claim in effect that the owner had failed to use the bpm.

Robert Angus Smith (see MacLeod) saw best practicable means as an elastic concept to be used only until fixed standards were established. However, after legislation in 1881 that did this for a couple of processes, this evolutionary procedure stopped, and it became the accepted view that it was better not to try to amend the statutes in this way but rather to work with non-statutory presumptive limits. Today there are only fixed legal limits for emissions of hydrogen chloride (the original target of the legislation) and sulfuric acid (imposed in 1881). But presumptive limits, used as indicative measures within the context of emission control in relation to best practicable means have been developed for a considerable number of emissions.

The early Alkali Acts of the nineteenth century were consolidated in the Alkali etc. Works Regulation Act of 1906, containing a schedule of carefully defined industrial processes and a list of "noxious or offensive gases" to be the concern of the Alkali Inspectorate. Since 1906 the list of scheduled processes has been considerably extended. The growth of the list, and particularly extensive additions made in 1958, has led to a growth in the size of the Inspectorate.

The Alkali Inspectorate, then, has a long history. Its name is a misleading survival from the past. The two other most significant features were developed a hundred years ago: its use of the best practicable means approach to regulation and its emphasis upon working **with** industry while keeping the prosecution power very much as a weapon of last resort.

STAFFING AND ORGANIZATION

According to the 1979 report of the Health and Safety Executive, Industrial Air Pollution, there were, at the end of that year, forty-seven inspectors. There was a headquarters staff of a chief inspector, three deputy chief inspectors, and three technical assistants (alkali inspectors). The remaining forty were divided between fifteen districts with a district inspector in charge of each district. There were also six sampling teams, each of them having two technical officers. There was also a limited number of support staff.

The picture therefore is of a district Inspector with one, sometimes two, assistants in each region, able to call upon the services of a sampling team. To put it another way, there is a "field level" inspector for about every fifty registered works.

In the 1973 Annual Report (1974) the relationship between the chief inspector and the field staff was described as follows:

> The Chief Inspector, with the help of his deputies, lays down the broad national policies and provided they

> keep within their broad lines, inspectors in the field have plenty of flexibility to take into account local circumstances and make suitable decisions. They are given plenty of autonomy and are trained as a team of decision-takers with as much responsibility and authority as possible. Nonetheless, they keep the head office staff well informed about the works under their control, so that the information can be assessed, compared and disseminated as necessary. It helps to formulate new policies, which are regularly discussed at annual staff meetings when all the inspectors from the United Kingdom gather for a three-day meeting and exchange notes.

The picture is therefore of a professional pattern of organization, combining autonomy with solidarity.

THE PATTERN OF WORK

The 1973 Annual Report of the chief inspector contained the following picture of the routine work of the Inspectorate:

> In practice, inspectors make routine, unannounced visits to inspect registered processes and to carry out their own emission tests where necessary. At least two visits per year are made to even the smallest, least offensive works under the inspectorate's control and at least eight visits per year to what are known as 'major potential offenders'. Usually far more visits than the minimum are carried out, many of a special nature to discuss developments and improvements with top management officials. All inspectors carry with them fairly simple sampling and analysing equipment which is used to check emissions to compare results with those of the works . . . .

This picture was confirmed by our interviews with emitters. A lead works, the subject of considerable local controversy, received visits at least once a month, other plants experienced much less regular surveillance. In 1979, according to the Inpsectorate's annual report, 14,099 visits were made to the 1,960 registered works. That is an average of 300 visits per inspector, or 7.2 visits per works. The annual reports mention many other activities, including special sampling, the careful study of particular industrial problems and a variety of educational and public relations tasks.

The statutes determining the work of the Alkali Inspectorate define industrial processes that are to be regulated. These are known as the scheduled processes. Works containing such processes have to be registered with the Inspectorate. Hence confusion can arise about the distinction between registered works and scheduled processes and there may also be processes that are not under Inspectorate surveillance. In 1979 there were 2,884 separate processes under Alkali Inspectorate surveillance. These included a large number of chemical processes, the more complex metal smelting proceses, the manufacture of electricity, the production of coke and smokeless fuels, oil refining and related processes, cement works, and aluminium works.

THE CONCEPT OF "BEST PRACTICABLE MEANS"

The modern Health and Safety at Work etc. Act of 1974 places the owners of registered works under a duty:

> to use the best practicable means for preventing the emission into the atmosphere from the premises of noxious or offensive substances and for rendering harmless and inoffensive such substances as may be so emitted.

But in order to understand what this really means, several issues need to be considered: namely, the position of the Alkali Inspectorate in interpreting bpm; the use made of both technical and economic considerations; the relationship between "preventing" and "rendering harmless" in the law; the concern with both overall technology and operating practice; the flexible character of bpm over time.

The Fifth Report of the Royal Commission on Environmental Pollution (1976) pointed out that:

> Although the law does not appear to say so explicitly, "best practicable means" is generally interpreted as "best practicable means to the satisfaction of the Alkali Inspectorate".

This position seems so far to have been left unclarified by the courts, which have also not explicitly interpreted the concept. The leading legal textbook in this field points out that only certain related expressions in other legislation - "all practicable measures" and "so far as is practicable" - have been elucidated in "reported decisions of the superior courts" (Garner and Crow, 1976). These decisions emphasized "the duty to have regard to the state of knowledge at the time and particularly to the knowledge of scientific people" (Garner and Crow, 1976). But in the case of bpm the Alkali Inspectorate seems to have been accepted as the arbiter of that "state of knowledge," having taken care to consult industry and other interested parties (see discussion on notes on bpm below).

The statement of the bpm principle in the law does not clarify the relationship between technical and economic considerations. Some other legal uses of it have done so. In particular in the section on the Control of Pollution Act 1974 dealing with noise it is stated that:

> "Practicable" means reasonably practicable having regard among other things to local conditions and circumstances, to the current state of technical knowledge and to the financial implications.

In his statement on this issue in 1973 (Annual Report, 1974: p. 11) the chief inspector pointed out:

> I have often said, and been criticised for it, that if money were unlimited there would be few problems of air pollution control which could not be solved technically. In this statement can be included the supply of manpower and material resources. We have the technical knowledge to absorb gases, arrest grit, dust and fumes, and prevent smoke formation. The chief reason why we still permit the escape of these pollutants is because economics are an important part of the word "practicable". A lot of our problems are cheque book rather than technical, and attitudes which take little account of the economics of scarce resources, on which there are many claims, can so easily get priorities out of perspective.

It is recognized that the first requirement of the law is that noxious emission should, as far as is practicable, be **prevented.** Only when this cannot readily be done does the second consideration, that they should be **rendered harmless**, come into play. Thus, the policy of dispersion through high chimneys is not the **primary** control device for industrial emissions under the laws administered by the Alkali Inspectorate. The 1973 report (Annual Report, 1974) put it like this:

> The alternatives of prevention or dispersion are not offered to industry. The inspectorate only considers dispersion when the best practicable means of prevention have been fully explored.

Section 27 of the Alkali Act 1906, as amended by Section 5(2) of the Health and Safety at Work Act, amplifies bpm by reference:

> not only to the provision and the efficient maintenance of appliances adequate for preventing such escape (of noxious gases) but also to the manner in which such appliances are used and to the proper supervision, by the owner of any operation in which such gases are evolved.

Hence, notes on bpm for individual industries contain guidance on "good housekeeping" in the day to day operation of plants and inspection is seen as concerned, among other things, with this issue.

An essential feature of the bpm approach to pollution control is that it allows for evolution over time. This is presented as one of its virtues, but it also provides ammunition for the Inspectorate's critics. As new abatement technologies develop and as industrial activities change, the regulatory process can continuously adapt to new circumstances. But the process of change involves two ingredients: change in the accepted criteria for the best practicable means as embodied in the notes published by the Inspectorate after negotiation with industry, and change in the ways those criteria are applied to individual firms. Critics of the Inspectorate see the first kind of change as involving a consensual negotiating process that always lags behind enforcement possibilities. But it may be questioned whether the redetermination of statutorily enforceable standards would proceed any faster.

The problem with the second kind of change is the fact that the Inspectorate obviously has to differentiate between the way it relates to new plants and the way it relates to existing ones. A newly established bpm will apply immediately to new plants and to new process units, replacements, enlargements, and any significant modifications to equipment in existing plants. Otherwise, the normal rule with regard to existing plants involves gradual upgrading, taking account of the need for equipment to complete its "economic life." This policy has been criticized by Social Audit, who allege that many firms in fact secure "expanding deadlines" (Social Audit, 1974: p. 12-13). There seem to be, so our local studies suggest, particular problems at a time of economic stagnation with both industries and firms with an uncertain economic future. In the former category come coking plants, using processes developed a long while ago, operating in a declining market, and likely to be replaced in the long run by new processes that make gas from coal. In the latter category come many medium and small metal manufacturing plants whose fortunes are dependent on the success of the British motor industry.

The main general considerations that affect the determination and enforcement of bpm have been outlined above. In doing so reference has been made to the "notes on bpm" prepared by the Inspectorate for each major emitter category. The process by which these are settled is described in the Alkali Inspectorate's 1973 Report (Annual Report, 1974: p. 12) as follows:

> Working parties and discussion groups are set up, consisting of representatives of the industry, its research organisation, if any, and the inspectorate. Outside specialist bodies are consulted when necessary and when available. The emissions are investigated by the partners, including the routes by which pollutants reach their targets, research and development being carried out by the industrial side with their own specialists and at their own expense and with inspectors holding a watching brief. The inspectorate frequently travels abroad, sometimes in company with industry representatives, to examine foreign technology. Results are reported to both the industry and the inspectorate. The chief inspector makes the final decision on any standards and other requirements, for he is ultimately responsible, but this only follows mutual discussions with industry representatives, whose approval is gained if possible.

More recently the Trades Union Congress, the Department of the Environment, and the Institution of Environmental Health Officers have been added to the parties consulted, but their actual input to the process seems so far to have been rather low. Once settled the "notes on bpm" are made available to the public. These notes are often elaborate, running to several pages and including guidance on good "housekeeping practice" within an industry as well as upon abatement technology.

In the application of best practicable means to individual enterprises the Inspectorate will have regard to local circumstances. These will include topographical considerations and the presence of other industry as well as special features of the regulated plant. Notes on best practicable means often contain two elements that merit further comment: "presumptive emission values" and "chimney height rules."

A discussion of presumptive emission values was provided by Dr. Mahler, at that time a deputy chief alkali inspector, at the 1966 International Clean Air Congress. Dr. Mahler stressed that "the setting of presumptive standards is entirely at the discretion of the Chief Alkali Inspector."

Dr. Mahler's emphasis on discretion is underlined in a more recent paper by another inspector (Health and Safety Executive, 1980):

> The requirement to use the best practicable means **operates continuously**, at all levels of emission, and the presumptive limit is the **maximum** that the Inspector will normally accept **as confirmation** that the best practicable means are being used. (author's emphasis)

In his paper, having stated that "No emission discharged in such amount or manner as to constitute a demonstrable health hazard in either the short or long term can be tolerated," Dr. Mahler went on to state a mixture of qualitative considerations, raising the issue of the balance between technical possibilities and cost discussed above and harder sounding scientific consideration. The latter included a formula for calculating chimney heights and relating them to emission rates and resulting ground level concentrations. In this formula the concentration danger levels accepted by the Factory Inspectorate are normally based upon the threshold limit values set for use in the United States by the American Conference of Government Industrial Hygienists.

There is, then, a complicated relationship between presumptive emission levels and chimney heights. Dr. Mahler described the final choice of chimney heights as "in practice arrived at by a blend of mathematics and the Inspectorate's experience of chimney heights that have produced acceptable conditions for given emissions in the past."

In concluding this long section on best practicable means it is worth reminding ourselves that its operation has two aspects that may be described as standard setting and implementation. The determination of "notes on best practicable means" and "presumptive emission limits" may be described as standard setting, their application to individual firms as implementation. But, the distinction normally made perceives the former as a policy-making stage subject to an open political process and resulting in the writing of standards into the law. Neither of these features are present in this case, the generalized bpm decisions are reached after private discussions. They are not legally binding, but might be produced in a court of law to prove that the Inspectorate is observing the spirit of the laws.

A justification for the discretionary character of the Inspectorate's enforcement standards has been offered by a chief alkali inspector as follows (Annual Report, 1974: p. 8):

> The concept of best practicable means is ageless and I submit that those who criticise it as being out-of-date because it was conceived many years ago, are really criticising the standards and requirements which have been set under it and the toughness of their implementation by the inspectorate. Best practicable means — or to give it its abbreviation of "b. p. m." — can always be modern if it is used properly. I have heard it said by a well-known authority from abroad, who has studied the international environmental control scene very carefully for the last 17 years, that when one applies all the so-called modern concepts of control, attempting to apply scientific principles and ideas on a grand scale, making use of computers, telemetering, air quality criteria, etc., one finally ends up with b. p. m.

What this seems to imply is that bpm is necessary because what is involved is the application of generalized standards to a complex scientific field. This accords with one of the arguments for administrative discretion identified by Jowell (1973), which is valuable where the concern of policy is with standards which are not susceptible to precise factual definition. He argues "the feature of standards that distinguishes them from rules is their flexibility and susceptibility to change over time." But what also seems present here are some unresolved political questions, and thus a situation that the author has elsewhere identified as a source of official discretion, in which complex political dilemmas are left as operational questions to be settled by public officials (see Hill, 1969: pp. 85-86; Rhodes, 1981: 154). This seems to be how Rhodes sees the position of the Alkali Inspectorate and explains its exposure to public criticism in recent years:

> The logic of its interpretation of what was intended by bpm has drawn it into considering, and answering — by default as much as anything else — questions which are essentially political in character. Questions like "How

> much can this industry — or this plant — afford to spend on anti-pollution measures?" or "If we insist on this particular measure will it force certain firms out of business and how therefore can we measure the resulting unemployment against the benefits of reducing pollution?" followed naturally from the inspectorate's cooperative approach to industry. In finding answers it has implicitly been deciding not only what degree of pollution is tolerable but at how fast a rate pollution should be diminished.

Rhodes goes on to explain the vulnerability of the Inspectorate to criticism partly in terms of the attempt to solve political questions with technological expertise, and partly in terms of its lack of economic expertise.

Regulatory Activities: Infractions and Prosecutions

The Annual Reports of the Inspectorate include data on infractions of the law and on prosecutions. In 1979 eighty-four infractions were reported and seven prosecutions were heard. There was a steady growth of reported infractions during the 1970s. There was also slight evidence of a greater propensity to prosecute. During the 1970s as a whole fifty-three prosecutions were completed.

The infraction statistics will probably not bear detailed scrutiny. It is far from clear under what circumstances inspectors report precise infractions, in relation to their general concern to improve standards by informal means. Furthermore, discovery of infractions is a haphazard process depending upon the intermittent visits of inspectors.

The Social Audit report discusses the Inspectorate's stance on infractions, quoting their 1952 report as pointing out that there is "no well defined dividing line between legal and illegal operation, and a decision as to whether a given set of conditions shall or shall not be treated as an infraction rests, to a great extent, with the District Inspector" (Social Audit, 1974).

Social Audit (1974) goes on to outline two reported cases where ". . . in one case a negligent works was threatened with prosecution and then took action to deal with the problem. In the second case there were also genuine technical difficulties — but no enforcement action was suggested. This works, which may have been causing as much or more local nuisance than the first, was allowed for economic reasons, to continue production." Social Audit also suggests that the stances of chief inspectors may make a difference. They point out how identified infractions fell in the middle fifties after the retirement of a long-serving chief inspector.

The Social Audit report particularly criticized the Alkali Inspectorate for a reluctance to use sanctions. One of these is "the theoretical power to close down an unsatisfactory works by refusing to renew its certificate of registration." They comment that the Inspectorate has never acknowledged this, reporting the following statement on this issue by the chief inspector:

> Once a works was accepted for registration under the Alkali Act annual renewal of the certificate would not be refused because a works did not continue to use the "best practicable means". On the contrary, the Inspectorate would be failing in its duty if it allowed such a thing to happen. (Mr. F. Ireland speaking at the Clean Air Conference, 1963.)

The other sanction is, of course, prosecution. The Social Audit report comments on the increase in the number of prosecutions in the late sixties and early seventies. From 1920 to 1966 there were only two prosecutions, but in the period 1967 to 1972 there were twelve successful prosecutions. As shown above prosecutions continued to increase in the 1970s.

Social Audit (1974: p. 19) suggests that much prosecution involves "stamping on mini-polluters." They point out that the rise in prosecutions in the 1960s involved particularly an attack on cable burners — metal recovery activities being carried out by small entrepreneurs operating often on waste land and seeking to evade registration. Our more recent data gave a similar impression. Social Audit describes this as "a policy-style operation most untypical of the Inspectorate" and contrasts it with the essentially "educational" approach adopted to large industry. They report:

> We asked Mr. Ireland what would happen if the same strict policy were applied to the other classes of registered works . . . . He replied that this would be quite unnecessary since large firms, concerned for their public image, will go to almost any lengths to avoid prosecution. "If we had to prosecute ICI, for example," Mr. Ireland conjectured, "heads would roll right, left and centre for the disgrace of it."

Inspection of recent reports shows that the description of the prosecution activities of the Inspectorate by Social Audit remains accurate. Metal recovery works have continued throughout the 1970s to be the main target.

The Royal Commission in Environmental Pollution broadly endorsed the Inspectorate's stance on the use of prosecution in terms of the importance of the cooperative relationship with industry.

> An aggressive policy of confrontation, involving prosecution for every lapse, would destroy this basis for co-operation; it would harden attitudes and dispose industry to resist the imposition of costly programmes for pollution abatement . . . . Industry is generally aware of its responsibilities in pollution control. If a firm has installed control equipment to the satisfaction of the Alkali Inspectorate and is striving by all reasonable means to maintain its emissions at an acceptable level, there is little to be gained by prosecution in the event of a pollution incident arising from, say, an unforeseeable breakdown of equipment. (Interpretation, 1976: para. 227):
>
> It should be noted, too, that prosecution is not the only sanction. Industry, and especially large industry, is concerned about its public image on environmental matters. Public opinion, expressed through complaints by local authorities, Parliamentary Questions, and so forth can be an effective sanction.

THE ALKALI INSPECTORATE AND THE PUBLIC

A key ingredient of criticism of the Alkali Inspectorate has been that it is an inaccessible, secretive, and uncommunicative organization. Some of this criticism is concerned principally with the legal structure within which it works, some with the way in which it is organized, and some with the way in which it chooses to operate. The earlier sections have dealt with these latter issues to some degree, particularly with the first two of the three points. In looking at the relationship with the public attention will be focused principally on the third, but in places it will be impossible to separate this from the other two. The contemporary operating style of the Inspectorate is clearly to some degree a function of the way the legal structure has been interpreted and the way the organization has been developed.

Any regulatory agency with a staff as small as the Alkali Inspectorate must be dependent to some degree on public complaints to initiate action. In the case of the Inspectorate this raises the problem that some of the emissions most dangerous to the public can be neither seen nor smelt, while some of the things about which people complain may be, relatively speaking, harmless. The case of cement dust emissions that forms a large part of the case-study material used in the Social Audit critique of the Inspectorate provides a good case in point. While in no way wishing to imply that it does not matter — a continual fall of dust upon people, washing, gardens, etc. is most unpleasant — the Inspectorate must have to make difficult decisions about the way it deploys its scarce manpower between dealing with issues like this and dealing with a variety of less visible but more noxious emissions.

In its Annual Report the Inspectorate provides some information about public complaints. There were 463 of these in 1979. A relatively similar total was received annually during the earlier years of the seventies.

In its 1978 Annual Report the Inspectorate made the following further observation of its data about complaints against registered processes: "About sixty of the complaints could be classified as attributable to dust or the 'physical' effects of smoke and fume, and the remainder to smell and 'chemical' aspects of fumes."

Cement works do come out high as complained about relative to their numbers. But in 1979 there was only one recorded infraction by these works. The campaign against metal recovery works seems justified by public complaints. However it is interesting to note in this case that in 1979 the number of infractions (thirty) was considerably in excess of the number of complaints (twelve). Several major causes of complaints hardly figure at all in the list of works responsible for infractions — electricity works, gas and coke works, chemical fertilizer works, and iron and steel works, are the prime examples.

The Alkali Inspectorate has come in for heavy criticism as a secretive organization. Our own failure to secure an opportunity to look at the enforcement work of the Inspectorate in any detail can only lead us to agree that this criticism is well founded. The issue of whether it is justifiable or not must rest upon an interpretation of the relationship the Inspectorate enjoys with industry. The annual reports provide only generalized data. Even firms that have been successfully prosecuted are not always named.

Social Audit similarly criticizes the Inspectorate for not giving information on emissions or details on situations in which firms have been allowed to operate at below "best practicable means" standards.

The Fifth Report of the Royal Commission on Environmental Pollution made a series of recommendations on these issues, as follows:

> the controlling authorities should be able to release data on emission to the public;
>
> when a firm has been notified of a breach of requirements the fact should be made public;
>
> registration of works should take the form of the "issue of consents", with "conditions defining the bpm for the works", available for consultation by the public (Fifth Report, 1976).

Since the Royal Commission reported, the only change in the situation is that part IV of the Control of Pollution Act 1974 has been brought into force. This enables the local government to provide emission data for the public, including but not exceeding the data made available by firms to the Alkali Inspectorate. Firms are safeguarded by a right of appeal to the Secretary of State that data revealing trade secrets should not be disclosed. There is also a provision requiring local authorities proposing to implement the Act to set up a consultative committee on which local industry and the Alkali Inspectorate are represented. In fact this provision has not, except to the most insignificant extent in a handful of authorities, been implemented. What is, however, most significant about this legislation is that while public criticism was of the secrecy of the Alkali Inspectorate the Act gave disclosure **powers** but not **duties** to the local authorities (Levitt, 1980).

The main response of the Alkali Inspectorate to criticism that it is uncommunicative, apart from a series of generalized public presentations of national policy from which this report has quoted freely, has been to support or accept the setting up of local liaison committees serviced by the local authorities where specific emissions are a cause for complaint. The Social Audit report (1974: 25-26) is skeptical about them:

> The Inspectorate's solution to the problem of informing the public has been to encourage the formation of local liaison committees in which representatives of the troublesome factory, the local authority, the Inspectorate, and, occasionally, members of the public, meet twice yearly for what Mr. Ireland describes as "frank confrontation". The real value of these committees has been questioned. They may provide some information (though they are under no obligation to do so) and ample opportunity for a heated situation to cool down. Public complaints which might

> otherwise have reached Ministerial level are in this way diverted.

From our limited experience we can make two comments on this view. First, a distinction should be made between committees providing for consultation between experts and officials and committees involving the public. While the above quotation implies that the former prevail, this is probably not so much the case today. The Inspectorate's list, however, does not make this distinction. However, inasmuch as the former is the case, and the participants in the liaison activity are regarded as privileged and bound to respect confidences, there is good ground for skepticism about the progress made toward public consultation. Hence, the 1976 Annual Report quotes, with what could well be regarded as misleading satisfaction, views expressed by an ICI manager:

> Until five years ago industry had tended to set itself apart. No one was convinced of anyone else's integrity. More recently two liaison committees covering the quarrying area near Buxton had been set up by the Alkali Inspectorate. These bring together the quarrying companies, public health officers and interested persons. There were few rules. The chairmanship was shared between the industry and the people. Although the public were entitled to know what went on, no good purpose would be served by selective reporting of controversial items. The two chairmen therefore approved statements which went to the district council and the press. Each member was bound not to abuse the confidence of the free discussion which had thereby become possible. When meetings were attended by responsible people, industry could and did respond openly. Now companies were prepared to disclose information which five years ago would not have been considered possible.

Who were those "interested persons" and who did they represent? How could they represent interests satisfactorily if bound to secrecy? What is the difference between "selective reporting" and the presentation to the press of jointly "approved statements"?

Students of public participation have highlighted in recent years the need to recognize a distinction between consultation involving the giving of information and consultation involving shared decisionmaking. The evidence available about liaison committees suggest they fall very much into the first category. Two of the liaison committees we have come across have faced problems with inadequate public participation. They have been kept going because the emitters regard them as worthwhile. How much is public involvement limited because people who are dissatisfied with environmental conditions want something done, not information? There is a limit to the appeal of regular meetings that provide reasons why things are not being done. Some of the local authorities that have not implemented part IV of the Control of Pollution Act similarly feel that there is little point in information sharing exercises if nothing is likely to be done. Hence, this second comment should be read not so much as a comment upon the Alkali Inspectorate's approach to information sharing as upon the emphasis given by the pressure groups in the late-1960s-early-1970s period to this subject. Clearly it was their intention that information sharing would somehow help to politicize, to intensify pressure for new control measures. There is no evidence that it has done this.

CONCLUSION

The standard criticism of the British system is that because it is private and discretionary the regulatory agency is in the control of the regulatees. The Alkali Inspectorate argues against this that, on the contrary, it can achieve much more effective pollution control through a system that is sensitively adapted to technological realities than through one that depends upon fixed and rigid standards and formal legal battles in the courts. The latter is likely to involve either the setting of standards at levels of emission well above those achievable in many cases or a marked enforcement deficit. The British system maximizes control and minimizes that disrespect for administrative action that arises where political goals and practical implementation achievements are markedly out of line.

The absence of hard data makes it impossible to evaluate this argument. Of course, ambient air quality data should in principle be usable for this purpose. However, the fact that the Inspectorate controls only some of the emission sources, and in particular the fact that progress in pollution control in Britain rests as much upon domestic smoke control policy as anything else, makes the use of such data difficult. Dispersion through high chimneys adds a further complication here.

Despite the absence of hard data, it is felt to be valuable to report the qualitative material included here for the light it throws upon the working of a system with several interesting characteristics. One charateristic is the determination of policy very largely through what conventionally is regarded as an implementation process in which statutory norms are virtually absent and politicians, and the general public, are hardly involved at all. This throws light upon the problems of drawing a decisive line between policy making and implementation. Related to this phenomenon is the close involvement of the regulatee interests in the implementation process. Their key interventions come neither in the law-making process nor in attempts to negate the impact of the law, but in complex interactions with the regulatory agency from which a consensual front is shown to outside society. Also related is the high discretion allowed the chief inspector and his staff, who are acknowledged by government and by the regulatees as professional experts whose judgment should be trusted in dealing with complex situations. Every pollution control system involves interactions between interested parties and strenuous efforts by economic interests to minimize limitations upon their activities. The British system does at least make this very clear. It is unfortunate that some of its spokesmen have tried to pretend that the Alkali Inspectorate is an entirely objective enforcement agency, perhaps because scientists like to present themselves as rationalists rather than pragmatists.

NOTE: This chapter is based upon work done as part of the comparative study of standard setting and implementation of sulphur dioxide air pollution control for the IIUG, Berlin, under the direction of Peter Knoepfel and Helmut Weidner. The author is grateful to Patricia Garrard and John Bowman for their assistance with the fieldwork.

REFERENCES

Annual Report of HM Alkali and Clean Air Inspectorate for 1973. 1974. (London: HMSO).

Fifth Report of the Royal Commission on Environment Pollution. 1976. (London: HMSO).

Garner, J. T., and R. K. Crow. 1976. Clean Air - Law and Practice (London: Shaw and Sons).

Health and Safety Executive. 1980. Industrial Air Pollution: Report for 1979, (London: HMSO).

Hill, M. J. 1969. "The Exercise of Discretion in the National Assistance Board," Public Administration.

Interpretation in the Fifth Report of the Royal Commission on Environmental Pollution. 1976. Cmnd. 6371 (London: HMSO).

Jowell, J. 1973. "The Legal Control of Administrative Discretion," Public Law (Autumn).

Knoepfel, Peter and Helmut Weidner. 1982. "Formulation and Implementation of Air Quality Control Programmes: Patterns of Interest Consideration," Policy and Politics, 10(1).

Levitt, R. 1980. Implementing Public Policy (London: Croom Helm).

MacDonagh, O. 1961. A Pattern of Government Growth (London: MacGibbon and Key).

MacLeod, R.M. "The Alkali Acts Administration 1863-84, The Emergence of the Civil Scientist," Victorian Studies, 9(2).

Rhodes, G. 1981. Inspectorates in British Government (London: Allen and Unwin).

Roberts, D. 1960. Victorian Origins of the British Welfare State (New Haven, Conn.: Yale University Press).

Social Audit. 1974. The Alkali Inspectorate (London: Social Audit).

IMPLEMENTING AIR POLLUTION CONTROL IN ITALY: THE IMPORTANCE OF THE POLITICAL AND ADMINISTRATIVE STRUCTURE

6

Bruno Dente and Rudy Lewanski

Italian public administration has often been described by both native scholars and visitors as a system that is highly fragmented (where even the simplest action involves several autonomous and uncoordinated agencies), highly legalistic (where the acts of Parliament are extremely detailed and lead to tiresome and complicated proceedings), and highly politicized (where the interventions of political parties systematically disrupt administrative activities).

Like most common wisdom this picture of public administration in Italy is too simplistic to come to grips with the complexities of actual policy making and implementation, even if it is granted that the characteristics noted above are in fact present to some extent. In the course of an analysis of data gathered as a part of an international research project comparing air pollution control policies in selected countries of Europe, the shortcomings of this traditional description emerged very clearly. The challenge for analysis was to separate, on the basis of the empirical findings, those elements of truth in the common understanding from those elements that were patently inaccurate or misleading.

In this chapter we briefly summarize the line of reasoning and the principal findings drawn from the examination of air pollution control policy in three Italian regions. In the light of the findings, the message for future research is that many general pictures drawn of the administrative system as a whole overemphasize structural characteristics that are of little descriptive, not to mention explanatory, value for understanding administrative action in a given local setting.

THE NATIONAL CONTROL PROGRAM

The national legislation, Act 615, presently governing air pollution control policy in Italy was passed in 1966. Its actual implementation, however, as far as industrial pollution is concerned did not begin until 1973, after the necessary executive regulations (Presidential Decree 322/1972) had been issued. The main features of the program can be summarized as follows.

The Substantive Content of the Program

The legislative program applies only to specially designated zones set up in particular areas of the country, selected according to the size of the city, the climatological conditions, and the geographic location in either the North or the South of the country. A second feature of the content program is that the most precise regulations are those with regard to the kinds of fuels industrial emitters are permitted to use. The same applies to domestic heating.

These two features of the program clearly demonstrate that the purpose of Act 615 was mainly a reduction of sulfur dioxide (and particulates) in those areas of the country where the ground level concentration of such pollutants was extremely heavy at the beginning of the sixties. As far as other pollutants and other regulations are concerned the program is much less precise. Furthermore, general emission standards do not exist, although the enforcement agencies can prescribe them on a case by case basis. Nor do air quality standards actually exist. It is true that clause 8 of Decree 322/1972 presents a list of maximum allowed ground concentrations on twenty-four hours and thirty minutes basis for eight different pollutants. But a careful analysis of the law indicates that such limits do not have any general impact. They do, however, have a function in connection with the regulation of individual emitters: if the ground concentration of a given pollutant, measured at the perimeter of the industrial plant, exceeds the limit set by the law **and** if it is possible to demonstrate that this is due to the contribution from the firm in question, then some action by the agency can be taken. In practice the effect of such a regulation is quite limited. For one thing, these limits are very high indeed (0.39 mg as a twenty-four hour average for SO_2), and in the second place, it is quite difficult to demonstrate that the contribution of a given industrial plant has caused the standard to be exceeded, especially if it is located in an industrial or residential area where other sources are present. Furthermore, the measurement methods prescribed in the law do not foresee the use of automatic monitoring networks. Finally, even if the demonstration could be made that fact does not significantly improve the position of the administrative agencies vis-a-vis the source in question.

The Implementation Agencies

The three main administrative actors responsible for the implementation of air pollution control policy are found at the regional, provincial, and municipal levels; no substantial enforcement responsibilities have been given to the national governent. At the regional level, Act 615 created a new body, the CRIA (Regional Committee for Air Pollution), composed of sixteen members representing the national administration, the regional administration, the provincial administration, and the associations of local authorities. Two representatives of the economic interests in the region are also present. As we will see, this body is formally responsible for the content of virtually every regulation of individual industrial sources. Nevertheless, its character as a collective body composed of representatives of different administrative offices has made it impossible for it to handle by itself all the work connected with these orders. Consequently, in all the regions, technical offices set up to act as the administative arms of the CRIA gradually became the real core of the regulatory system.

At the provincial level the main actor is the Provincial Laboratory (LPIP), a technical agency within the Health Administration responsible for the chemical analysis of industrial emissions and often in charge of operating the automatic monitoring networks. The LPIPs, however, do not have any administrative powers.

At the local level the municipalities are responsible for all direct contacts with the industrial polluters. Although they have some regulatory authority of their own — namely the possiblility to authorize the use of certain fuels - in the normal case the municipalities act as a kind of intermediary between the industrial emitter and the regional offices.

The Procedural Arrangements

Two points here are of special interest. The first is that the CRIA (and obviously the regional technical offices too) does not have, at least in theory, any contact with industrial emitters. Formally all permit or clean-up proceedings must pass through the municipality, which is the one authority that receives the technical reports and declarations every factory is required to submit and that has the legal authority to issue the final order (even if its technical content must conform to the decision reached by the CRIA). Furthermore, if the regional authorities want any further information on a case in hand, they ask the Provincial Laboratory to make an inspection and send a report of the findings. Consequently, as far as the formal situation is concerned, the most important regulator has no direct contact with the regulatee.

The second important point to be noted is that if the procedural arrangements are quite complex in the normal cases of the authorization of new plants or abatement measures for existinng ones, they are much more so with regard to enforcing compliance with the orders issued. In such cases the procedure followed involves no less than a dozen different steps to be taken by several different agencies, including the setting up of a special commission at the provincial level and the intervention of the prefect in those cases where the closing down of the polluting factory is ordered. If one adds the problems involved in monitoring compliance where there are no general emission or immission (air quality) standards and also considers that apart from the possibility of closing down the factory by prefectorial order, the administrative sanctions available lack any economic significance, then it is not surprising that little enforcement action of this kind takes place.

THE EMPIRICAL STUDY

What follows is drawn from the principal findings of a research project examining the characteristics of the implementation process in connection with the national program for the control of industrial air pollution with reference to sulfur dioxide. The research was carried out in three different Italian regions and in three municipalities within each of these regions. (In one case, the city of Turin, the unit of analysis was limited to a single district because of the size of the metropolitan area.)

The investigated regions are comparable in terms of urban and industrial structure. They are all located in the Po valley in the North of the country, one of the most highly polluted European regions and by far the most threatened Italian area. The regions also have similar climatic conditions, while their political characteristics, as we will see, vary considerably.

The sample of municipalities within these three regions was selected according to different criteria. The first and most obvious was the inclusion in the control zones to which the antipollution legislation applies. The second very important criterion was the availability of data on air quality over at least a portion of the time period under investigation. In a situation of high institutional fragmentation and generally low administrative effectiveness in general (characteristics that are partly prestructured by the legislative control program, as already pointed out, and partly a general feature of the Italian situation), a study aimed at documenting implementation shortfalls and analyzing the factors accounting for them would have proved to be extremely costly and, at the same time, of limited practical use. For this reason our efforts were focused on singling out those factors that explain those cases where the implementation systems formed relatively well.

Although the ultimate dependent variable of the comparative study is the impact of public policy on the quality of the air over the period investigated, the difficulties involved in determining to what extent changes in air quality can be attributed to the outputs of environmental agencies meant that the judgments of the relatively good or bad performance of the regions are made more in terms of the ability of the agencies to change the behavior of the industrial firms and not necessarily with regard to a clear-cut reduction of ground concentrations of the pollutant investigated.

As far as the independent variables are concerned there is, first of all, the character of the decision processes through which regulatory actions were taken. Here we considered the following factors: degree of closedness or openness of the decision process (as indicated by the number of actors participating); the extent to which the decision process is characterized by bargaining or authoritarian interactions (as indicated by information from the interviews, plus more hard data such as changes in the content of regulation during the process itself or the presence or absence of formal administrative or judicial sanctions); and the episodic or systematic nature of the processes (as indicated by similarities and differences between the regulation content for comparable emitters).

The second group of variables deals with the characteristics of the actors involved, particularly the environmental agencies. In addition to those factors traditionally considered relevant for determining the kinds of output produced, such as personnel and resources, the structure of the national control program suggests that attention should be paid to the relationship between these different agencies themselves. We have therefore defined a typology of different kinds of relationships found in the course of the investigation in order to see (also with an eye to eventual modifications of the present program) whether a particular network can be singled out as optimal in the sense of ensuring greater effectiveness in the implementation of pollution control policies.

THE ACTORS

From an analysis of the national legislative program, however, it is possible to draw up a first list of administrative agencies who are formally involved in the control policy. Previous research suggests some additional actors as well as some of the relevant dimensions to be analyzed. Since one of the objectives of the exercise was to examine the relevance of the political actors, we, therefore, tried to distinguish between the political and the technical components at the different levels of the administrative hierarchy.

The Political Actors

As we have already pointed out, the national program envisages a shared competence between the regional, provincial and municipal levels of administration. In the Italian context the relevant administrative offices are responsible to the elected government bodies at the same level. There is always a good chance that those will all have different political majorities. However, the general impression is that the party affiliation of the political heads of departments has very little influence on regulatory decisions. Not only does the political composition of the government at a given time seem to be of little significance for administrative action, but the change or stability in the party alignment does not have any discernible impact.

According to Italian political/administrative tradition, the powers of issuing binding orders regarding the behavior of individuals are entrusted to the political head of the administrative structures. In our case this is usually the mayor; since the provincial administration does not have any regulatory powers. Every order, prescription, permit, or administrative sanction issued by the administration must have the signature of the mayor. In practice, these politicians have made little use of the potential formal powers and the influence these formal powers would seem to give them. The general lack of interest in air pollution on the part of politicians is hardly surprising when one bears in mind that the Italian political parties pay very little attention to the environmental policies in general and, insofar as they are concerned at all, they are worried about protecting some other economic interest like agriculture or, especially, tourism.

Since none of our localities was an agricultural or tourist area, the representation of the economic interests connected with industrial activities seemed by far the prevalent concern of the political actors. This did not, however, go so far that they explicitly took the industrialist side in the more dramatic issues. Rather the policy as a whole was given low priority. This lack of consideration of environmental issues is also reflected in the extreme weakness of the environmentalist groups and organizations that, if they exist at all, are solely concerned with politically dramatic campaigns like anti-nuclear power. A day-to-day monitoring of environmental quality in order to improve the present situation as well as to prevent a further deterioration seems totally absent. This is remarkable when one recalls that air pollution in many of the localities studied is extremely bad.

The same is true for the trade unions. Although they have an expressed policy against industrial pollution, they are in reality much more interested in improving working conditions inside the factories. Consequently they are more interested in investments to this end than in those concerned with reducing industrial emissions.

Nevertheless we did find that the public plays a quite important role with frequent interventions at various stages of the control processes. These interventions take the form of the individual protests of persons from the immediate area against the various nuisances caused by the industrial processes. In general the complaints tend to be concerned with smoke and smells. Although these protests seldom lead to a level of controversy great enough to interest political officials in taking up the defense of those individuals affected by pollution, the importance of these protests in setting activities in motion should not be underestimated. As we will see, they can have very definite consequences for the form and the outcome of the regulatory process itself.

The Administrative Actors

The national program itself specified the structure of the administrative organization of air pollution control implementation, creating a new body, the CRIA, and entrusting the already existing local government structures, notably the municipality and the Provincial Laboratory with the main administrative and technical tasks.

As a collegiate body the CRIA meets more or less frequently with the official representatives participating with varying degrees of regularity. A general idea of the activities of these bodies can be obtained from the following table.

	Lombardy	Piedmont	Emilia Romagna
Number of meetings (yearly average)	6.6	5.0	8.3
Number of decisions (yearly average)	803	68	140
Members present (average)	63.8	61.7	63.3
Personnel of the technical office	22	3	9

The first impression that can be drawn from the table is that there are significant differences in the working of the committee among the three regions and that the main reason seems to be the number of technical staff in the offices. Bearing in mind that the industrial structure is broadly comparable between Lombardy and Piedmont, while Emilia Romagna is more agricultural, the difficulties faced by the Piedmonteses in coping with pollution is clear in relative terms, without considering the adequacy of the individual decisions taken to deal with the situation in the region.

The second self-evident feature is that it is simply not possible for a body meeting every two months for two to three hours and composed on average of ten people to deal with the number of issues it confronts. This means that, at least when the amount of regulatory activity is considerable, the CRIA functions as a mere ratifying body for the proposals coming from the technical staff. CRIA meetings are therefore much more concerned with general policy debates or specific big issues (such as the monitoring networks or the authorization of big new projects) than with the individual regulatory activities that should be their main task.

While the law provided for the representation of all the relevant existing agencies on the regional committee in order to provide the technical skills implied in air pollution regulation, the crucial strategic decision regarding the subsequent fate of the control policy proved to be the staffing of the technical offices attached to the CRIA with officers from the regional administrations. The decision regarding the staffing of the regional offices was important because the kind of skills these officials possess has had significant consequences for the prevailing orientations of the different agencies.

The three regions have consequently developed different philosophies that, ceteris paribus, are bound to influence the prevailing type of output. In Piedmont, the lack of sufficient technical personnel meant that the role of the secretary, a full time administrative official, was crucial. This lack of technical skills and subsequent dominant role of an administrative official engendered a legalistic orientation that can be summarized as follows: the responsible authorities have the task of prosecuting illegal behavior of the emitters (regardless of how serious the consequences of the emission are for the air quality); the formal aspects of the process (submitting reports, respecting deadlines, etc) are given equal — if not more — weight than the more substantive ones; court intervention is regarded as a necessary part of the regulatory process.

In Emilia Romagna the staff of the technical offices grew slowly but steadily from 1972 onward. The most prevalent professions, especially at the beginning, were meteorology and chemistry. In this region, the least polluted area in our sample and the one with major tourism and agricultural interests, the result has been an air quality oriented strategy that can be summarized as follows: the purpose of the policy is to improve the situation where ground level pollution is high and in other cases to prevent the situation from getting worse; intervention, therefore, can be limited to the regulation of emitters located in the threatened areas and to the prevention of new firms being located there; new sources, even a big emitter, located in an area with relatively low levels of pollution would not be regulated. An obvious precondition for this type of regulatory activity is the establishment of an effective monitoring system. This was the principal policy objective of the regional office between 1974 and 1979.

In Lombardy the staff of the technical offices is far bigger. In fact a whole department of the Milano Engineering Faculty was hired, at first as consultants and later as permanent officials. Some years ago the number of staff was slightly higher (about twenty-five people) consisting primarily of engineers. Today the situation has stabilized at approximately fifteen technicians working full time in the office (the rest is administrative and clerical staff). This situation, plus the very bad pollution of the region and the fact that the provincial administration of Milano in 1970 already had a monitoring network in operation led to an emission-oriented strategy: the objective of regulatory activity is the greatest possible reduction of the volume of emissions regardless of the actual quality of the ambient air; the consequence is a systematic clean up of the existing factories stressing the importance of abatement technology and changes in fuel consumption.

The structure and organization of the provinicial level agency, the Provincial Laboratory, is less important from our point of view. In practice, the impact of the LPIP activities on the control processes, at least in the field of SO_2 pollution, is quite limited. In any case it is worthwhile to emphasize that the relations with the regional offices are very good in Emilia Romagna, where the monitoring network was a regionally financed policy; full of conflict in Lombardia, where the region made an effort to create its own network; and almost nonexistent in Piedmont where, on the other hand, there are conflicts with the city of Turin.

The other core actor in the process of controlling air pollution in Italy is the municipalities themselves, which are responsible for providing information for the decisions by regional offices on the content of the orders and which have the formal authority for issuing the orders themselves to the individual polluter. As far as the relative position of municipal offices vis-a-vis other actors is concerned, the situation can be summarized as follows:

Strong municipal offices, in terms of size of staff, exist in only one situation, the city of Turin, which set up a specific section dealing with air pollution in 1966. This office is staffed by one medical doctor, one licensed chemist, and one technician for each of the sixteen districts of the city. This office is responsible for both domestic and industrial air pollution as well as for running the monitoring networks. The office in the city of Piacenza is much smaller (one chemist and two technicians) but, when measured against the size of the town in terms of population, the industrial structure, and the level of pollution, it can be regarded as actually quite strong, even though it deals also with water pollution.

Medium-strong municipal offices exist in two cases. Here the officials primarily in charge of pollution control (an engineer in one case, two chemists in the other) have the technical skill needed to understand the problem being dealt with.

Weak municipal offices exist in all the other five cases. Here a situation exists where there is either no specific office at all dealing with pollution in general, let alone air pollution, or the office that does exist is staffed only by administrative personnel and therefore lacks the technical expertise to perceive the problems as well as the resources to acquire outside advice.

These categories are, of course, quite rough but do give an idea of the general situation. In the first case the offices tend to regulate the emitters effectively, in the second case they ask the regional offices to do so, and in the third case they are not even able to provide adequate inputs to the decisions of the CRIA.

Before entering the analysis of the results of control policy, a third category of actors besides the political and the administrative officials, namely the courts, must be added. In order to understand the importance and the limits of judicial intervention in the Italian case the following factors must be taken into account: in a situation of general ineffectiveness of the regulatory activities carried out by the national or the local administration, the courts in the sixties and seventies have gradually become a very important actor (at least in the eyes of public opinion and mass media) in protecting the so-called general interests (i.e., protection of health, of nature, of architectural and artistic goods, etc.). Even if judicial intervention in the field of air pollution has been less important than in the field of water pollution, there is an expectation that the courts will be active in this field as well. As a result of these factors, the courts do indeed tend to intervene in some cases, not so much to impose judicial sanctions but rather to raise the level of public consciousness, thus pushing the administrative offices to act and stimulating the industrial polluter to do something in order to improve the situation. Thus, while the number of court interventions is quite high, the actual number of polluters found guilty at the end of the first degree trial is relatively small.

THREE MAIN TYPES OF INTERACTION PROCESSES

Leaving aside the interventions by other categories of actors — at both the administrative and political level — that are involved in less than the 15% of the processes investigated and whose intervention is sometimes of little significance, we can draw a first general picture of the processes actually taking place. Figure 6-1 refers only to the clean-up process (sixty-six in total). The numbers in brackets indicate the frequency of the particular actor's intervention. Since we have investigated only those processes that actually took place, the 100% municipal intervention does not mean that all industrial polluters have been regulated, let alone successfully dealt with. Behind this general pattern, however, the research findings indicate two important points. First, the intervention of the Provincial Laboratory does not have any clear-cut consequence for the outcome of the process. Even though the involvement of these laboratories is more likely when the technical complexity of the industrial process is higher, the specific characteristics of the pollutant SO_2 and its origin from combustion processes make such interventions, concerned almost solely with the chemical analysis of the emissions, more or less useless. It is possible and even likely that with regard to other kinds of more

Figure 6-1

Actors Involved in the Clean-Up Process

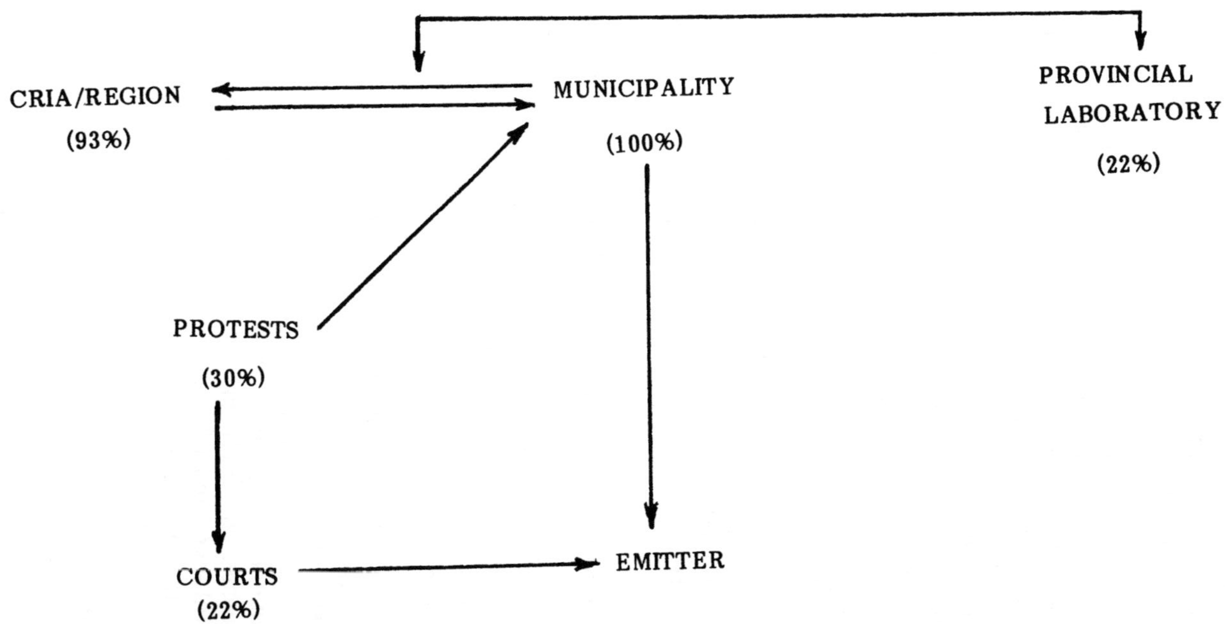

complicated, sophisticated pollution the intervention of the Provincial Laboratories does make a difference. The second point is even more important. Intervention by courts and the presence of popular protests are highly correlated. In virtually all the fifteen cases of court interventions we find popular protests (normally addressed to the municipality but sometimes to the court itself).

The main analytical consequence of these two points is that the general pattern can be both simplified and, further, differentiated according to two different types of processes. First, there is the normal pattern, i.e., that occuring in the majority of the cases. This can be sketched as in figure 6-2.

This is a very closed process, substantially excluding intervention by other actors. As we will see, the effectiveness of the process, in terms of outcome and even impact, depends on the double link between the two core actors. However, the relative closedness of the process does not have clear cut consequences for the other dimensions; thus we find some processes of this type that are highly formal and authoritarian, while others are highly cooperative and involve a substantial amount of bargaining. Furthermore, these processes can be quite episodic and scattered over time, just as they sometimes are linked with each other in a systematic attempt to depollute a given area or a given industrial branch.

Two further points deserve mention. The fact that the network is simple does not mean that the process itself is simple. That may indeed be the case but it is equally possible that the control process, while involving only two actors, is long and complex and divided into several phases, each with different formal or informal interventions by the implementing agencies. Finally, one must also note that if this is true with regard to the clean-up processes, which are aimed at abating pollution by existing industrial sources, the same goes for the majority of permit processes; i.e., the authorization of almost all new plants.

The actor network of a second type of clean up process, already referred to, is sketched in figure 6-3. Here the degree of openness of the process is much greater than in the previous case, primarily because other actors (mainly health authorities) tend to intervene more frequently. In these cases the process is not only open but, in general, also quite authoritarian and normally episodic. The first characteristic is understandable because of the need of the implementing agencies to play by the book when the attention of the public and of the judicial system has been raised, a situation reflected in the absence of direct contacts between the emitter and the regional administration that is one of the main features of the national program. Furthermore, the intervention of the courts with

Figure 6-2

Normal Inaction Process

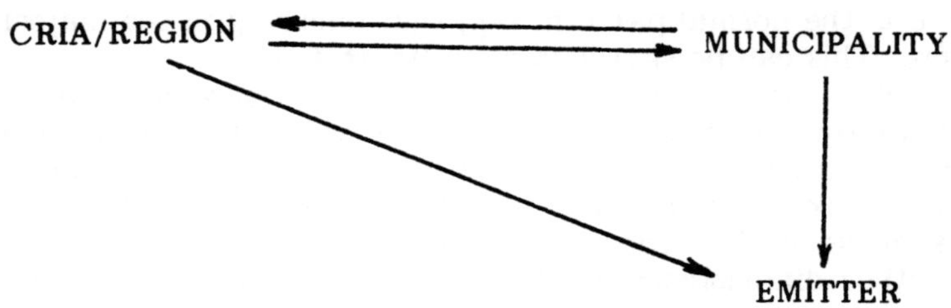

Figure 6-3

A More Open Interactive Process

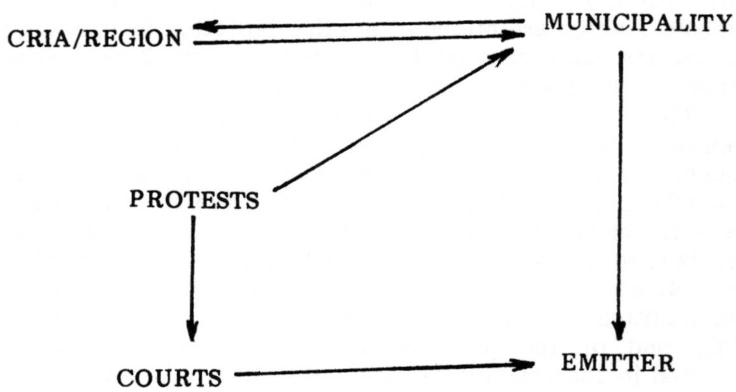

the presence of penal sanctions, actual or threatened, leads to a more rigid relationship between the regulators and the regulatee. The episodic character of this type of control process is the result of the nature of popular protests, which are related to specific nuisances to the neighborhood. The absence of intervention on the part of environmentalist groups or organizations, due to their extreme weakness in Italy, means that public intervention is unsystematic and associated more with the perception of pollution than with its real degree.

There is a third typical interaction pattern that occurs in some special cases. As we have already indicated, the closed relationships that take place in the majority of the clean-up processes is also the rule in the normal permit cases. When a small or medium sized industry applies for a permit for a new plant or for an enlargement of the existing one, the relations are normally only with the relevant municipal and regional offices. But when a major plant is concerned — as an electric power plant, or a refinery — the situation changes almost completely (see figure 6-4).

In fact these processes are far more complex than indicated in that they are vey long and normally conflictive, with many different actors intervening autonomously at their own initiative or following specific request from the municipal political representatives. The main feature of this proces is that it is the only one, among the ones we studied, where the political actors play a significant role. What is even more interesting is that such an intervention seldom occurs in connection with measures to abate pollution of an existing plant, even a large one, but only when a new permit is requested. In this case the process tends to be very open, highly conflictive (even if this doesn't exclude a substantial amount of bargaining), and obviously highly episodic. The most important thing is that the central role played by the politicians at the local level means that the technical conditions contained in the final permit can go considerably beyond those recommended by the CRIA.

In terms of maximizing investments for environmental protection — maximizing the protection costs involved in new plants — the political intervention is very effective, even in absence of previous strong popular protests. Of course, the politicization of the issue, implied in the role played by politicians, creates widespread alarm in the population and stimulates the intervention of environmentalist organizations or political groups. Nevertheless, it must be emphasized that the structure and outcome of the process are not significantly different whether the interventions take place before or after the process actually begins. Thus it is difficult to determine if the politicians were stimulated by the public concern or vice versa.

Figure 6-4

Interactive Clean-Up Process for Major Emitters

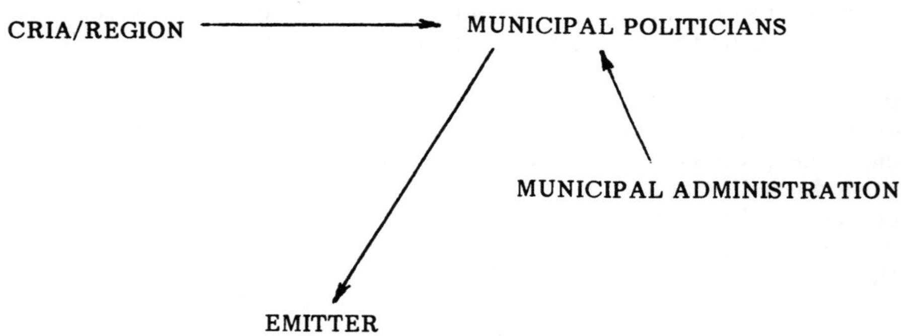

It is also interesting that such politicization occurs mainly at the local level. Only in cases of greater significance — such as power plants when the need to increase the national energy production is stressed — is the regional political system likely to intervene. Even then every effort is made to avoid getting embroiled in conflict with the local politicians. When the issue is less dramatic, regional politicians are absent from the process and the political parties do not attempt to involve higher levels of government in the issue.

THE OUTCOMES OF THE CONTROL PROCESS

Both the protagonists and the outside observers share the view that the impact of the enforcement agency activity on the quality of the air has been very small if not completely marginal. The improvement of the situation that has occcurred in Italy — as in other European countries — since the late sixties is seen as a consequence of the changes in domestic heating fuels imposed by legislation and, subsequently, as an effect of the energy crisis of the mid-seventies. Neither factor is influenced at all by public policy in the field of industrial air pollution control.

Nevertheless, even with these caveats in mind, something can be said regarding the performance of the implementing system concerned with the control of industrial air pollution. A careful and thorough analysis of the outputs of the implementing agencies, and a comparison of them with the structure of the implementation field (the quantity and quality of industrial emitters), shows a number of different situations that can be categorized as follows:

High level of program implementation: The regulatory activities of the agencies have resulted in issuing orders to all or most of the polluting industries and in securing substantial changes in the emitters' behavior (e.g., changes in fuel, abatement equipments, increasing the height of chimneys, etc).

Medium level of program implementation: The regulatory activities have concentrated on a few emitters, in general the biggest and those causing the major nuisances with regard to the source, and simple changes in behavior were achieved.

Low level of program implementation: The regulatory activities are either completely absent or were unable to change the behavior of the industrial actors substantially.

It is interesting to note when examining such measurements of the dependent variable that variation is found not only between regions but also between localities within each region.

Of course there are several factors that could explain the

variations observed. The actual amount of pollution and the structure of emissions (e.g., the concentration or dispersion of the polluting industries) are two of the most obvious. In this final section, however, we will concentrate on two groups of variables: the character of the implementing system as a set of relationships between administrative actors and the characters of the control processes.

The first conclusion we have drawn is quite straightforward: the strength of the implementing agencies in administrative terms accounts for a good deal of the variation in the final performance. A weak regional structure is simply not able to cope with the complexities of regulating industrial sources. The size of staff and its technical skills are most significant in preparing regulations that contain conditions that can be met by the industry and that are appropriate for improving the emission situation.

The same is true for the strength of the municipal offices. Lack of personnel and/or skill means that it will be impossible to carry out substantial emitter inventories, to stimulate the regional activity and to oversee the enforcement of orders issued. But the absolute strength of these agencies is not the only variable that has a significant impact on performance. As we have seen in the previous section, two-thirds of the control processes are of a very closed type, with only two intervening actors involved. In such cases the strength of the link between the local and regional offices is most important, i.e., their ability to cooperate and share responsibilities for the final policy outcome. The nature of this link in turn depends on the power situation between these actors. If the two actors are both weak, the resulting performance will be very poor. On the other hand, if they are both strong — or at least adequate in terms of coping with the problems they face — the result will be significantly better.

Two more interesting situations are found when the distribution of the power is unequal. If the regional offices are far stronger than the municipal ones, no systematic clean-up of the given locality will occur. For one thing the regional officials will be busy with those municipalities able to provide substantial inputs to regional activity . Where the environmental administration is in general relatively weak, the result will be that in those areas where the municipal offices are not able to stimulate the regional agencies, the pollution problem will simply not be dealt with at all. Secondly, if the regional offices do intervene, it will be much less systematic and in general with regard only to the major polluters or the industrial branches that are dealt with throughout the region as a whole.

On the other hand, a situation where inequality of power is to the advantage of the local offices will probably create a condition where, once it becomes clear that the regional administration is unable to solve all the problems raised locally, the municipal administration will give up the idea of a joint effort and will concentrate its own efforts either on the most important polluters or on the problems it feels able to solve alone. Again, in a situation where environmental agencies are weak, these will be the simplest cases. In both situations no systematic clean up will occur and the general level of implementation performance will be low to medium, as it was in the reverse case.

The case where a municipality is too strong in comparison to the regional offices is of peculiar interest because it seems to prove that not only must the resources available for the implementation of a public policy be adequate, they must also be evenly distributed among the different intervening agencies. In the area of air pollution control we do not have the usual case of coordination but rather a division of labor laid down by the national program that presupposes active cooperation between different actors. Where this is not forthcoming, the result is not someone doing more than required, but everybody doing less than possible.

The consequences of these different networks for the type of control processes are quite clear. A generally weak network will not only prove highly ineffective in terms of the quality of its outputs but will also tend to adopt a formal/authoritarian pattern of operation and a case by case approach. At the other end of the continuum a strong network will generate processes characterized by a systematic pattern and strong bargaining with the industrial plants. In this case both the municipality and the regional offices will have direct access to the controlled firms, while in the case of a weak network virtually all contacts will be made through letters and official documents (if only because it takes less time to write an official letter than to go to the industrial premises or meet an industrial representative in public offices).

A large degree of informality will also be found in those processes with a regional dominated network; the difference will be that in this case no systematic approach — at the local level — will be possible and that the monitoring of the industries compliance will be lacking.

A more complex situation will occur where a municipal dominated network is found. Here too no systematic clean up will be done because the municipal offices lack the legal power, let alone the skills, to cope with the complex industrial structure. Consequently attention will be on the most important and the simplest cases, removing from the agenda all the problems requiring more sophisticated analysis. With these emitters the relation will probably be quite informal, involving a substantial amount of bargaining. But where major problems occur, the lack of cooperation with the regional offices will probably lead to the formalization of the issue and to the request for intervention by different agencies such as the Provincial Laboratory, other agencies, possibly the judicial system and, of course, the regional offices too. This shift from a highly informal pattern of operation, with the municipal offices acting as a sort of environmental consultant to the industries, to a highly formal relationship, including sanctions, court prosecutions, etc., seems typical of a municipal dominated network where every intervention has a specific story and is not linked to any attempt to reduce pollution systematically in the locality.

Until now we have concentrated our attention on the normal, closed processes, noting that when protests occur, the pattern of interaction among the different actors will differ considerably from the usual pattern. We have already pointed out how the open process is much more episodic and formal. From this point of view its performance can be regarded as sort of intermediate between the better results obtained by the equally strong network and the total lack of impact of the evenly weak one. On this point it should be noted that the lower effectiveness of a formal process is obviously a consequence of the inadequacies of the national program that was aimed more at protecting the industries against an excess of regulation than in providing substantive powers to the administration itself. Playing by the book, therefore, proves almost invariably less effective than bargaining, where the officers are able to raise different issues and play at different tables for different stakes.

From this point of view, it appears that the presence of popular protests is an asset for public policy only when both the bottom level and regional administrative actors are very weak. In this case the open process that takes place is able to generate some results. It is not, however, necessarily more effective in those processes than the informal bargaining that takes place on a case by case basis in a regional dominated network or in a systematic way in an evenly strong network.

CONCLUSION

If we examine the results of the analysis carried out in air pollution control policy against the conventional wisdom about Italian public adminstration, some surprising conclusions emerge. The importance of bargaining and informality in enforcing regulatory policies is clearly at odds with the generally assumed legalistic pattern of administrative operation in Italy. Of course a high degree of legalism is present in the national program, and when it seems the easiest way to deal with a problem (because of the weakness of the implementing agency or because of the intervention of popular complaints and/or the judicial system) it actually takes place. However, not only is it not an unavoidable feature, but the most surprising finding — because it contradicts a whole literature on Italian bureaucrats — is the willingness shown by the administrative officers to enter into bargaining proceses.

The same goes for the problem of fragmentation between administrative agencies. Here, too, the ancient Italian tradition of sharing competences between different agencies marks the national legislative program and can be regarded as an incentive toward fragmentation. Under certain conditions, it also seems to be the case in the course of the control processes as well. But again this outcome is not unavoidable. When an adequate balance of power between administrative actors occurs, the result will be a much more integrated network than envisaged (or hoped for). The sources of fragmentation seem to be contained less in the national program itself and much more in the staffing and organization of the agencies. In our study we found evidence of cooperative administrative networks where the different partners shared responsibilities and common values over the actions to be taken.

Only slightly different is the politicization issue. We did indeed find intervention by political actors in administrative processes. Even more important, when politicians do intervene, they are the unchallenged masters of the situation. No administrative agency, regardless of its administrative strength or technical skill, is likely to prevail against political interventions. On the other hand, not only are these political interventions infrequent, but they occur strictly in one kind of process: permit procedures for big plants. No interest is shown in the day-to-day control policy, which is primarily concerned with the abatement of pollution from existing sources. In this sense politicization does not disrupt administrative routine, a finding in striking contradiction to the current wisdom.

Summing up, the general picture of Italian public administration contained in textbooks and the observations of foreign scholars certainly has some validity. But this picture seems to reflect much more the reality of legislation than the reality of actual administrative operations. This is understandable since the weakness of Italian political sciences and the traditions of European continental countries gave a virtual monopoly of the study of public administration to the legal profession.

The traditional approach is also dangerous from a policy oriented point of view. If it is true that the inadequacies of legislation do not necessarily affect the outcome of public policy, the reverse, unfortunately, is also true: good laws are not a sufficient — and sometimes not even a necessary — condition for good implementation. Only through the analysis of the reality of the policy process can the factors be recognized that are actually important for determining what the impact of policy will be at the bottom line.

7 STATE AND LOCAL RELATIONS ON ENVIRONMENTAL REGULATIONS IN THE FEDERAL REPUBLIC OF GERMANY

Jochen Hucke

THE IMPLEMENTATION PROBLEM

This chapter examines some of the difficulties confronted in obtaining a sufficient degree of waste and sewage disposal at the local level in the FRG. It focuses on the decision-making processes within the local communities as well as on the relations between state and local administrative agencies in connection with the implementation of these programs.[1] If one were to look at the conditions under which the implementation programs in environmental policy are effectively carried out, one would expect to find the following situations which are in fact realized in the Federal Republic of Germany:

a) There are clear standards to guide implementation: as specified by the German water resources law (Wasserhaushaltsgesetz, abbreviated WHG), sewage is to undergo at least biological treatment. The standards for solid waste disposal laid down in the waste disposal law (Abfallbeseitigungsgesetz, abbreviated AbfG) prescribe either controlled dumping or composting or incineration to be done in such a manner as to avoid endangering and damaging the soil, landscape, ground water, and health.

b) The responsibilities for environmental protection in these fields are clearly defined. Local communities are responsible for waste and sewage disposal as a part of the public services they provide for their citizens. Their activities in this connection are supervised by special technical state agencies (Amter fur Wasser- und Abfallwirt- schaft, abbreviated WWA) as well as by the state district governments (Regierungsprasidien, abbreviated RP), which exercise general administrative and legal supervision over local communities.

c) The administrative offices in charge are staffed with specialists for waste and sewage disposal. Within the local administrations special departments are responsible for these tasks. They employ engineers and technicians for planning and carrying out the tasks involved.

d) The communities are able to raise the revenue needed for these environmental protection tasks. According to law (Kommunalabgabengesetze, abbreviated KAG) citizens must utilize the public waste and sewage disposal facilities and must be charged fees that cover the cost of these services.

However, despite these seemingly favorable conditions, significant implementation deficits can be found in practice; such as:

a) In more than one-third of German local communities, irrespective of the size of city, sewage disposal does not meet the standards of biological treatment.

b) In solid waste disposal the more expensive but also environmentally more compatible solutions such as composting, recycling, or incineration are seldom chosen. In fact, the prevailing modes of disposal often do not meet the requirements of orderly deposition.

c) The procedures for making decisions on improving the environmental protection services are extremely long and drawn out. In some of the cases examined it took more than ten years to reach a binding decision on building or expanding a sewage or waste treatment plant. Frequently, the plants were already too small and overloaded at the time of their completion. This was due to the fact that the increases in production and consumption leading to a higher degree of waste and sewage had been underestimated at the time the plans were made.

d) Many plants suffered from follow-up problems after their completion; e.g., neighbors were disturbed by bad smells and noise, areas for the disposal of sewage sludge were lacking, the sludge contained a dangerous degree of heavy metals, etc.

These problems in conection with problems of cost, site, and technical equipment of waste and sewer plants reflect a relatively low degree of rationality in the decisions regarding the provision of environmental protection services at the local levels. Viewed more generally, these implementation deficits suggest that local communities in fact typically act as externalizers, although one would not necessarily expect them to do so given the favorable conditions for implementation mentioned above. Indeed local communities, by providing for the disposal of refuse and the treatment of sewage, do act to eliminate dangers to the health of their citizens within the city limits. However, they are less concerned with the negative consequences for the environment outside their borders that can result from the inadequacies of their waste and sewage treatment facilities. It is in connection with these negative spillovers beyond a community's borders that state control over local goverments comes into play. It is the task of the designated state agencies, concerned with enforcing environmental laws, to induce the cities to make a greater effort to meet the goals of environmental protection. The nature of the interactions between these levels of government will be described in the following sections.

THE IMPLEMENTATION STRUCTURE FOR ENVIRONMENTAL REGULATION

Waste and sewage disposal have traditionally been tasks of local self-government. In Germany they developed parallel to the urbanization and industrialization during the second part of the neneteenth century. In many cases, the cities' activities in this area were the result of severe public health problems such as widespread illness and epidemics. The decisions taken at that time with regard to sewage disposal often had far-reaching consequences for subsequent development of the city. Thus, the building of sewage collection systems and the point of discharge into the nearest river frequently determined the site of the sewage plant that is often still in use today.

The basic regulatory structure in this field of environmental protection has also not changed much over time. In order to discharge sewage into a river and to dispose of their waste, local communities need a permit from the state that is granted on the basis of a formal procedure. The administrative responsibility for issuing such permits lies with the RPs and WWAs which specify certain conditions regarding the degree of environmental protection to be met, such as emission standards, etc. These state agencies also have the right to demand an improvement in the level of environmental protection in those cases where the cities do not take the initiative themselves.

At the same time, over the years the requirements concerning the degree of environmental protection has been tightened substantially. Especially since the increased attention to environmental policy in the early seventies, the standards of the WHG have been made markedly more stringent. For waste disposal, which had formerly also been regulated under the WHG, the AbfG introduced a separate set of regulations to govern this area. These laws specified that biological sewage treatment and orderly waste disposal were to be the minimum standards to be met by the local communities. Since many of them did not meet these standards, it was the job of the state administrative agency to see that the laws were enforced.

A brief description of the internal implementation structure of local communities will make clearer the implementation processes resulting from these legal requirements. According to German constitutional law, local communities have the right to selfgovernment within the framework set by the relevant state laws. This means that while they are legally bound to meet the requirements laid down in federal and state laws, they are at the same time to a certain degree free to decide how and when to fulfill these obligations. The relevant local decisions are made by the members of the elected councils, the Gemeinderat, who are responsible for determining the local budget and for controlling the work of the local administrative officials.

Typically the local administration consists of about thirty departments staffed with professional personnel. These departments include those specifically concerned with waste and sewage disposal. Each department is headed by an official whose job it is to cooperate with the other departments, with the citizens and with the state agencies with regard to routine matters. At the same time, there is another organizational link between the administrative offices, the Gemeinderat, state agencies, and the public. This is the top of local government, the Burgermeister (mayor) and the Dezernenten, the political officials in charge of directing the work of the different administrative offices.[2] The main functions of those officials are to control the departments and to cooperate with the Gemeinderat, the public, and with state agencies when more important cases are involved.

Figure 7-1 shows the structure of implementation for state and local actors. In order to appreciate the manner in which the laws in question are carried out, the problems confronted in implementing them, and the deficits, it must be kept in mind that formal authority and professional skills are unequally distributed among the actors involved in such a way that hinders effective implementation in two ways:

a) As far as the relationship between state and local agencies is concerned, the formal responsibility for enforcing the environmental laws lies with the state agencies. In practice, however, it is local communities that have to make the building decisions and provide the money for environmental protection in their jurisdictions.

b) At the local level, formal decisions are made by the elected representatives, i.e., the Gemeinderat and the political executives. In fact, these actors depend on advice and recommendations from professional officials of the administrative departments.

The following sections discuss the consequences of this pattern of structural differentiations for the process through which environmental protection sources are provided and for the results achieved.

MOBILIZING LOCAL EFFORT: THE FUNCTIONS OF STATE AGENCIES IN THE PROCESS OF IMPLEMENTATION

The tightening of legal standards for environmental protection

Figure 7-1

Typical Implementation Structure for Waste and Sewage Disposal

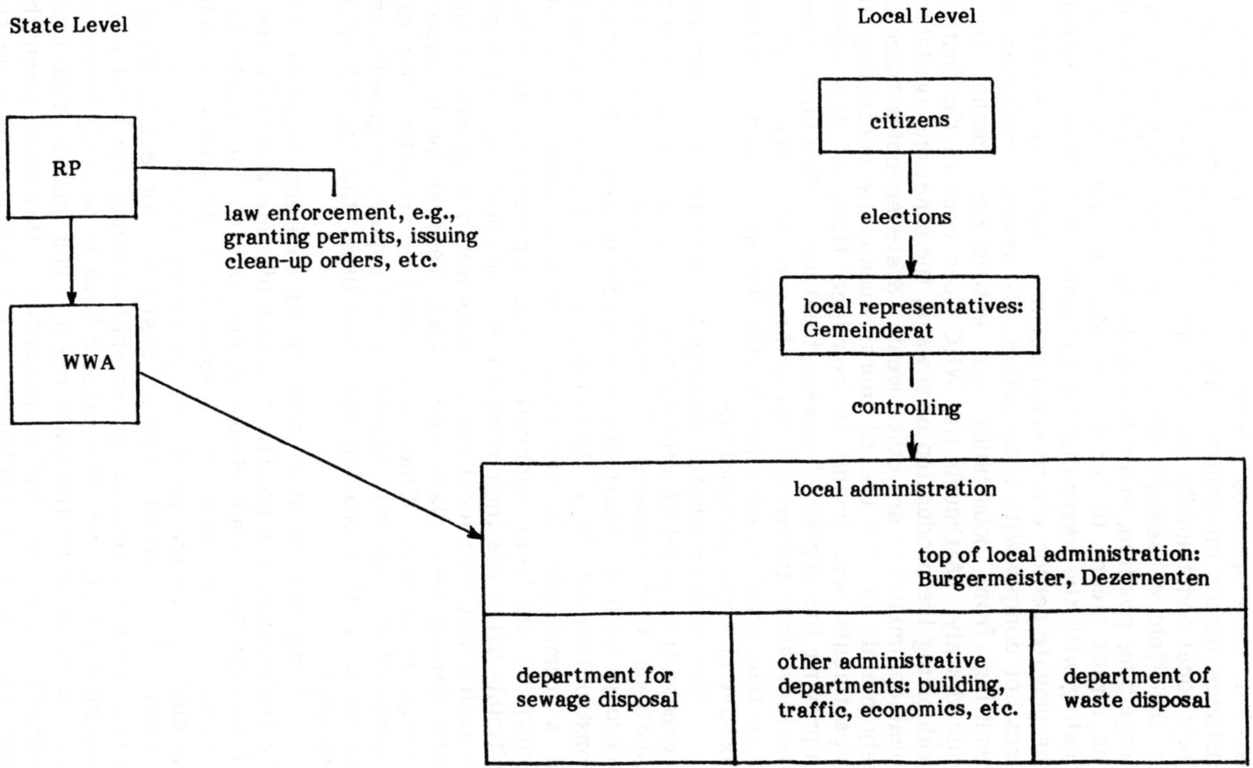

did not automatically induce the local communities to increase the level of their services. Since this would have meant in the first instance higher investments and increased fees for their citizens, most local communities delayed taking further measures. Especially in the field of sewage disposal, they felt they were in a good bargaining position, since the state agencies did not actually have the direct means to force the cities to increase their efforts in dealing with the waste disposal problem. In contrast to dealing with the private sector where state agencies can close down a firm that does not comply with their orders, the sewage production of a city, resulting from households and enterprises, cannot be stopped immediately. Although the WHG does contain the instrument of prohibiting the production of sewage, the sanctions available against local communities are quite weak. State agencies therefore must rely mainly on the use of moral suasion by contacting the local departments and trying to convince them of the necessity of improving the degree of sewage treatment. This kind of persuasion strategy alone turned out not to be very effective. State agencies have thus tried to combine it with the application of some kind of positive or negative sanctions.

The most successful strategy for inducing local communities to increase their level of activity has been a form of indirect negative sanctions that consists of combining environmental protection approval with licensing new construction areas. In Germany, new construction outside of the built-up area is possible only on the basis of a formal plan for the area to be developed. These plans are drawn by the local communities and approved by the RPs. These officials often use their competence for approving this construction in such a way that local communities would be granted approval for their development plans only if they were willing to improve their sewage treatment. Since most local communities are extremely interested in economic expansion and population growth, especially for reasons of improving their tax base, the log-rolling strategy seldom fails.

Compared to this strategy of indirect negative sanctions, strategies using the positive sanction of state grants for the building of sewage treatment plants turned out on the whole to be less effective. All states have established programs to induce the building of sewage plants by providing grants covering up to 50 percent of investment costs. State aid for constructing sewage plants has the effect of appreciably reducing the local fee paid for sewage disposal, since the citizens have to pay only those costs that are not covered by the state grant. This makes state grants very attractive for the local communities. However, since the funds available are much smaller than the number of applications, the instrument of state grants has tended to retard rather than stimulate local activity. When asked to improve their sewage disposal, local communities often argue that they are waiting for state grants that are not available at present.

Table 7-1 shows that in solid waste disposal the situation is different from that of sewage treatment. Initiatives for improvement are mainly taken here by the local administrations themselves, while in sewage treatment it was the task of the state agencies to mobilize the cities' efforts. This difference can be explained by the respective problem structure in each program area.

Table 7-1

Source of Primary Initiative in the Implementation Processes Examined

Initiator	Waste Disposal	Sewage Treatment	Total
Local administration	13	4	17
State administration	4	26	30
Professional experts (consultants, etc.)	3	2	5
Local politicians	2	3	5
Local civic movements	0	1	1
Private firms	3	0	3
Total	25	36	61

In sewage treatment local communities can continually externalize their sewage by releasing it into the nearest river, while in solid waste disposal they need new dumping grounds when the old ones are filled up. Here it is in their own interest to look for new dumping areas early and to get a state license for dumping to keep down the price of the land to be bought. This in turn puts state agencies in a better bargaining position. Since local communities are in need of new dumping areas, they will be more willing to accept the conditions concerning the degree of environmental protection laid down in the license.

Generally, negotiations over the time limits and the degree of relatively close working relationship between state and local administrative agencies. Though their interests differ concerning the timing and degree of improvement, there are also things that those actors have in common. Both have the same professional background in terms of technical training and their functions as public administrators. Both are interested in arriving at an equitable solution of the case at issue. In general, this tends to result in strengthening the position of local administrators within the implementation structure described because:

a) Local administrative officials are involved in all of the relevant decision-making processes with regard to both the state and the local context itself. They possess the information needed to deal with the cases and are able significantly to influence the result of the implementation process.

b) Since the state administrators are interested in reaching a solution, they will ultimately be willing to accept some reductions of their demands concerning the degree of environmental protection.

THE LOCAL IMPLEMENTATION PROCESS: THE DOMINANT ROLES OF THE EXPERTS

Table 7-1 indicates that initiatives for implementation processes come almost exclusively from administrative officials (state and local) or from private experts (consultants, firms). Local politicians or citizen groups are almost completely absent, although their general interest in environmental protection has risen considerably over the last few years. This can be explained by the fact that waste and sewage disposal are considered to be technical issues requiring a good deal of expert knowledge. Consequently political decision makers tend to rely heavily on the skills of their administrative staffs. Since the extent of effective political control over these officials is quite limited, local administrators have a wide range of discretion in deciding when and how to inform politicians about events going on in their fields of operations. In many cases, local administrative officials alone or together with state agencies initiated the planning of improvements in environmental protection services. The Gemeinderat was briefly informed about the results of planning at a much later point. Consequently the degree of political direction of the planning process has been quite low. In many cases, political approval, when it was absolutely necessary, was sought in connection with the Gemeinderat's decision on a particular investment for a waste or sewage plant. At this late stage in the decision-making process, the possibilities for a political connection were very limited, since this would have meant going through the whole time-consuming planning process once again. In fact, in many cases the Gemeinderat could do little more than agree to what the administrative officials had planned. As can be seen in table 7-2, the extent of political participation in the implementation processes is higher in the smaller communities. This may be the result of the relatively higher visibility of political processes in these communities.

Table 7-2

Degree of Political Involvement in the Implementation Processes at the Local Level

	Degree of Involvement				
	High		Low		
	Waste	Sewage	Waste	Sewage	Total
More than 100,000 inhabitants	3	1	9	10	23
Less than 100,000 inhabitants	4	5	0	1	10
Total	7	6	9	11	33

In the larger communities there is a higher degree of functional specialization and differentiation between the political and the administrative structures. The fact that implementation is dominated by the local administrative officials and not by the local political decision makers need not, in itself, be problematic. When political representatives can rely upon the professional competence of their administrative staffs, they can relax political control. However, in the area of waste and sewage disposal the actual degree of political control appears to be insufficient, since effectiveness of the measures taken by local administrators is in many cases too low. This can be seen when the results actually achieved in implementation are compared with what an adequate solution would involve if the requirements of environmental protection had been properly considered:

- The site of the waste or sewage treatment plant should be far outside the built-up area in order to prevent nuisances from emissions and to provide room for further expansions of the community without coming into conflict with the waste or sewage plant.

- The size of the plants should guarantee sufficient reserve capacities for future increases in waste and sewage production resulting from economic and population growth of the community.

- The time frame for planning processes should cover a period of at least twenty years.

- The most advanced technology available for environmental protection should be used.

- Possibilities for intercommunity cooperation should be considered in order to reduce costs and to reach better technical and capacity solutions.

- More than one alternative solution should be investigated in order to come up with an optimal solution.

Only a few of the implementation processes investigated came even close to meeting these requirements. Most showed a very limited degree of this kind of rationality, as indicated in table 7-3. Decision-making was dominated mainly by some kind of bounded rationality and muddling through as this has been described in Lindblohm's models.

The primary objective of most local administrators was to keep costs down in a twofold sense. First of all these administrative officials tried to keep the immediate investment costs for improvements in environmental protection as low as possible by looking for sites near the built-up areas (thus minimizing investments for channels, etc.), by limiting the size of the plants built, and by seeking variances from stringent technical requirements on environmental protection. At the same time, they tried to limit the effort devoted to planning and detailed preparatory studies by considering only a limited number of alternatives for decisions about site, technical system, and inter-community cooperation. Especially with regard to sewage disposal, there was a strong tendency to work from decisions made years ago by improving existing plants, even when these sites had subsequently become inadequate because the property was too small for new buildings and was surrounded by residential areas. The effects of this low-level decision (when measured against an optimal location and construction decision in terms of maximum environmental protection) was poor performance. Of the fifteen sewage plants that went into operation before the end of our research, nine suffered follow-up problems of inadequate functioning, nuisances for neighbors, etc. The same was true for four of fourteen waste disposal plants.

Table 7-3

Indicators of the Relative Degree of Rationality in Implementation Decisions

	Degree of Rationality	
	High	Low
Searching for alternative sites for plants (yes/no)	11	9
Searching for technical system alternatives (yes/no)	11	29
Adequate size of sewage plant (yes/no)	2	16
Considering inter-community cooperation (yes/no)	11	35

While it is easy to attribute the administrators' tendency to limit the effort spent on detailed investigations to bureaucratic routines and the lack of effective political control, their concern with reducing investment costs is more difficult to explain. Given the low degree of political control together with the administrators' professional skills, their interest in keeping their work load as low as possible, and the state agencies' pressures for improvement, one would rather expect that local officials would push for solutions of the highest technical quality. This would save them much subsequent trouble with poorly functioning equipment and spare them negotiations with state agencies. Even though local fees for environmental services would rise with the technical improvements introduced, one would further expect that the officials would be able to gain citizen approval for such measures, since several public opinion polls have shown a certain willingness to pay more for environmental protection.

In fact, however, local administrators do not take advantage of these favorable conditions. In most cases they anticipated that they had to be frugal under any circumstances. They saw themselves defending what in their opinion were the community's real interests against more far-reaching demands of the state agencies. Consequently they never really put their potential influence concerning higher investments within the local decision-making structure to the test.

There seem to be three reasons for this behavior. First of all, local administrations act as technical experts and not as environmentalists. The issue of saving money, therefore, is more important to them than the arguments for improving environmental quality. Secondly, local agencies are convinced that they have to defend local autonomy against state intervention. Therefore they try to weaken the demands made by their state counterparts. Lastly, the internal division of labor with local administration also has consequences for the position and behavior of these officials. Waste and sewage disposal departments stand merely at the edge of local attention. Politicians and the local public expect that these officials will do their work effectively and will not become an issue of local politics where attention is primarily focused on problems of housing, economic growth, and schools. Departments responsible for these functions play the dominant role within local administration and are able to mobilize money for their programs. The waste and sewage disposal departments consequently have more difficulty in getting access to those at the top of the local administration who would have to support their demands for more investments in the Gemeinderat. Furthermore they often do not want to jeopardize their reputation for efficiency which has been earned by being moderate in their demands for and use of public funds.

SUMMARY: LIMITS TO IMPLEMENTATION AND POSSIBILITIES FOR IMPROVEMENT

There are several reasons for the implementation deficits discussed above:

a) The instruments available for supporting the states' demands for improving local environmental services often are too weak. Strategies of direct negative as well as positive sanctions turn out to be ineffective; a greater degree of success has been achieved by indirect negative sanctions (e.g., threat of stopping further community growth).

b) Political control over local administration is too weak. Local politicians rely too heavily on the skills of their administrative officials.

c) Local administrators are not diligent enough when planning and considering alternative schemes for providing environmental protection services.

d) Local waste and sewage departments engage in costsaving activities instead of trying to mobilize more money for their activities.

Any attempt to improve this situation should tackle both the instruments available to influence the state-local relationship and the conditions of local decision making. First steps to strengthen the states' position have already been undertaken. The introduction of effluent charges seems to have increased the communities' willingness to make investments for sewage disposal. Furthermore, the funds available for state grants have been increased in connection with the economic stabilization program, thus reducing the number of local communities waiting for financial assistance.[3]

At the local level increased effectiveness could be expected from a stronger activation of the local political system. This means that political representatives as well as local civic movements that have shown an increasing interest in environmental protection during the last years, should also worry about things that in the past may have seemed to be trivial matters in their eyes, like waste and sewage disposal. Evidence from some of our cases shows that the results of implementation can be improved when local representatives ask more often and in more detail for information about what is being done and about the alternatives that should be taken into account. Increased political attention will in turn strengthen the position of local waste and sewage departments in administrative bargaining and may cause them to drop their general cost-saving strategies.

NOTES

1. Data reported here are drawn from an empirical study financed by the German Research Foundation and carried out by the author together with Axel Muller and Peter Wassen in 1978-1979. Case studies on forty-six decision-making processes concerning the construction or improvement of waste and sewage disposal plants were conducted in eleven local communities of different size on the basis of official records and interviews. For a full report see Jochen Hucke, Axel Muller, Peter Wassen, Implementation kommunaler Umweltpoltik, Frankfurt/New York, 1980.
2. There are certain differences in the local political structure between the northern and southern parts of Germany. In southern Germany elected representatives themselves form the top of the local administration, while in northern Germany there is a city manager (Stadtdirektor) in charge of administrative

management along side the political office of mayor (Burgermeister).

3. In its program of investments for the future (Zukunfts-investitionsprogramm, ZIP), the federal government spent 16 billion DM for the improvement of sewage treatment, from 1978 to 1980, especially in the Rhine area.

THE ROLE OF EFFLUENT CHARGES IN DUTCH WATER QUALITY POLICY

8

Hans Bressers

INTRODUCTION

In the overpopulated country of Holland, the natural environment is very heavily burdened. Care for the environment is becoming more and more part of government policy. One of the means by which the public authorities can try to achieve a reduction of pollution is by imposing charges upon those who bring about pollution. This method is being used in the Netherlands, albeit formally the charges are not used as a means to induce polluters to pollute less but as means to pay the cost of abating the effects of pollution.

The use of effluent charges as a regulatory instrument is a much disputed affair, as much in the Netherlands as in the United States. The range of opinions goes from heated pleas in favor to direct rejection of such charges. One of the most important arguments that can be used for or against a given policy is its assumed effectiveness. Given certain aims, the question about effectiveness of a certain measure is in principle an empirical one. This chapter considers some of the evidence from the experience with the Dutch water quality charges to examine the relations between charges and the treatment of discharge by the most seriously polluting industrial branches. Of the various effluent charges used in the Netherlands only those within the framework of the Pollution of Surface Waters Act, 1970, will be examined, since this charge system has been in operation the longest time.

Section 2 of this chapter offers a brief survey of the goals, means and degree of goal-attainment of Dutch water quality policy. The next section considers the various functions the effluent charge can have as a policy instrument. Section 4 examines the ways in which charges can stimulate a decrease in pollution according to the theory, and considers the question of how to investigate whether the Dutch water quality charges do, indeed, have such an effect on the treatment of industrial effluent. Section 5 analyzes data bearing firstly on the relation between charges and the treatment of industrial water pollution and, secondly, on the question of whether the high correlation found can be rightly interpreted as a strong causal relation. In Section 6 we conclude that effluent fees do, in fact, have a strong stimulative affect on pollution control.

A BRIEF SURVEY OF DUTCH WATER QUALITY POLICY

Three principles of Dutch water quality policy are of importance when discussing the effectiveness of effluent charges: the stand-still principle, the preference for combatting pollution at the source, and the polluter-pays principle.

The stand-still principle can be regarded as the main goal of the policy. In the Dutch interpretation it implies that regulatory efforts are aimed at "reducing the total extent of existing pollution, by both dealing with particular problem areas and preserving as much as possible the present level of environmental quality in relatively unpolluted areas".

Consequently, the object of the 1969 legislation is to make surface waters cleaner. But Dutch government also has certain preferences regarding the way in which this goal should be attained. Specifically, it prefers to combat pollution at the source. In the case of water quality policy this means that a reduction of the amount of pollution in industrial waste water is to be preferred to eliminating this pollution in central sewage treatment plants after discharge. However, this is more theory than practice. In the past decade an enormous effort has been made to extend regional treatment capacity with the result that the amount of organic pollution removed from industrial effluent increased from 26% in 1975 to 46% in 1980, thereby to a large extent making up arrears bringing the Netherlands in line with the advancements of other countries who use the regulatory approach.

In order to combat pollution at the source the 1970 Pollution of Surface Waters Act prohibits all direct discharges of effluent into surface waters without a license. Indirect polluters who discharge into a sewerage collector must observe the conditions imposed by municipalities which in turn face demands upon the quality of discharges from their treatment plants from the water authorities. Direct dischargers are required to have a permit in which conditions for the discharge are formulated. This rather complex permit system has resulted in similar responses as in other countries: it serves more as a power base for negotiations than as a means for straight-on implementing standards.

The third principle, "polluter-pays", is the basis for the effluent charges of the Pollution of Surface Waters Act. Officially, the sole purpose of these effluent charges is the collection of the money needed to finance purification measures taken. Given the ambitious program of expanding the purification capacity, the charges involve large amounts of money. The revenues from the charges in 1971 amounted to about $20,000,000, about $140,000,000 in 1979 and about $300,000,000 in 1980 (U.S. dollars). In the

Netherlands each firm has to pay a fee roughly according to the amount of water pollution it produces. The amount of pollution is measured in pollution-units, called inhabitant-equivalents. An inhabitant-equivalent is meant to be the equivalent of the amount of organic pollution of waste water one person normally produces. The fee per pollution unit rose sharply during the period that the charge system has been in effect (from about $4 to about $15-$20) with some differences from one region to another. This differentiation is not, however, based upon different environmental standards, but on the regionally different costs of building and maintaining purification plants. Given the official "goal" of these charges (i.e., to raise revenue) effect they may have in reducing the pollution of industrial waste water can be viewed as a positive side-effect.

In 1969 the Dutch surface waters were polluted by dozens of millions inhabitant-equivalent (ie) of organic pollution. Surface waters, especially flowing ones, have the capacity to purify themselves from these organic wastes. But the enormous quantity of pollution by far surpassed this self-cleaning capacity in most places in the country. As a consequence waters lacked oxygen and became biologically "dead". Of the total amount of organic pollution about 32.6 million ie were produced by industry. Fourteen branches of industry accounted for 90% of this, or roughly 29.2 million ie. It was these branches of industry at which the water quality policy had to be directed if organic pollution was to be combated at the source. The effects of these policies have been remarkable. By 1975 the organic pollution produced by the fourteen branches had already been decreased by 14,800,000 ie's. In 1980 the total was 9,090,000 ie's. The average improvement during the whole period was 69%, of which 49% was achieved between 1969 and 1975 and 20% during the period 1975-80. During this last period 39% of the pollution value remaining in 1975 was removed. The question remains, however: Can this goal-attainment be regarded as a side effect of the Dutch effluent charges?

EFFLUENT CHARGE AS INSTRUMENT OF ENVIRONMENT POLICY

The effect of environmental charges is usually divided into three functions:[1] a revenue function, a regulatory function and an allocative function.

Revenue Function

In the Dutch environment law pollution charges are justified by their function as revenue charges.[2] Viewed in these terms, these charges are intended to raise money for financing measures to improve environmental quality. The amount of revenue to be collected will be determined by the amount necessary to pay for these measures.

Regulatory Function

In addition to a function in connection with operationalizing the principle "the polluter pays", these charges can also be used as restraining or regulating charges. In this case the amount of the fee to be paid by a firm will also depend on the amount of pollution caused by its production. Thus the charges will have a differential impact on the costs of different production activities. Those forms of production or products previously creating a relatively high level of pollution will become relatively expensive in comparison with those forms of production involving relatively minimal amounts of pollution, which will, therefore, become relatively less expensive. Thus, the charges can stimulate a move to processes and products which cause less pollution. Gradually, the Dutch government has begun to recognize this regulating function of effluent charges.[3] This does not mean that the present system effluent charges is optimal for this regulatory function. In order to obtain optimality the level of such charges should be derived from the costs of industrial effluent needed to meet quality objectives and not from the need to finance the construction of purification works.[4] Other factors responsible for the fact that the Dutch effluent charges are not optimal as regulatory charges are:

- that the pollution level from the smaller industrial discharges is computed on the basis of the number of employees, the level of production or the level of water consumption which means that in such cases the amount being charged is not directly related to the level of pollution;[5]
- that for polluters producing less than 10 (formerly 20) pollution units (including all households) a scale of set charges which does not vary with pollution loads is in force, which means the charge can be viewed as a revenue charge only;[6]
- that the system of general charges is applied only to biologically treatable waste. In many, but not all, cases a charge is imposed for heavy metals but only rarely for other pollutants.[7]

Allocative Function

The third possible function of charges to be mentioned here is the allocative function. This function is employed in the economic theory of the "externalities".[8] Externalities are to be looked upon as influences, positive or negative, operating outside the market and working as side-effects on the production conditions or the satisfaction level of other economic units.[9] Since real costs and assets do not play a part in the decision-making of economic actors, externalities are looked upon as market imperfections.[10] A remedy often suggested to deal with these imperfections is to charge for externalities whenever possible.[11] Sometimes this is possible by putting a charge upon production factors with harmful externalities for the environment. In this way the price mechanism as a decision-making model will, theoretically, lead to an optimum allocation of production factors.

After initial enthusiasm over the possibilities for dealing with "soft" environmental interests in the context of a "hard" economic weighing of costs against benefits, nowadays there is presently a good deal of skepticism regarding the use of such economic incentives. In this connection the work of R. Hueting in the Netherlands is illustrative. In his dissertation (a brave attempt to attach prices to negative environment effects, thus creating a "new shortage"), he reaches the conclusion that while the connection between environment and economy has been made theoretically, the quantitative elaboration (for the Netherlands) appears to be only partially possible.[12] Outside Holland, Baumol and Oates, among others, have opposed allocative charges since these are not feasible in light of the lack of necessary information. Instead they advocate a system of regulating charges based upon a well developed environment standard.[13]

Valuation of Regulative Function of Effluent Charges

In the Netherlands the system of water quality charges has been designed to meet a revenue raising function. However, in relation to the treatment of industrial effluent the regulative function has come to be particularly important. Regulative charges are one of the possible instruments to influence the decision-making process in firms in such a way that the amount of pollution they cause will be reduced. Opposition to the use of charges as such an instrument of regulation has always been very strong in Holland. In part this can be explained by the fact that many civil servants and politicians are not familiar with the underlying economic theory, by the resistance of firms and their representatives to any and every increase of costs, the fear that the autonomy of the firm could be curtailed, in the conservative camp, and, on the progressive side, by the distrust of the market mechanism.[14]

A sound appreciation of effluent charges as an instrument of regulation must be based, however, on an understanding of theoretical and empirical arguments used to justify this function. Economists, in particular, have written much about the efficiency and effectiveness of effluent charges.[15] However, the discussion tends to stop with theoretical arguments. As a result pleas made in favor of the introduction of regulatory effluent charges as the most important instrument of environmental policy cannot be backed up with the experience of actual practice.[16] Nevertheless, critical remarks are made about their expected effectiveness and efficiency. In the statement of the Dutch government on "Instruments of Environmental Policy" effluent charges are considered to be less suitable in these situations where:

- the cost of collecting the necessary information is very high (although these will be at least as high in the case of nonfiscal regulation, such as a permit system);
- the price elasticity of the demand is low, so that price changes will only have slight effects. (Viewed over a longer term, technological development stimulated by these changes in the cost structure will have results for the level of industrial water pollution. Moreover, out of considerations of competitiveness, the firms will try to reduce their costs to a minimum, even if the demand for a certain product is not decreasing.)
- in view of the possible dangers, damage or hindrance to the immediate surroundings, highly toxic waste must be subjected to precisely stipulated limitation.[17] In my opinion this last factor represents a particularly significant argument against using effluent charges as the primary instrument for promoting the treatment of industrial effluent discharges.

A theoretical disadvantage, which has been of small practical importance for the Dutch situation in the immediate past, is that pollution will increase when charges per production unit remain the same while production and consumption increase.[18] For this reason continual adjustment of the level of the effluent charges would be necessary with all the costs of decision-making that these recalculations would involve. With a permit system this would not be necessary because the maximum amount of pollution allowed would be stipulated in the license. Consequently, any production increases that occur cannot lead to increases in the amount of pollution produced. Since, in the Dutch case, the level of the charges does not pretend to be attuned to the "acceptable" amount of pollution anyway, this argument has been of minor importance. Moreover, by tying the level of charges to the cost of building new treatment plants, these charges are constantly rising much faster than production and consumption. Furthermore, one has to ask if the licenses would not be continually adjusted as, on one hand, the standards per production unit became more restrictive as a result of technological developments, and because, on the other hand, in many cases the authorities will not want to lose the added employment from an expansion of production by refusing to allow any increase in pollution.

Another criticism that is sometimes hurled against the effluent charge is that this could be construed by polluters as "buying the right to pollute".[19] It is feared that viewed in this way the effluent charge will hamper the treatment of industrial waste water. This argument against effluent charge, as being a counter-productive sanitation clean-up instrument is advanced especially by environmentalists.[20] However, irrespective of the theoretical arguments pro and con, how do things work out in practice? Can we say that effluent charges are an effective instrument for reducing industrial pollution as economic theory would have us believe? Or is it more so that polluters see it as a means of buying off their responsibility for protecting the quality of the environment, as some environmentalists fear? These are empirical questions. With regard to such queries, Lettie McSpadden Wenner points out that there has been very little empirical research into the effectiveness of effluent charge. What there is does not allow for hard conclusions.[21]

In the following sections we have tried to make a modest contribution to increasing the empirical knowledge of the effectiveness of effluent charges. Effectiveness will be interpreted here in terms of the effect of these charges on the realization of a specific end, viz: the treatment of industrial water pollution. We first look closely into the theoretical assumptions regarding the operation of charges and operationalization of the variables involved. In the last part of the chapter information concerning the most polluting industrial branches in the Netherlands will be interpreted in light of this discussion.

THE OPERATION OF EFFLUENT CHARGES: THEORY AND OPERATIONALIZATION

The pollution restraining effect of environmental charges is brought about by the price mechanism. The supposed effect of the price mechanism in turn is based upon a number of assumptions generally accepted by economists. These include the following:

1. The person making decisions is fully informed about cost and benefits, providing him therefore with all conceivable choice alternatives;
2. The person making decisions is "subjectively rational" which

means that in making decisions all perceived costs will be weighed against the benefits and that alternative will be selected with the highest net assets. Since all environmental charges are calculated on a per unit of pollution basis, they will have the effect of increasing the costs for products and forms of production in proportion to the amount of pollution these cause. On the basis of these assumptions, a number of consequences can be expected from the use of such charges.

A Decreasing Demand

The first effect will be a higher price for products whose production generates a relatively high amount of pollution. Depending on the price elasticity of the demand for the products in question, this will, to a certain extent, lead to a decrease in the demand for the product in question. As a result, the production of these products, and consequently the pollution they cause, will also decrease.[22]

Reduced Charges as Possible Benefits of Abatement

Charges also influence the decision-making process in firms. In formulating their response to pollution control (charges) the individual factory will consider the relative costs of (a) paying charges, or (b) undertaking abatement measures. Theoretically it can be demonstrated that the firm will get its highest net benefit by reducing pollution to such an extent that the cost of the last treated pollution unit equals the saving on the charge for this unit.[23]

Technical Development

Thirdly, out of concern for their competitive position, firms will try to develop techniques enabling them to save on charges by polluting less.[24] In this way, the induced cost increase can be counteracted. Expressed in terms of decision making this means trying to create new and attractive choice alternatives. In terms of economic theory it means trying to lower the marginal cost curve of pollution abatement.[25] This effect of a system of charges is also realized via the decision making process within the firm.

On the basis of the above theoretical considerations the following variables can be derived for constructing a model for explaining the extent of the pollution abatement effort:

Y	- the extent of pollution abatement (dependent variable),
X1	- the amount of charges per pollution unit or the marginal benefits of abatement,
X2	- the marginal costs of abatement,
X3	- the increase or decrease of production.

(X1, X2, and X3 are independent variables).

Sanitation of Pollution (Y)

The dependent variable will be measured in terms of the precentage decrease in the organic pollution produced by the various branches of industry.

Effluent Charges (X1)

According to the above model, the impact that charges will have on the abatement of pollution should be a function of the amount of the charge per pollution unit. There are, however, reasons to doubt if the level of charge is the only or even the most important aspect of the charge affecting the abatement effort. If we consider abatement of discharge to be the result of a decision by a single, rational actor, as is usually done in economic theory, it has to be assumed that his decision will be the result of weighing the marginal costs against the marginal benefits per pollution unit (i.e., the level of charges). However when decisions are seen as products of a complicated organization, which seems to be more likely, other aspects of the decision making process must be taken into consideration.[26] Disjointed incrementalism is no monopoly of state bureaucracy. All large organizations are unlikely to make quick changes to catch small net benefits.[27]

The above indicates that the effect of charge in limiting industrial discharge is not caused in the first place by marginal net benefits.[28] In order to convince firms to modify their present mode of production, the relative burden of the amount of charge on the firms costs structure is of greater importance. This "pressure of charges" can be determined by multiplying the amount charged per pollution unit by the amount of pollution units produced. In order to correct for differences in the level of production between firms and thus to calculate the burden of the change in proportion to the size of the firm, this figure must be divided by the production value.[29] In this way it is possible to determine what part of the production costs is caused by water quality charges. The formula showing the way in which this "charge factor" influences the decision making process of the firms looks like this:

$$\frac{\text{amount of pollution units}}{\text{production value}} \times \frac{\text{level of charge}}{\text{per pollution unit}} = \frac{\text{pressure exerted}}{\text{by charges}}$$

Although the level of charge per unit varies considerably from one regional water authority to another,[30] the differences in average levels of charge per pollution unit from one branch of industry to another will be much less, since most branches of industry are spread out over many different areas. This means the averge differences between various branches of industry with regard to the relation between pollution and production value will be relatively constant.[31] Consequently, when water quality charges significantly affect the extent of discharge abatement, then differences in the extent of abatement between branches will also correlate with the number of pollution units produced divided by the production value. This factor will therefore be considered as an indicator of the sensibility of the industrial branches to the pressure of charges and will be called the "charge factor" forthwith.

When a correlation can be shown between two phenomena, this does not necessarily mean that there exists a causal relation. Only in a perfect experimental research design, where all possible disturbing factors can be controlled can causality be proved. But even when we cannot employ such a research design, there are ways to prove plausability of causality. One of the ways this can be done is to take care that the indicator for the independent variable is distinctive enough to suggest a possible causality between this variable and the dependent variable.[32] As far as could be determined there is no other plausible explanation for any correlation found between the charge factor and degree of abatement than that these charges have led to the observed abatement effort. It is, of course, possible that a high degree of pollution will attract extra attention from the authorities, environmentalists and public opinion and that this "publicity" will lead to abatement activity. However, it is difficult to explain why this attention would be directed towards the pollution per unit of production value, instead of the overall extent of pollution as such.[33]

The Cost Factor (X2)

The (marginal) abatement cost will have a negative impact on the extent to which the amount of pollution discharged is limited. This factor can therefore be used to help explain differences between the amount of abatement in various branches of industry. The operationalization of the variable "abatement cost" is difficult. The curve of marginal abatement cost per branch of industry is unknown. Moreover, it would be difficult to analyze in a model a variable whose value not only varies from one unit of investigation to another, but also within a given unit. However, there are estimations by the Dutch Central Bureau of Statistics of the total cost of abatement per branch of industry.[34] By dividing these costs by the number of pollution units produced the average costs of abatement per branch can be obtained. These average costs should be interpreted as indicating the height of the marginal cost curve.[35] As far as is known these marginal cost curves are curvilinear. Assuming that the shape of the curves is just about the same for a given amount of abatement the average cost will correspond to the marginal cost.[36] The correlation between the average cost of abatement and the marginal cost of abatement is even more obvious when we consider that most branches of industry treated between 50% and 100% of their effluent during the investigation period, thus "paying" for a considerable part of the marginal cost curve.[37]

Production Increase (X3)

Generally an increase of production will lead to a higher pollution value of the industrial discharge while a production decrease will lead to reduction in pollution. It is, however, possible to correct the value of the dependent variable, the extent of abatement, for the amount production has increased or decreased during the same period. Production increase does not always result in a proportionate increase of pollution. This is the case, for example, when new investments are made to prevent pollution. Likewise, a production decrease need not always lead to a proportionate reduction of pollution when, for example, full production does not produce more pollution than a lower level of production with the same equipment. Therefore, it is better to consider an increase in production as a separate explanatory variable. This has the additional advantage that it will then be possible to consider the influence of charges and costs on the level of production. This variable is operationalized as the percentage increase or decrease in the amount of production (figure 8-1).

Model

The model used to explain the extent of pollution abatement contains three independent variables. These are:

Figure 8-1

Model of the Explanation of the Extent of Abatement

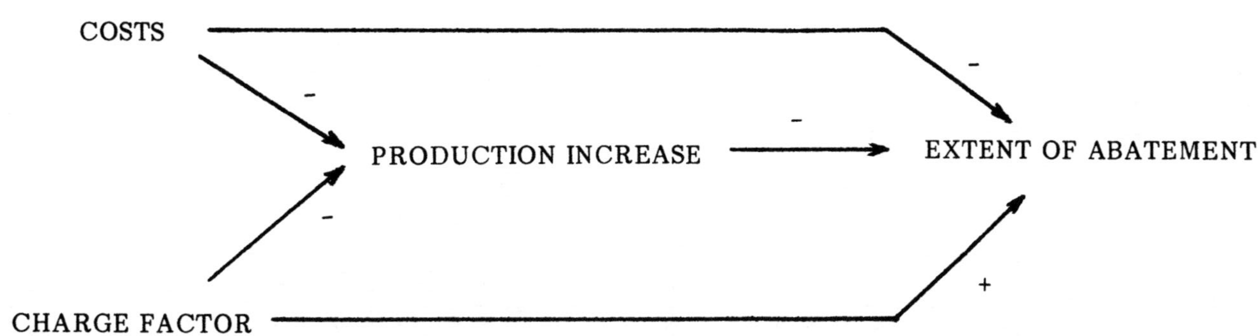

1. The number of pollution units per production value of one billion Dutch guilders;
2. The average cost of abatement per pollution unit;
3. The percent increase in production.

Given our theoretical assumptions, it is to be expected that the first factor will correlate positively with the extent of abatement, and the second and third negatively. The fact that for some relations between the variables we have used average cost instead of the marginal cost will mean that it will be necessary to correct for curvilinearity.[38]

Data Collection and Selection of Research Units

The information on abatement costs has been taken from the Central Bureau of Statistics publication called "Water Pollution Related to Production and Investment 1969" (1977). The figures on pollution by various branches of industry in 1969 and the production value of these branches in millions of guilders in that year were also taken from this study. Data on pollution in 1975 were taken from the Indicative Multi-Year Programme on Water Pollution 1980-1984. The remaining data were calculated on the basis of other published and nonpublished CBS information.[39] The fourteen branches of industry that were the most polluting in 1969 were chosen as research units. In that year these branches of industry together accounted for more than 90% of the biologically treatable industrial pollution. For this reason, the study can be viewed as a semi-population analysis of industrial water pollution in the Netherlands for the period 1969-1980. The analysis is restricted to pollution by biologically treatable waste.

THE EFFECTIVENESS OF DUTCH EFFLUENT CHARGES

Effectiveness can be defined as goal-attainment resulting from a given policy. There is no doubt that a certain amount of goal-attainment has been achieved. During the period 1969-1980 industrial discharge of biologically treatable waste decreased markedly. The fourteen industrial branches analyzed produced almost 79% less organic pollution in 1980 than they had in 1969. The question remains, however: to what extent can the amount of pollution abatement realized be attributed to the system of effluent charges? In trying to answer this question on the basis of the data we have gathered, we will first look at the period as a whole and then compare the years 1969-1975 and 1975-1980.

Correlation Analysis

The average amount of abatement per branch of industry during the whole period was 69%. According to the model outlined above, the level of abatement by the industrial branches should correlate negatively with the abatement cost and production increase, and positively with the charge factor (the pollution divided by the production value), the factor through which according to the model, the effluent charges have an impact. Also the necessary correction for curvilinearity should lead to stronger correlations.

These expectations all seem more or less to hold. The average abatement cost has a negative correlation with the amount of abatement of r=-.50, s=.034.[40] Increase in production shows a slight negative correlation with the amount of abatement (r=-.21, s=.236). On the other hand, the charge factor (the relation between pollution and production value) correlates strongly with the amount of abatement (r=.73, s=.002). When there is no correction for curvilinearity this correlation is much lower: r=.35. The above correlations all point in the expected direction. In order to get an idea of the extent to which differences in amount of abatement can be statistically "explained" by each of the three independent variables, the correlation coefficients can be squared. Then the differences in production increase explain only a small part of the amount of abatement: 4%. That part of the differences in sanitation that can be explained by the differences in average cost of treatment is somewhat larger: 25%. By far the most important of these three factors is the effluent charge which can account for 53% of the variation.

Regression Analysis

The next step is to see which part of the variance in the amount of treatment can be explained statistically by the three factors together and what must be attributed to each individual factor.[41] To do this a multiple regression technique has been used. Table 8-1 gives a summary.

Table 8-1

Explained Variance in Treatment

multiple correlation	0.79 (Pearsons R)
% explained variance	63% (R^2)
standardized influence (beta) of	
a. factor of charge	0.61
b. cost of treatment	-0.25
c. production increase	-0.30

Apparently the influence of the charge factor does not decrease much when the influences of the other two factors are taken into account.[42] The model with the three independent variables appears to be able to "explain" almost two-thirds of the differences in the amount of pollution abatement between various branches of industry.

The model presented above (see figure 8-1) suggests the possibility that abatement cost and charges also affect the amount of abatement by means of their influence on increases or decreases in the level of production. The charge factor and abatement cost variables appear to have a fairly low negative influence on production increase. In Figure 8-2 the model is presented again, this time with the beta values. Furthermore, the effect of cost on abatement is partly balanced out by the influence of this factor on the production increase (-.25 - (-.36 x -.30) = -.14). The indirect effect of the charge factor via its consequences for the level of production results in an increase of influence by (-.16 x -.30) = .05.

Two Out-Liers

In the construction of the above model, some potentially important factors were not included. These include:

— the level of charge per pollution unit (because it was assumed this would on the average be fairly constant between various branches of industry),

Figure 8-2

Elaborated Model for Explaining the Amount of Abatement

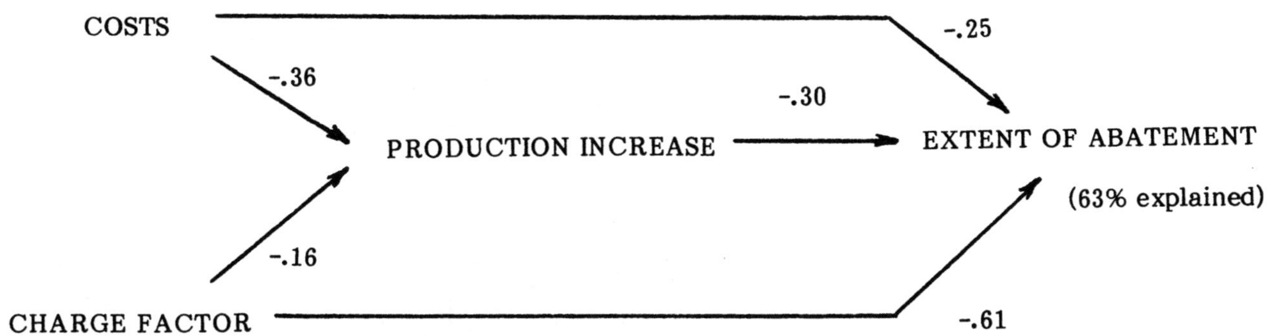

— nonfiscal regulation via the licensing procedure.

With two of the industrial branches investigated there is good reason to expect that the omitted factors do in fact influence the amount of abatement undertaken. One of these branches is the starch industry. For some time this industry had expected that it would be allowed to discharge its untreated effluent directly into the coastal waters by means of a pipeline leading into the sea. In anticipation of this solution, these firms were charged a lower effluent charge than was the case in other industrial branches. In the meantime, policy has changed and untreated discharges are no longer to be permitted. However, since the industry has expected to be spared the necessity of limiting the pollution in its discharges, it did not pursue alternative abatement strategies with the consequence that the amount of pollution reduction realized by this industry is less than would have otherwise been technically possible.

Another branch of industry occupying a special place is stock-farming. This branch consists of many thousands of relatively small "firms" for which the charges have hardly ever been calculated precisely in line with the amount of pollution they cause (especially that caused by cows and pigs). Accordingly, the impact of charges on the amount of abatement realized by this industrry will be small. On the other hand, this branch of industry has been subjected to a most stringent policy of nonfiscal regulation in the form of various prohibitions and control measures. In contrast, in other industrial branches the limits placed on the amount of organic pollution permitted in their discharge is often very weak. The reason that strict limits are placed on stock farms is that they are usually not connected to the sewerage system with the result that their discharges cannot be handled in treatment installations. This effluent is usually discharged directly into surface waters such as ditches which have a limited self-cleaning capacity.

When the correlation analysis and regression analysis is repeated for a group of twelve branches of industry (excluding the above two), the influence of the charge factor is even more noticeable. For this group of twelve branches the amount of abatement carried out between 1969 and 1980 correlates with the factors discussed as follows:

a. the charge factor
$R=.84$; expl. var $(R^2)=70\%$; $s=.001$

b. the cost of abatement
$R=-.48$; expl. var $(R^2)=24\%$; $s=.055$

c. production increase
$R=-.24$; expl. var. $(R^2)=6\%$; $s=.222$

Taken together in a regression analysis the three factors account for more than three quarters of the difference between the industrial branches in the amount of pollution reduction. The standardized influence (beta) of the charge factor in this analysis is .83. This means that the inclusion of abatement costs and production increase does not reveal the correlation between charge factor and pollution decrease to be spurious.

The Periods Compared

The various results so far show an especially strong relation between the charge factor and the amount of abatement; here the model is able to explain almost two-thirds of the variation in the amount of abatement. A further step is required in order to test our assumption that the relation is causal. Indications for such a relation might be derived from the accuracy of the predictions made on the basis of a causal relationship between these factors. In order to do them we divided the total period from 1969 to 1980 into two (1969-1975 and 1975-1980) and examined the following "predictions" regarding the way in which these periods could be expected to differ.

Charges - Pollution

It was expected that the influence of the charge factor would be greater in the second period than in the first. Only in the second period were the charges collected generally throughout the whole country. Moreover, they increased very quickly. At the same time, it could be assumed that the charge factor would also have an influence on the level of abatement in the first period because all firms knew already in 1969, when the Pollution of Surface Water Act was passed, that they would be charged in proportion to the amount of pollution they caused. Also various water quality inspectors visited all firms in their jurisdictions to check on their awareness of the above policy and to inquire about the amount of pollution they proposed to deliver to the treatment plants in the future. Consequently, in combination with the direct influence of the relatively low charges of that period, an anticipatory infuence of the charges on the behavior of the factories was likely.

Costs - Pollution

It was assumed that the influence of the cost factor would

remain constant during the two periods. The cost of abatement measures would thus have a constant limiting effect on the amount of abatement itself. At most it could be expected that in the recession period 1975-1980 more attention was paid to costs than in the period 1969-1975

Production - Pollution

The effect of the factor production increase on abatement could be expected to be much smaller during the second than during the first period. While a very big production increase occurred during 1969-1975, production remained quite stable for the period 1975-1980.

All three of the predictions appear to be largely right. The Pearson correlations between charge factor and pollution decreases are .61 and .65 respectively. The abatement costs correlate -.46 and -.54 respectively and the production increase -.20 and .13. As expected, the (Pearson) correlation of abatement with the cost of abatement measures does not differ much from one period to the other, although there is a slight increase. The effect of production increase is also, as expected, somewhat smaller. The predicted increase in the influence of the charge factor during the second period, as compared with the first, is quite small, less than was expected.

CONCLUSION

The so-called "charge factor", i.e. the sensitivity of industrial firms to the pressure of effluent charges and defined by dividing the amount of pollution produced by a given industrial branch by the production value for that branch, appears to correlate strongly with the amount of abatement. Moreover, all these relationships seem to confirm the expectations derived from the theoretical assumptions made. On the whole, the model explains some 63% (in the group of 12 even 76%) of the differences (variation?) in the amount of abatement carried out in the different branches. If the observed relationships are causal, then it would seem that effluent charges have been a very effective instrument for achieving a reduction in pollution by industrial effluent in Holland.

At this point then the question remaining to be answered is to what extent can these relationships be regarded as causal relationships? On the basis of the above analysis it can be concluded that:

1. The indicator for the pressure exerted by effluent charges has been chosen in such a way that there is hardly any other plausible explanation than that effluent charges are leading to abatement.

2. All relationships point in the theoretically expected direction.

3. The original relationships did not disappear when the effects of other factors were taken into account. This suggests that the relation between charge factor and abatement is not spurious.

4. When two industrial branches are excluded from the group examined (two industries for which it could be expected that the charge influences would have a less strong effect), the measured relationships between charge factor and amount of abatement was greater.

5. Assumptions regarding differences that could be expected between the relationships in the two periods turned out to be correct.

Given this evidence, therefore, we can draw the following conclusion: there are solid indications for a strong effect of effluent charges on the amount of abatement activity with regard to industrial discharges containing biologically treatable substances. Two qualifications of the general conclusion are, however, in order.

In the first place, the word indication in the conclusion has been used advisedly. In order to be more certain about the circumstances under which charges are effective, additional research would be necessary, involving a closer look than was possible here at the actual decision-making processes of the individual firms.[43] The above analysis underscores the importance of such investigations. Secondly it should be noted that while it can be shown that charges can be an effective instrument to stimulate abatement of industrial water pollution, it cannot therefore be concluded that such charges are in this respect superior to other types of instruments.[44]

In Holland, as in other countries, the primary policy instrument for reducing the amount of pollution in industrial waste water has been a permit system. Other analyses have shown that these permits and related policy instruments such as abatement plans drawn up by water authorities and individual firms have played no significant part in reducing organic pollution in industrial waste water. Furthermore, the experiences in other areas of environmental policy in Holland give reason to doubt whether a permit system could have stimulated the level of abatement activity with regard to industrial discharge actually observed.[45] Moreover it should be noted that the Dutch effluent charges formally are revenue-raising charges. It is possible that if these charges were set more with an eye to their function as regulative charges, their effect on the amount of abatement carried out would be greater.

This conclusion rests, however, on the assumption that the conditions that make this policy instrument effective in Holland would also hold where the effluent charges were geared more explicitly to their regulatory function. This may not be the case. The Dutch effluent charges are officially justified on the basis of their destination function. This has some disadvantages, but also an important advantage. Firms trying to avoid paying the charges would be regarded as tax-dodgers. The legitimacy of the instrument is based not only upon environmental values, but also upon the general liability to taxation. Perhaps the kind of effluent charges that are optimal from the point of view of economic theory would not be the most practicable ones. From a public administration point of view, the implementability of a policy instrument is no less important than the optimalization of its theoretical effects.

NOTES

I would like to thank Bas Denters, Pierre Coumans, Professor Andries Hoogerwerf, Jeroen G. Janssen and Jaap van Selm for their valuable comments on earlier versions of this chapter; also Janny van Vuren, Charles Mason, and Ken Hanf for their help with the translation.

Literature marked with a D is in Dutch. Titles are translated.

1. D. E. James, H. M A. Jansen and J. B. Opschoor, Economic Approaches to Environmental Problems, Amsterdam, 1978, p. 216. Governmental statement: Instruments of environmental policy, D, Second chamber of Parliament, Assembly-year 1974-1975, pp. 142-143.
2. Explanatory Memorandum to the Pollution of Surface Waters Act, D, Second chamber of Parliament, Assembly-year 1964-65, pp. 11-12.
3. Hans Bressers, "Policy Analysis and Development of Water Quality Policy," D, in Bestuurswetenschappen, 1979 (3), pp. 70-82.
4. See for instance, A. Myrick Freeman III, Robert H. Haveman, and Allen V. Kneese, The Economics of Environmental Policy (New York, 1973), pp. 97-98, and William J. Baumol and Wallace

E. Oates, "The Use of Standards and Prices for Protection of the Environment," in Peter Bohm and Allen V. Kneese, The Economics of Environment (London, 1971), p. 56.

5. This happens according to tables with conversion coefficients. The tables most used are those of central governmental charges and the model of the Union of Water Authorities.
6. Industries discharging less than (usually) 10 inhabitant equivalents are — for purposes of the collection of charges — considered to be private households and, as a result, pay for the fixed number of 3 or 3.5 ie's. Since the number of ie's is fixed in such cases there is no incentive to decrease pollution.
7. A charge on heavy metals is not generally applied and is in any case relatively lower than the charge on organic waste, since it covers only the cost of measurement and of eventual damage to the sewage treatment plant.
8. William J. Baumol and Walkace E. Oates, The Theory of Environmental Policy (Englewood Cliffs, NJ, 1975), part 1.
9. This definition is by P. Hennipman, Welfare Economics and Economic Policy (D, Alphen aan den Rijn, 1977).
10. See, for instance, David Collard, Prices, Market and Welfare (London, 1972), p. 3.
11. By economists in the tradition of Pigou.
12. R. Hueting, New Scarcity and Economic Growth, D, (Amsterdam, 1974), p. 264.
13. Baumol and Oates, 1971, op cit and 1975, op cit; see also, James, Jansen and Opschoor, 1978, op cit, p. 218.
14. This is illustrated by the study by J. van Puttens "Haagse Machten" (Powers in the Hague), D, (The Hague, 1980), pp. 121-123, about how the system of charges which was initially a central element of the Selective Investment Regulation gradually got weakened until there was only a weak reflection left of the original plans.
15. See, for instance, Allen V. Kneese, The Economics of Regional Water Quality (Baltimore, 1964); Lawrence J. White, "Effluent Charges as a Faster Means of Achieving Pollution Abatement," in Public Policy vol. 24 (Winter, 1976), pp. 111-125; Stuart S. Nagel, "Incentives for Compliance with Environmental Law," in Lester W. Milbrath and Frederick R. Inscho (eds.) The Politics of Environmental Policy, pp. 74-94; Krister Hjalte, Karl Lidgren and Ingemar Stahl, Environmental Policy and Welfare Economics (Cambridge, 1977), p. 59; and the economic literature mentioned before. Very enlightening is the article by Lettie McSpadden Wenner, "Pollution Control: Implementation Alternatives," in Policy Analysis, Winter 1978, pp. 47-65.
16. White 1978, op cit.

17. Governmental statement: Instruments of environmental policy, D, op cit, pp. 152-153.
18. Compare McSpadden Wenner, 1978, op cit, pp. 50-52.
19. Nagel, 1975, op cit, p. 79
20. Such as the Dutch section of Friends of the Earth International.
21. McSpadden Wenner, 1978, pp. 63-65.
22. Compare for instance Hjalte, Lidgren and Stahl, 1977, p. 59.
23. Compare Freeman, Haveman and Kneese, 1973, op cit, p. 99
24. This could be other means of production as well as cheaper ways for treating discharges.
25. Compare James, Jansen and Opschoor, 1978, op cit, p. 225.
26. Compare Graham T. Allison, Essence of Decision (Boston, 1971).
27. Walter A. Rosenbaum, The Politics of Environmental Concern (New York, 1976), quotes the former American Secretary of Interior Walter Hickel while speaking about the promotion of pollution sanitation by industries: "You've got to hit them with a two-by-four to make them believe you."
28. Local authorities I spoke to sometimes indicate that industries often pay more than necessary by not taking measures that would bring them net benefits. Among other things, which are mentioned in the text of the chapter, the investment should not only be profitable, but should be more profitable than other possible investments.
29. It would be more correct to divide the amount of charges paid by the added value in production but there are not suitable data for this.
30. In 1979 these varied between $6 and $19 per pollution unit. However, both extremes were the charges of very small water authorities. Eighty percent of the individual firms paid between about $11 and $16. The differences between the average level of the charges paid by the various branches were probably even less.
31. The ratio of the highest and the lowest average charges paid by the various branches is 2:1 at a maximum and probably less. The ratio of the highest and the lowest value of the factor pollution/production value is about 700:1!
32. Compare Michael Scriven, "The Methodology of Evaluation," in Ralph W. Tyler, Robert M. Gagne and Michael Scriven (eds.) Perspectives of Curriculum Evaluation (Chicago, 1967), pp. 39-83.
33. If we took individual firms as our units of analysis, it is possible that heavy polluting industries per product unit would get extra attention because they pollute more than similar industries. Public opinion and government may consider this pollution unnecessarily heavy. Our analysis is carried out per industrial

branch and, therefore, this possible explanation for the influence the factor may have on amount of abatement is not plausible.

34. Dutch Central Bureau for Statistics, Water pollution in relation to production and investment 1969, D, (The Hague, 1977).
35. See on the theoretical points James, Jansen, and Opschoor, 1978, op cit, p. 218; Myrick Freeman III, Haveman and Kneese, 1973, op cit, p. 99; and for empirical data, Central Bureau for Statistics, General Environmental Statistics, D, 1975 (SO2-redution Holland); Allen V. Kneese and Charles L. Schultze, Pollution Prizes and Public Policy (Washington D.C., 1975) (with regard to sugar production and oil refining) and Hjalte, Lidgren and Stahl, 1977, op cit, pp. 60-63 (SO2 reduction in Sweden).
36. This correlation would be perfect when (1) the curves do not intersect and (2) industries have identical starting points as far as abatement activity is concerned.
37. The fact that the average abatement costs are placed, as an independent variable, next to the factor of charge may cause problems. It may be that the cost of abatement will not only influence the amount of abatement itself but also the extent to which charges will lead to abatement measures being taken. In other words, at low cost and correlation between the charge factor and abatement might be stronger than at higher levels of abatement costs. In this case it would not be correct to consider the two variables as independent variables. The normal test using a multiplying factor in the regression equation was not possible because the variables had been transformed to correct for curvilinearity of relations. However, when regression was applied to partial populations, such as those with high costs and those with low costs, highly similar outcomes resulted when the influence of the two outliers (which were disturbing factors especially in small partial groups) was taken into account.
38. The amount of pollution units per unit production value will correlate with the amount of abatement. There is reason to expect a decrease in this correlation when moving along the line of 0% towards 100% abatement. The marginal cost of abatement is initially low, but increases curvilinearly when nearing the 100% abatement. The pressure of the charges first leads to much abatement (caused by the low marginal cost) but when increased sanitation has led to increased marginal cost, the marginal effect of the increase will not even be possible. This expected curvilinear form of the correlation can be transformed into a linear form and thus be made suitable for statistical analysis by taking from the root or the logarithm of

the explanatory variable. This function has the form of y=x or y=L09.x. This last approach was chosen because empirically this appeared to be the best approach to the relationship. When looking at the impact of the average cost on the amount of abatement, a comparible problem occurs. Now, however, the correlation is negative, so that an analogue transformation would mean that one would have to take the root or the logarithm of a negative figure, which is not possible. A good approach to the expected curvilinear form of the relation is given however by a function with the form $y=a-bx^2$, squaring the average cost to obtain a linear relation. The fact it is a declining curve does not matter because a B-coefficient can also be negative. There is no reason to expect curvilinearity in the impact of the production increase on the amount of sanitation. The impact that production increase will have on pollution per industrial branch is not exerted by means of abatement and the marginal cost that go together with it, but by means of an increase in the amount of produced goods (or a decrease). It does not matter therefore, for the relation between production amount and pollution, that the marginal cost of sanitation has a curvilinear path.

39. An appendix with a more detailed account of data sources can be obtained from the author. Please write to Hans Bressers, Department of Public Administration, Twente University of Technology, P. O. Box 217, Enschede, Holland.

40. The significance of the correlations is shown, although most of the population of polluting branches is included in the research. This is meant not to show whether or not the population has the same relations as the sample, whether the relations can be explained by chance or are worthwhile to interpret causally.

41. Though fourteen branches are a very small number when making use of techniques for multi-variant analysis, I believe this to be justified because it is the only way to make full use of this data. Furthermore, correlation and regression analysis with various combinations of seven to twelve branches showed a remarkable consistency in the results. For this reason the reliability of the analysis seems to be good. Even in this small sample the beta of the charge factor is significant (Compare the ratio of standard errors and B's). Finally, what is important here is not the precise regression equation, but the fact that the impact of the charge factor is shown not to be spurious.

42. Partial correlation analysis was also used in order to find out how much of the relation is maintained when other phenomena are held constant. This leads to identical results: Correlation of

abatement, with relation other two factors constant, with

charge factor	0.63
cost of abatement	-0.30 (Partial R)
production increase	-0.43

43. Given the fact that the operation of the charges is on the level of individual firms while the analysis in this article is at the level of industrial branches, there are some methodological problems. In research which has not yet been published, I also found the same strong indications for an impact of the effluent charges in an analysis based upon the comparison of water authority areas instead of branches of industry. This would indicate that the relation found in this article is not an artifact of the level of analysis. See Hans Bressers, Policy-Effectiveness and Water Quality Policy, D, (Euschede, The Hague, 1983), chapter 6.
44. Giandomenico Majone in "Choice Among Policy Instruments for Pollution Control," Policy Analysis (Fall 1976), pp. 589-613, claims that even different methods of policy implementation would probably have identical results when lower relations remain unchanged. Investigations in France showed that charges became the subject of negotiation just as well as permit conditions (Kneese, quoted by McSpadden Wenner, 1978, op cit).
45. For the Dutch situation, see Ministry of Public Health and Environment, "Advice on Combined Granting of Licenses Based on the Air Pollution Act and the Nuissance Act," D, 1976; Investigation on the Coordination of Environmental Legislation, D, 1977; Test Project License Procedures Based on the Air Pollution Act and the Nuissance Act. D, 1977; and the Ministry of Economic Affairs, Possibilities to Improve the Governmental License Procedures, D, 1976.

POLICY ALTERNATIVES IN SOVIET ENVIRONMENTAL PROTECTION

9

Charles E. Ziegler

INTRODUCTION

A number of developments over the past decade or so illustrate the increasing salience of environmental problems for Soviet policy makers. In the mid-1960s, controversy over the potential pollution of Lake Baikal appears to have stimulated and legitimized environmental protection as an issue for discussion in the Soviet press (for a more complete discussion of the Baikal controversy, see Goldman, 1972; Zumbrunnen, 1974). The output of scholarly books and articles by philosophers, economists, biologists, physicists, and sociologists reflects the broad range of organizations concerned with these questions. Support is also evident in high places — Brezhnev's report to the Twenty-fifth Party Congress in 1976 emphasized the importance of environmental protection and announced that 11 billion rubles would be allocated for the purpose during the tenth five-year plan (Brezhnev, 1976). N.K. Baibakov, Chairman of the State Planning Committee, recently outlined planned capital investments of 1.8 billion rubles for the implementation of environmental protection measures in 1981 (Pravda, October 23, 1980, p. 3). Greater organizational commitment is evident in the elevation of the former Hydrometeorology Service attached to the Council of Ministers to a State Committee on Hydrometeorology and Oversight of the Environment. The committee's director, Dr. Iu. Izrael, claimed his organization had approximately 10,000 personnel working on environmental problems as of early 1979 (Christian Science Monitor, February 7, 1979: p.3).

Despite the considerable support for environmental protection evidenced in budgetary allocations, press coverage, scientific research and bureaucratic reorganization, Soviet policy makers appear to be uncertain about the precise form environmental policy should assume. Uncertainty regarding environmental decisions is closely tied to the broader problem of economic reform in the Soviet Union (for a more extended discussion of this, see Ziegler, 1979). Constraints on labor and capital resources have slowed extensive economic growth in the past two decades, resulting in programs and pronouncements designed to achieve more efficient use of extant resources. The programs of the last two Party Congresses reflect the determination to stimulate intensive economic growth through technology and efficient management practices. Economic reform has been accepted in principle by the Soviet leadership, although there is substantial disagreement over the actual measures to be adopted.

In an attempt to stimulate greater efficiency in utilizing natural resources, labor, and capital, leaders at the highest level have urged the use of economic levers and incentives in the place of administrative actions (see Brezhnev, 1976, p. 23). With the encouragement and legitimacy conferred by such pronouncements, Soviet economists have advanced innovative proposals embodying market or other economic incentives to environmental protection. This chapter examines the alternative approaches to environmental policy problems — economic and administrative - available to Soviet policy makers. The approach adopted, in the form of national environmental legislation enacted, gives some indication of the capacity of the Soviet system to entertain new ideas and incorporate them into public policy.

The first section of this chapter describes some of the more innovative, nonincremental solutions to environmental pollution advanced by Soviet economists. The second part outlines the actual response of the Soviet government to pollution problems, which consists largely of incremental administrative arrangements. Several of the more important environmental laws will be reviewed in this section. The concluding section makes some general observations about the openness of environmental policy debate in the USSR and the selection and implementation of alternative environmental strategies.

POLICY ALTERNATIVES: ECONOMIC INCENTIVES AND DISINCENTIVES

As Charles Lindblom (1977, p. 239) has observed, "Communist systems rely on authority far more than do the market-oriented polyarchies." Soviet leaders use some market mechanisms (to allocate labor, for example), but they prefer to exercise control through authority rather than through exchange. The willingness to experiment with and use market mechanisms in the post-Stalin era is a central aspect of Soviet "liberalization."

Previous research indicated that private ownership of natural resources is the only major economic incentive decisively rejected by Soviet decision makers (Ziegler, 1982). Virtually all other types of economic incentives would appear to be ideologically acceptable. Since the mid-1960s Soviet economists have proposed a variety of economic solutions to environmental problems. One category of solutions attempts to force polluters to internalize external costs generated in the production process. To the extent that economic levers have become part of policy, the governmental response has been to adopt from the other broad division of economic incentives — paying polluters to stop polluting.

Paying Polluters

Prior to 1975 the Soviet government expected polluting enterprises and organizations to pay for environmental protection measures using money from the enterprise development fund. The fund is a sum of money set aside for capital investment and for enterprises to use to make improvements in organization and production techniques. The effectiveness of the fund in raising efficiency has been weakened by the small size of the fund and by overly centralized control through the ministry (Nove, 1977). Ministry officials are reluctant to invest in projects that may tend to reduce overall output or that incur continuing costs. Measures aimed at preventing waste or purifying discharges do both. By 1975, the national economic plan did include specific budgetary allocations for preventing pollution, mandating the expenditure of funds (Izvestia, December 5, 1974: pp. 1-2).

If enterprise directors did not use monies from the fund, they were expected to divert part of their general budget to pay for the construction of purification facilities, to restore strip-mined land, etc. Directors were understandably reluctant to jeopardize plan fulfillment by shifting resources away from "productive" activities. Success and failure in the Soviet system of central planning are based largely on physical output. Additional criteria have been added since the 1965 economic reforms, but the quantitative indicator retains its position of primary importance (see Ryavec, 1975). The rational enterprise director will devote all available resources to maximizing production of the limited number of products, since their output constitutes the major criterion of success. Salary bonuses, recognition, and promotion are contingent upon these criteria.

The bonus system is a form of economic incentive that has become institutionalized in the Soviet system. Logically, in a system where the productive resources are owned and operated by the state, bonuses awarded to individuals should be greatest in the sectors having the highest priority. There is empirical evidence that such a correlation does exist in the Soviet Union (see Matthews, 1978, p. 24). The largest bonuses go to the military and intelligence sectors, then heavy industry, and finally light industry. To the present time, bonuses have not been awarded for success in environmental protection efforts, although Soviet authors have suggested the adoption of this practice (see e.g., Bakaev, 1977).

Although bonuses are not awarded for protecting the environment, they may be denied for failure to comply with environmental directives. A 1979 resolution of the State Committee on Labor and Social Questions and the Central Council of Trade Unions stipulated that executive personnel of organizations and enterprises failing to implement environmental plans and measures would forfeit a minimum of 25 percent of whatever bonus they had earned. This applies to factory managers, heads of urban services organizations, and their deputies, and chief engineers. If these individuals violate state plans for the national economy they may lose the full amount of any earned bonus (Ekonomicheskaia gazeta, 1979). Since bonuses often amount to one-third or even one-half of managerial salaries, this could be a significant incentive if applied consistently.

The incorporation of environmental protection into the state plan in 1975 was one indication of the increasing importance of this policy area for the Soviet leadership. This change in policy was partly symbolic and partly functional. Symbolically, the official status of environmental protection was elevated from a local or regional matter to a position of national importance. It reinforced the earlier national commitment symbolized in the September 1972 session of the Supreme Soviet on conservation and the environment.

Functionally, specific sums were to be allocated and spent for the protection of air and water. Theoretically, enterprises and organizations would no longer be expected to pay for equipment and maintenance costs out of the basic fund. In recent years, however, directors have been pressured by the Kremlin to use money from the basic fund for environmental protection. Furthermore, the amounts allocated for environmental protection are apparently insufficient, given the weakness of the present infrastructure when compared with what is needed for a successful policy. Serious pollution violations often occur because obsolete factories and plants cannot utilize modern abatement equipment (Pravda, June 17, 1975; Podgorodnikov and Travinskii, 1974).

Capital investment in environmental protection grew rapidly in the two years following the 1972 Supreme Soviet session, peaked in 1975, declined over the next two years, then rebounded slightly. Table 9-1 indicates the pattern of national expenditures. Brezhnev (1976) announced that 11 billion rubles would be spent for environmental protection in the course of the tenth five-year plan. The data presented in table 9-1 suggests that unless expenditures increased drastically in 1980, just under 2 billion rubles remained unspent.

Table 9-1

State Capital Investments in Measures for the Protection
and Rational Utilization of Natural Resources
(in comparable prices, millions of rubles)

	1968-70	1971-72	1973	1974	1975	1976	1977	1978-79	1976-79
Total (USSR)	1200	857	1143	1528	2084	1887	1783	3813	7383
Water Resources	—	—	917	1242	1383	1430	1390	2865	5685
Atmospheric Basins	—	—	116	152	154	183	172	332	687

Sources: Narognnoekhoziaistvo SSSR v 1977g: statisticheskii ezhegodnik (Moscow: Statistika, 1978) pp. 348-445; Narkhoz 1979, p. 445; Narkhoz 1980, p. 417.

Originally, plans had provided for expenditures of 5.8 billion rubles in 1976-1978, including 4.7 billion for construction and installation (Poletaeva, 1979). Several union republics — the Russian Soviet Federated Socialist Republic, Georgia, and Belorussia — failed to allocate the full amount of capital investment. The USSR Ministry of Coal Industry and the USSR Ministry of Ferrous Metallurgy also did not spend the full amounts allocated to them in the plan (Poletaeva, 1979).

How can we explain these failures to utilize the full amounts allocated? The source of the problem may be found in the balance of economic priorities existing in the Soviet system of central economic planning. A certain sum may be allocated, say, for the construction of purification installations, but construction enterprises must first fulfill their assignments for priority projects (see Podgorodnikov and Travinskii, 1974). At present there is only one organization, the All-Union Gas Purification and Dust Trapping Association, whose sole task is the production and distribution of antipollution equipment. Created nearly four decades ago, the association was assigned to the USSR Ministry of Chemical and Petroleum Machine Building Industry by the Supreme Soviet in 1972. Earlier reports (Pravda, March 24, 1969, p. 3) indicated that the association was unable to meet the demand for air pollution equipment, but its performance has improved in recent years.[1]

No such organization exists to manufacture equipment for treating effluent discharged into waterways. Several institutes carry out basic research on water pollution and purification equipment, such as the All-Union Research Institute for Water Supply, Sewage and Hydrological Engineering Equipment (Pryde, 1972). Construction is generally the responsibility of the relevant construction ministry.

In sum, the construction and installation of purification facilities is a low-priority item for virtually all organizations within the economic bureaucracy. These organizations have higher-order tasks that require time and attention; environmental protection is strictly secondary as an organizational goal. It does not "pay" for an enterprise to devote the 20-30 percent of its basic fund that is often necessary to purify effluents adequately (Khachaturov, 1968, p. 13). The easiest solution is simply not to make use of the limited funds that have been allocated (Izvestia, March 2, 1973, p. 3; June 18, 1975, p. 5)

The Polluter Pays

The second broad range of alternatives involving economic

incentives assumes that polluters should pay the social costs incurred through production. The theoretical framework on which this assumption is based has been developed by Western economists within the context of market economies. As I will demonstrate shortly, these principles of economic theory are also applicable to the command economy.

Theoretically, pollution and resource waste occur when the market mechanism fails to produce an accurate valuation of natural resources. If it is possible to better the lot of at least one member of society without diminishing the well-being of any other member, then resources are being used inefficiently. Resource allocation, in economists' terms, has fallen short of Pareto optimality. The Pareto optimum is the theoretical point at which all productive resources are utilized (and valued) just equal to their most valuable alternative use. This alternative value, or opportunity cost, is determined through supply and demand in a competitive market economy. Since the value of all resources is maximized, social welfare is maximized and resource "waste" (inefficient use or pollution) reduced to a minimum (Bator, 1958).

In practice, environmental resources are often undervalued because they are not exchanged through the market. These resources have opportunity costs, although the opportunity costs are not reflected in the market price. Thus, firms using the undervalued resources pay only part of the cost. The remainder "spills over" into other sectors in the form of technical or physical effects. Economists refer to these phenomena as technological external diseconomies (see Freeman, Haveman, and Kneese, 1973; Kneese, 1977).

Official Soviet doctrine maintains that the elimination of private capital confers a systematic environmental advantage on the USSR by eliminating external diseconomies (Voprosy filosofii, 1973). Most Soviet writers, however, acknowledge the existence of tensions between national priorities and the interests of ministries, departments, and enterprises. One writer candidly argued that "national economic altruism cannot be a realistic basis for branch economic policies" (Leksin, 1977). Symbolic appeals to promote the general welfare were acknowledged to be ineffective. The solution he proposed, however, involved an increased role for central planning and coordination rather than using economic incentives.

Other Soviet economists have advocated schemes that would force enterprises to absorb some or all of the external costs incurred in production.[2] One, V. Shkatov, suggested the adoption of differential rents determined by a scale of cadastre (an official register of land or natural resources) prices for natural resources. The cadastre would indicate the quantity and value of natural resources such as land, oil, and mineral deposits, and would take into account the location and transportation costs of these resources.[3] Users of natural resources would pay for them according to a system of "polar prices." Under conditions of maximum ease of extraction, transportation, and value, enterprises would pay a positive sum. Under difficult conditions enterprises would receive a payment from the state, and under average conditions the price for resources would be zero (Shkatov, 1968).

Application of this system of polar prices to the use of natural resources would partly compensate for the inefficient exploitation of resources encouraged by the absence of fixed costs for extraction firms (Goldman, 1972). Shkatov suggested that the principle of polarity could also be applied to effluents. The release of one cubic meter of heavily polluted water, for example, might result in a charge of three kopeks subtracted from profits or from the basic fund. Conversely, a premium of two kopeks could be paid to the enterprise per cubic meter of fully cleaned waste water (Shkatov, 1968).

Other Soviet economists have argued that pollution problems exist because the principles of economic accountability do not apply to pollution control. A record is kept of the outlays provided for environmental protection, but there is no mechanism for measuring success in terms of actual results. The authors of an article in Voprosy ekonomiki in 1972 suggested imposing a pollution charge on enterprises to induce adoption of a least-cost approach to pollution (Federenko and Gofman, 1973). N. Feitelman (1978), writing in the same journal six years later, also supported the idea of an environmental pollution charge factored into the unit costs of production. Feitelman stressed the need for an economic valuation of natural resources — he specifically mentioned the possibility of allowing enterprises to sell incidental resources not provided for in the plan — and urged that fines be revised to reflect external costs more accurately.

Enterprises and associations may sell valuable by-products to other enterprises and keep the income for themselves. The red tape involved in obtaining departmental and ministerial approval for such an exchange can be overwhelming, though. Boris Komarov (1980) related the case of a chemical plant in Kranoiarsk territory that attempted to sell the valuable fluorine it was pumping into the atmosphere. Both the seller and potential buyer were departments within the Ministry of Chemical Industry. Nevertheless, the Krasnoiarsk plant continued to pollute the atmosphere with fluorine for over five years until final approval was granted.

As industrialization spreads throughout the world accompanied by the increasing consumption of fossil fuels, policy makers are finally realizing that even the earth's atmosphere is a limited resource, though renewable to a point. The concept of selling rights to use increments of atmospheric resources has recently gained acceptance among U.S. policy makers, and has been implemented by a number of states (Federal Register, vol. 43, no. 118 (June 19, 1978, p. 26381). In the Soviet Union, no such charge for the use of air as a "dumping ground" has been implemented in any systematic way, and charges for the use of water have only been introduced experimentally. The present policy toward water usage involves supplying the user with water free of charge or requiring the user to pay a minimal fee to the state (Lozhansky, Kuzin, and Pichakhchi, 1977).

The practice of fining enterprises and enterprise directors for violations of environmental laws is another means of forcing the polluter to bear the costs. Inspectors of the Sanitary Epidemiological Service may fine individuals 50 to 100 rubles and an enterprise 500 rubles. Smaller fines may be imposed by the chief sanitary physician (Kelley et al., 1976). Soviet officials have complained about the

> . . . erroneous and incomplete application of fines and compensations for damages and low efficiency of credit and financing system stimulation. . . Analysis of the data on efficiency of fines for discharge of untreated or insufficiently treated effluents into streams and/or water bodies has demonstrated that the sums of fines per one violation are much lower than the cost of harmful effects inflicted on the national economy (Lozhansky et al., 1977).

In the mid-1970s, a document was drawn up for the economic valuation of natural resources entitled "Basic Regulations on Methods for the Economic Valuation of National Resources in Large-Scale Plan and Design Calculations." It was reported that a number of branches had begun to implement these regulations by 1975,[4] but later publications indicate that the intent of this document was never fully realized (see Feitelman, 1978; Lozhansky, et al., 1977). Wasteful use of cheap or free natural resources lowers unit costs for enterprises and raises profits (Tupytsia, 1977). The overall effect is to subsidize firms that waste resources while economically penalizing forms that adopt stringent environmental standards.

Economic concepts of opportunity costs and externalities can be applied to both market and command economies. If prices are viewed in the generic sense of "terms on which alternatives are offered" rather than simply as exchange ratios in a market, accounting prices or provisional valuations may be established in a nonmarket economy for the purpose of allocating resources (Lange and Taylor, 1966). Soviet economists have almost uniformly supported the concept of an economic valuation of natural resources to reflect their most valuable alternative uses. These same economists recognize that externalities exist in the Soviet socialist economy. They locate the source of these external costs in the functional divisions of the ministerial system, which suggests that externalities result from the distribution of **organization** rather than the distribution of **property**. The implication is clear — administrative reorganization is needed to realize the effectiveness of economic approaches. In the following section Soviet administrative organization is analyzed as it relates to environmental protection.

ADMINISTRATIVE ORGANIZATION: INCREMENTAL SOLUTIONS

Soviet national environmental legislation is based on the premise that adequate institutional mechanisms exist for enforcing environmental protection. An important 1973 joint resolution of the Central Committee and the Council of Ministers instructed the Union Republic Central Committees and Councils of Ministers, the area (krai) and regional (oblast) Party committees, the autonomus republic Councils of Ministers, area and regional executive committees, and USSR ministries and departments to intensify supervision and to establish systematic control over the implementation of environmental protection measures (Pravda, 1973). The Hydrometeorological Service, an organization attached to the Council of Ministers, was instructed to organize a nationwide monitoring and control system for levels of air, water, and soil pollution. The USSR State Committee for Science and Technology was given the responsibility for coordinating research on conservation and the rational utilization of natural resources. A Chief Administration for the Development and Production of Gas Purifying and Dust-Trapping Equipment was formed under the aegis of the USSR Ministry of Chemistry and Petroleum Machine Building for supervising the operation of purification equipment (Pravda, January 10, 1973, p. 1).

A 1978 resolution of the CPSU Central Committee and the USSR Council of Ministers went further toward centralizing environmental protection than any previous legislation, yet it did not vest control in a single superagency as many environmentalists had suggested (Pravda, 1979). The most notable change was the elevation of the Main Hydrometeorological Service to a State

Committee on Hydrometeorology and the Environment (Gosudarstvennyi Komitet po Gidrometerologii i Kontroliu Priorodnoi Sredy or "Gidromet" in Soviet parlance), currently headed by Dr. Iuri Izrael.

By making this agency a state committee, the Soviet leaders have granted it autonomy from the ministerial system (Gidromet was formerly under the control of the Ministry of Health). The function of state committees, such as the People's Control Committee (KNK) and the better known Committee for State Security (KGB), is to provide the Council of Ministers with a horizontal control over the entire ministerial structure. The new responsibilities of the State Committee on Hydrometeorology and the Environment were to organize a monitoring system for the natural environment, regulate air use in urban and industrial centers, to draft and monitor norms for permissible levels of air pollution, and to monitor the siting of facilities in order to prevent atmospheric pollution. The new state committee was furthermore

> given the right to check on the observance of enterprises, institutions, organizations, construction projects and other facilities, regardless of their departmental affiliation, of norms and rules in the field of atmospheric protection, and also to submit proposals on suspending the operation of industrial facilities that are violating established norms until the necessary measures have been carried out (Pravda, 1979).

But the laws also vested supervisory powers over the fulfillment of state plan assignments in several ministries in addition to Gidromet — the Ministry of Land Reclamation and Water Resources, the Ministry of Agriculture, and the Council of Ministers' Committee for the Supervision of Industrial Supervision and Mine Safety.

It should also be noted that Gidromet was primarily assigned responsibility for **air** pollution. Primary responsibility for water pollution remains with the Sanitary Epidemiological Service of the Ministry of Health, although this responsibility is shared with the Ministry of Land Reclamation and Water Resources, the Ministry of Agriculture, the Ministry of Fish Industry and others. Similarly, the duties of protecting forest resources and the soil are divided among several ministries and agencies. In sum, although there has been limited movement toward centralization of environmental protection, responsibility remains divided among a substantial number of organizations.

In addition to the two joint resolutions discussed above there have been six major environmental laws adopted in the past decade. These are the Principles of Water Legislation (1970), Principles of Land Use (1968), Principles of Mineral Legislation (1975), Principles of Forestry Legislation (1977), and the laws on air quality and the animal world (1980).[5]

These legislative enactments are remarkably similar in structure and emphasis. State ownership is proclaimed as the basis for utilizing the natural resources in question. The legislative goals stated include both the protection and preservation of these resources, combined with their most efficient and complete exploitation.

Water use in the USSR is free of charge in most cases (subject to a fee in special instances), and water use is available to state, cooperative, and public organizations, enterprises, and institutions, and to citizens. Users have the right to use water for the purposes for which it has been granted only; they must utilize water rationally and are obligated to take steps toward completely eliminating pollutant discharge into bodies of water. Protection of water quality and conservation of water constitute the obligations of enterprises, organizations, and institutions using water. Regulation is coordinated among the relevant agencies, the executive committees of local soviets, and in certain cases specially empowered state agencies. Violators of USSR and Union Republic water legislation are criminally or administratively liable in accordance with the relevant legislation. Users are **not** required to make restitution to the state for losses.[6]

Use of the earth's interior is assigned free of charge, aside from special instances established by the USSR Council of Ministers, to state, cooperative and public organizations, institutions and enterprises, and to citizens. Because of the nonrenewable nature of mineral resources, the legislation stipulates that utilization must be scientifically substantiated and rational. Users are responsible for the fullest possible recovery of minerals and for preventing pollution of the earth's interior. In actuality, mineral resources are often underutilized because of the low fixed costs of extraction. A mining concern subject to diminishing marginal returns at one location need not worry about absorbing the fixed costs of purchasing a new site, since land is a free good (Goldman, 1972). Furthermore, the enterprise pays only about 40% of the geological prospecting costs; the state picks up the rest (Yakovets, 1979). Both factors provide an incentive to waste natural resources. On the conservation side, enterprises that have higher rates of return due to favorable conditions are subject to higher turnover taxes (Kaser, 1970). This is similar in effect to Shkatov's system of polar prices discussed above. Violations of mineral legislation may incur criminal, administrative, or other liability in accordance with USSR and Union Republic legislation. The "other" liability mentioned here apparently refers to material restitution. Enterprises, organizations, institutions and individuals (officials and other personnel) are held materially liable, in Article 50, for violations.[7] Supervision over the use of the earth's interior is exercised by the relevant agencies the soviets and their administrative and executive agencies, with the assistance of public organizations whenever possible.

Of the six pieces of legislation, only the "Principles of Forest Legislation" embodies a charge for the use of a natural resource. Standing timber is allocated through payment of a fee based on fixed rates. At least one Soviet writer has complained that the rate per tree does not fully reflect timber value (Tupytsia, 1977). Nevertheless, instituting a fixed charge for a resource represents a new departure for Soviet policy. Although it is going too far to argue that this clearly signals a rethinking of the form of Soviet environmental policy, there does appear to be a chronological progression toward greater use of economic incentives.

Forest users may be state, cooperative and public enterprises, organizations, and institutions, and individual citizens. They may use forest resources only according to the authorization granted them by the state. Forest users are required to make the fullest and most rational possible use of timber and must clean up timbercutting areas and recondition exploited land areas at their own expense. As with the use of mineral resources, actual Soviet timbering has been incredibly wasteful. Thousands of tons of lumber rot each year because of inadequate storage and transportation (Komarov, 1980).

In the case of land use, usufruct is granted free of charge to collective and state firms, industrial and public organizations, and citizens. Land users are obliged to use the land rationally, to protect and improve soil fertility, and to take the necessary steps against erosion and contamination. State control over land use is exercised by the soviets and their executive and administrative organs and by the relevant state agencies. Violators of the land legislation are subject to criminal or administrative liability in accordance with USSR or Union Republic legislation. In addition, enterprises, institutions, organizations, and citizens are obligated to compensate the state for any damage caused from violations of the legislation.

Efficient land use in the Soviet Union is hindered by the same factors that preclude the most efficient exploitation of mineral resources. These include a fragmented bureaucratic approach to land utilization and the absence of scarcity prices. According to one student of Soviet land use policy, the task of assigning more rational values to land use received increased attention in the late 1970s (Krisch, 1980).

The laws on air quality and animal protection both went into effect January 1, 1981. The air quality legislation contains a small article empowering the Union Republics (and the USSR) to establish material and moral incentives for implementing the laws (Art. 21, "Law...on Air Quality," p. 11). Violators of air quality legislation are obligated to make recompense for any damages caused through air pollution. Aside from these modest provisions, the legislation relies on administrative arrangements to achieve compliance. It should be pointed out, however, that the administrative procedures and penalties are considerably more sophisticated and far-reaching than earlier legislation. The adoption of maximum allowable emissions standards is a significant step forward from the usual Soviet practice of setting maximum permissible levels of concentration of pollutants in the ambient air.

The use of the animal world is assigned free of charge, although USSR and Union Republic legislation may establish charges for the use of animal resources (Art. 11, "Law...of the Animal World," p. 11). Compensation for damages may be required of users, but the evidence suggests that poachers generally are not subject to large fines. In any case, those guilty of poaching tend to come from the ranks of the privileged, the economic and political elite. They are likely to avoid paying fines through their connections and influence (Komarov, 1980).

CONCLUSION

The economic alternatives discussed in this chapter appear to merit serious consideration by Soviet policy makers — they all fall within the parameters of acceptability of the system.[8] Soviet leaders are willing to have a variety of alternative strategies proposed and discussed in the official press, though few of the economic solutions proposed for solving environmental problems have actually been implemented. The willingness to entertain and on occasion experiment with alternate strategies indicates a certain flexibility on the part of the Soviet leadership. Flexibility at the top levels of the Party and government, however, may be frustrated by the bureaucrtic intransigence of local Party and state organizations.[9] Central decision makers are constrained in their selection and evaluation of alternatives as a result of certain pathologies in the structure of the Soviet command economy. For example, policy makers often receive distorted information on environmental performance through the ministerial structure or find that ministries and departments conveniently disregard environmental regulations (Ziegler, 1980).

These findings should not surprise students of Soviet politics or students of administrative organization. The complex of penalties and rewards found in the Soviet planned economy reflects the "bias" of that system toward production rather than environmental protection. The commitment of the Soviet leadership to environmental protection, although substantial, is obviously secondary to the commitment to industrial development. Viewed from this perspective, bureaucratic obstructionism is eminently rational, for it serves the interests of both the organizations and the individual members. Plans are fulfilled, deadlines met, bonuses earned. The implementation of environmental protection measures may in most cases be delayed in deference to more immediate and more crucial goals.

Given the inability of the Soviet leadership to agree on a specific approach to environmental problems, as suggested by the vague, general character of the earlier environmental legislation, this policy arena has been opened to input by such groups as the environmental economists (Schwartz and Keech, 1971).[10] Open debate means accessibility, but it also means competition with the established bureaucratic interests in the ministerial structure. In the Soviet Union, the key political resource is organization. Soviet reformers may have complete access to the press and the top leadership, but they do not have the organizational resources that would enable them to compete effectively with the economic bureaucracy.

The result, in terms of policy outputs, is at best an incremental process of change. Over time, a series of incremental changes may yield major differences in policies. The new air quality law, for example, is a fairly sophisticated piece of legislation incorporating effective administrative regulations (such as the maximum permissible emissions standards). This law, which will be implemented primarily through a newly empowered state committee (Gidromet), could go far toward reducing air pollution in the Soviet Union. Much will depend on the resistance of pollution organizations to the new regulations and on the extent of the powers granted to Gidromet. At the time of this writing, it is too early to ascertain the scope of Gidromet's authority to regulate pollution violators. The future of this organization should provide a valuable clue about the effectiveness of Soviet environemental protection efforts.

NOTES

* An earlier version of this chapter appeared under the title, Policy Alternatives in Soviet Environmental Protection, Carl Beck Papers in Russian and East European Studies (University of Pittsburgh) No. 102.

1. The deputy director of the Gas-Purification Administration of the Ministry of Chemical and Machine Building Industry recently reported that the output of gas-purification equipment had increased by 2.5 times in the period 1975-1978. See Iu. Krovitskii, 1978.
2. We must realize that an accurate valuation of **all** external costs would be extremely difficult and subject to widely varying interpretations of "value." The reason for this is the market failure mentioned earlier. Since market processes do not apply to most environmental exchanges, the opportunity costs of environmental resources cannot be calculated.
3. The USSR Council of Ministers adopted a resolution in 1977 ordering the Ministry of Agriculture and the Union Republic Councils of Ministers to conduct a State Land Cadastre. See Izvestiia (July 1, 1977), p. 2.
4. V. Zhamin, "Ekologiia i ekonomika," Voprosy ekonomiki, No. 7 (July 1975), pp. 91-101. The author does not identify the compilers of this document. The Central Mathematical Economics Institute, however, has been researching questions of resource valuation since 1974.
5. The "Principles of Land Legislation of the USSR and the Union Republics" (Pravda, December 14, 1968, pp. 2-3) is reprinted in Philip R. Pryde, Conservation in the Soviet Union, (London; Cambridge University Press, 1972), pp. 184-199. The "Principles of Water Legislation of the USSR and the Union Republics" (Pravda, December 12, 1970) is reprinted in ibid, pp. 224-240. The "Principles of Legislation of the USSR and the Union Republics on the Earth's Interior" (Pravda, July 11, 1975, pp. 1-2) translated in Current Digest of the Soviet Press, Vol. 27, No. 29 (August 13, 1975), pp. 11-17. The "Principles of Forest Legislation of the USSR and the Union Republics" (Izvestiia, June 19, 1977, pp. 2-3) translated in ibid, Vol 29, No. 25 (July 20, 1977), pp. 9-16; The "Lw of the Union of Soviet Socialist Republics on Air Quality," (Pravda, June 27, 1980, p. 2), translated in Current Digest of the Soviet Press, Vol. 32, No. 28 (August 13, 1980, pp. 9-12, 19); The "Law of the Union of Soviet Socialist Republics on the Protection and Utilization of the Animal World," (Pravda, June 28, 1980, pp. 1,3), translated in Current Digest of the Soviet Press, Vol. 32, No. 29 (August 20, 1980), pp. 10-14, 24.

6. An article requiring users to make reimbursement for losses that would have held officials and other employees individually materially liable for losses, was included in the draft legislation but was deleted from the final law. Article 4.6 specifically states that no compensation is required for losses caused by unauthorized use of water. See "Principles of Water Legislation of the USSR and the Union Republics," reprinted in Pryde, 1972.
7. Article 50 is virtually identical to the article on material liability deleted from the water legislation.
8. This author agrees with E.E. Schattschneider's statement that "All forms of political organization have a bias in favor of conflict and the supression of others because **organization is the mobilization of bias**" (The Semisovereign People, Hinsdale, Ill.: Dryden Press, 1960), p. 69. The essence of political power, Schattschneider argues, is the power to define alternatives. Soviet leadership, in my estimation, is considerably more flexible in entertaining alternatives than previously believed.
9. John Hardt found that local and regional party organizations constitute an institutional barrier to the successful introduction of Western technology into Soviet economic systems. See John P. Hardt, "Imperatives of Economic Reform and Communist Political Systems," in Teresa Rakowska-Harmstone, ed., Perspectives for Change in Communist Societies (Boulder, Colo.: Westview Press, 1979).
10. Schwartz and Keech suggest that policy problems may be delegated to an interactive rather than a synoptic process of problem solving when the Soviet leadership is unable to reach a consensus. See Joel J. Schwartz and William R. Keech, "Public Influence and Educational Policy in the Soviet Union," in Roger E. Kanet, ed., The Behavioral Revolution and Communist Studies (New York: Free Press, 1971), pp. 176-177.

REFERENCES

Bakaev, V.E. 1977. "Stimulirovanie ekonomiiu vody," Ekonomika i organizatsiia promyshlennogo proizvodstva, No. 4 (July-August).

Bator, Francis M. 1958. "The Anatomy of Market Failure," The Quarterly Journal of Economics (August): pp. 457-476.

Brezhnev, L. I. 1976. "The Report to the CPSU Central Committee and the Party's Immediate Tasks in the Field of Domestic and Foreign Policy," translated in Current Digest of the Soviet Press, Vol. 28, No. 8 (March 24).

Ekonomicheskaia gazeta. 1979. "To Protect Nature," in Current

Digest of the Soviet Press, Vol. 31, No. 42 (November 14).
Federenko, N. and K. Gofman. 1973. "Problems of Optimization in the Planning and Control of Environment," Voprosy ekonomiki, translated in Soviet Review, Vol. 24, No. 2 (Summer).
Feitelman, N. 1978. "Sotsial' no-ekonomicheskie problemy ekologicheskogo ravnovesiia v zapadnoi sibiri," Voprosy ekonomiki, No. 10 (October).
Freeman, A. Myrick III, Robert H. Haveman, Allen V. Kneese. 1973. The Economics of Environmental Policy (New York: John Wiley and Sons.
Goldman, Marshall I. 1972. The Spoils of Progress: Environmental Pollution in the Soviet Union (Cambridge, Mass.: MIT Press).
Kaser, Michael. 1970. Soviet Economics (New York: McGraw Hill).
Kelley, Donald R. et al. 1976. The Economic Superpowers and the Environment (San Francisco: W.H. Freeman).
Khachaturov, T. 1968. "Ekonomicheskie proablemy ekologii," Voprosy ekonomiki, No. 6 (June).
Kneese, Allen V. 1977. Economics and the Environment (Middlesex: Penguin).
Komarov, Boris (pseud.). 1980. The Destruction of Nature in the Soviet Union (White Plains, N.Y.: M. E. Sharpe).
Krisch, Henry. 1980. "Utilization of Land in the USSR," paper presented at the Annual Meeting of the AAASS, November, Philadelphia.
Krovitskii, Iu. 1978. "Po dolgosrochnoi programme," Ekonomicheskaia gazeta, No. 18 (April).
Lange, Oscar and Fred M. Taylor. 1966. On the Economic Theory of Socialism (New York: McGraw-Hill).
Leksin, V.N. 1977. "Narodnokhoziaistvennaia effektivnost' i interesy otrasli," Ekonomika i organizatsiia promyshlennogo proizvodstva, No. 4.
Lindblom, Charles E. 1977. Politics and Markets (New York: Basic Books).
Lozhansky, V. , Kuzin, and Pichakhchi. 1977. "On the Role of Administrative, Economic and Technological Measures in Protection of Surface and Subterranean Water Against Contamination and Depletion," UN Water Conference, Mar del Plata, Argentina.
Matthews, Mervyn. 1978. Privilege in the Soviet Union: A Study of Elite Life-Styles under Communism (London: Allen and Unwin).
Nove, Alex. 1977. The Soviet Economic System (London: Allen and Unwin).
Podgorodnikov, M. and V. Travinskii. 1974. "Konflikt na beregu reki," Literaturnaia gazeta, No. 4 (January 23).
Poletaeva, P. 1979. "Delo vazhnosti gosudarstvennoi," Ekonomicheskaia gazeta, No. 6 (February).

Pravda. 1979. "On Historical Measures to Intensify Conservation and Improve the Utilization of Natural Resources," in Current Digest of the Soviet Press, Vol 31, No. 1 (January 31).

Pravda. 1973. Translated in Current Digest of the Soviet Press, Vol. 25, No. 2 (February 7).

Pryde, Philip R. 1972. Conservation in the Soviet Union (London: Cambridge University Press).

Ryavec, Karl W. 1975. Implementation of Soviet Economic Reforms: Political, Organizational, and Social Processes (New York: Praeger).

Schwartz, Joel J. and William R. Keech. 1971. "Public Influence and Educational Policy in the Soviet Union," in Roger E. Kanet, ed., The Behavioral Revolution and Communist Studies (New York: Free Press).

Shkatov, V. 1968. "Tseny na prirodnye bogatstva i sovershenstvovanie planovogo tsenoobrazovaniia," Voprosy ekinomiki, No. 9 (September).

Tupytsia, Iu. 1977. "Ekologicheskie faktory v izderzhkakh proizvodstva," Voprosy ekonomiki, No. 7 (July).

Voprosy filosofii. 1973. "Krugli stol Voprosy filosofii: Chelovek i sreda ego obitaniia," No. 1.

Yakovets, Iu. V. 1979. "The Intensification of Production and the Evaluation of Resources," Ekonomika i organizatsiia promyshlennogo proizvodstva, No. 9 (September) in Current Digest of the Soviet Press, Vol. 31, No. 50 (January 9, 1980).

Ziegler, Charles E. 1982. "Soviet Environmental Policy Parameters: The Macro Value Framework," Studies in Soviet Thought, Vol. 23, No. 3 (April).

Ziegler, Charles E. 1980. "Soviet Environmental Policy and Soviet Central Planning: A Reply to McIntyre and Thornton," Soviet Studies, Vol. 32, No. 1 (January).

Ziegler, Charles E. 1979. "Disaggregated Pluralism in a Socialist System: Environmental Policy in the USSR," Ph.D. Dissertation (Urbana: University of Illinois).

Zumbrunnen, Craig. 1974. "The Lake Baikal Controversy: A Serious Water Pollution Threat or a Turning Point in Soviet Environmental Consciousness," in Ivan Volgyes, ed., Environmental Deterioration in the Soviet Union and Eastern Europe (New York: Praeger).

III
STUDIES COMPARING IMPLEMENTATION PRACTICE

IMPLEMENTING AIR QUALITY CONTROL PROGRAMS IN EUROPE: SOME RESULTS OF A COMPARATIVE STUDY

10

Peter Knoepfel and Helmut Weidner

INTRODUCTION

When it comes right down to it, what difference does environmental policy make for the actual level of environmental quality? And if it has no significant impact, which factors are most important in determining the condition of a given environmental medium? In most studies of the implementation of public policy it is, at least implicitly, assumed that the policy or program at issue would, if carried out effectively, make a difference with regard to the objectives being pursued. In the following report on the preliminary analysis of data collected in connection with a research project examining SO_2 air quality control policy in six European Community countries and Switzerland, it is this assumption that is examined critically (for a comprehensive presentation of the research concept, see Knoepfel, 1982; Knoepfel, Weidner, and Hanf, 1980a and 1980b). In addition, the extent to which and the manner in which different interests are incorporated in control programs, thus enjoying privileged status (or relative disadvantage) during the implementation phase, is also considered. In particular we address, on the basis of the initial results of the comparative analysis, the following questions common to other studies of the implementation process:

1. In what ways does the structure of environmental control programs affect the ability of different actors involved in the implementation process to promote their particular interests? How do these different actors attempt to assert their interests in earlier stages of the policy process (e.g., during the program formulation phase) so as to prestructure the implementation game to their advantage? (See, for example, Bardach, 1977; Sabatier and Mazmanian, 1982.)

2. Is it possible to attribute changes in emitter behavior (viewed as the observable impact of policy implementation outputs) directly to implementation activities when environmental quality data are taken as the indicator for tendencies in emitter behavior?

3. Is there any evidence that the institutionalization of public participation in the enforcement process strengthens the position of environmental actors in implementation activities?

Owing to the limited space available, we will present the results of our project concerning these questions in abbreviated form. Since the comparative analysis has not yet been completed, the results reported here may be subject to minor modifications later. Nevertheless, the conclusions present should hold true for the approximately fifty local implementation areas (LIAs), the smallest units in our analysis of the SO_2 quality control programs, selected from twenty regions in Italy, France, the Federal Republic of Germany (FRG), the Netherlands, Belgium, the United Kingdom, and Switzerland.[1] A more extensive discussion of the project design, including the set of variables examined, along with the final results of the comparative analysis of the data, will be published in two volumes currently in preparation (Knoepfel and Weidner, forthcoming).

THE SERENDIPITY EFFECT OF CROSS-NATIONAL COMPARISON

Before turning to the results of the empirical study, we want to discuss, on the basis of four examples drawn from the research, the way in which a cross-national study can often be an important precondition for a deeper understanding of the policy processes in a given country. Various dimensions of the problems under investigation, as well as factors influencing the behavior of actors involved, which ultimately turned out to be of general relevance across the countries studied, were found in concrete national settings only because they had been stumbled upon in other regions or countries and then subsequently discovered elsewhere as well. Once the research had been sensitized to a given phenomenon in this manner, it was possible to look explicitly for similar or equivalent structures or behavior in other national settings. This process of serendipity can be illustrated with the following examples.

Activities by Environmentalists and Other Citizen Organizations

We had not expected to find citizen organizations whose efforts were focused exclusively on the SO_2 problem active at the local level. Even when the search was broadened to include organizations active in the area of air quality control in general, we were not much more successful in finding groups with this special interest. However, information drawn from case studies in North-Rhine Palatinate in Germany and in Holland suggested that it would be necessary to include, as potentially relevant actors, those groups concerned with environmental protection in general. This turned out to be quite important for the subsequent analysis of the interaction processes through which the different enforcement outputs were generated. Moreover, this broadened definition of potentially relevant actors also made it possible to predict more accurately what kinds of implementation processes we would be likely to find in the individual LIAs.

Analysis showed that public concern for air quality in general and SO_2 pollution in particular tended to develop from opposition to specific industrial development projects. In this sense, the implementation process itself, for example, in connection with the granting of a permit for the construction of a new plant, significantly influenced the activities of the citizens in the locality by raising the level of information about the project, by expanding their experience by participation in the formal permit process, and by providing a focus for mobilizing opposition and concern. In the course of these activities, the more general opposition became successively more structured and ultimately focused on the debate over specific pollutants. This pattern of development often led to efforts by citizens to influence decisions on particular pollutants such as SO_2, even though there had previously been little public sensitivity to air pollution problems. It should, however, also be noted in this connection that enforcement agencies themselves often reinforced this development in that they placed questions of SO_2 control at the center of their negotiations with the emitter. In any case, this general underlying pattern of growing awareness and increased focus on air pollution can be found in the other countries studied.

Intervention by Central Authorities in Local Enforcement

Investigations in the French LIAs of Creteil and Fos-Etang de Berre-Martigue revealed different types of interventions by central authorities in important implementation processes. These ranged from the formal take-over of permit decisions in the case of major development projects to recommendations by central authorities to the formally responsible agency or prefecture. In many cases these interventions by central ministries were in response to initiatives from the local level. On the basis of the French experience we developed a typology of central interventions that also contained several types of informal activities. Using this extended typology we were then able to detect similar forms of central influence on local implementation processes in other countries. However, only in a few instances were we able to identify interventions by the central government comparable to the subtle French pattern. This suggests that in the other countries under study the de facto autonomy of local or regional units in implementation processes must be considered relatively high.

Strategies Employed by Administrative Agencies as a Substitute for Participation

Some cases examined in the Swiss canton of Basel-Landschaft indicated that when dealing with complex licensing decisions in the industrial sector, where there were no legally binding technology standards, the responsible agencies would systematically collect information on abatement technologies used in identical or similar plants. This practice was justified in terms of the principle of equal treatment under the law and by the desire to ensure that environmental policy measures did not distort market competition among emitters. This kind of silent presence in permit procedures of emitters not directly effected is also found in the Netherlands. In fact, in both countries this state of affairs reflects a component of political-administrative culture highly devoted to the principle of equality of law that far exceeds what is formally required by air pollution control laws themselves. To a certain extent this practice can be viewed as equifunctional to the legally supported cooperation between the British Alkali Inspectorate and industries, which is often criticized as being a cozy relationship.

Quite different circumstances were found by the French and Italian research teams on the basis of their interviews with agencies and emitters and an analysis of comparable licensing decisions. The fact that within the same LIA emitters were treated differently (for instance, by granting variances for the use of fuels with high sulfur content) was nowhere met with criticism. Special arrangements, individually different considerations of equity, and even openly unequal treatment owing to political relations (especially with respect to power plants, which enjoy — comparatively — markedly preferential treatment) are apparently quite consistent with the political-administrative cultures of these countries. In Switzerland comparable plants are consulted. In France it is the central ministry that is consulted, while in Italy individual scientists are contacted.

Substitution of Collective-Oriented Decision Making for Individual Implementation Processes

One of the basic hypotheses of implementation theory states that in addition to, or even instead of, formal licensing or sanction processes, certain informal procedures develop that are often more effective and that can lead to a quasi-contractual relationship between emitter and agency. This hypothesis — which has been confirmed by several empirical studies — was also included in our initial research design. As it turned out, we were able to find constellations of this kind, though with varying degrees of intensity. Focusing on individual bargaining processes as suggested by implementation theory tended, in the beginning, to blind us to the informal collective mechanisms of regulation that had, over time, become institutionalized. It was only after intensive discussions over the findings from the French LIA Fos-Etang de Berre-Martigue that our attention was called to the existence of such meta-structures. For emittees involved in such relationships the most important substantive element of the formal licenses was the requirement to switch to low sulfur fuel oil in periods of severe air pollution. The installation, maintenance, and operation of corresponding alarm networks lie with the Secretariat Interministeriel Permanent des Pollutions Industrielles (SIPPI) which is supervised by the local industrial association (AIRFOBED). The definition of special protection zones, in which smog alarms may be accompanied with special directions for industrial combustion processes, in effect tends to reduce the load of individual licensing decisions. However, in some cases this relief may go so far that air quality control only takes place in local smog situations; i.e., individual licensing procedures are replaced by the incorporation of emitters into a collective alarm system.

When we first noted this mechanism, we treated it as a unique phenomenon that could be explained by the features of French industrial development policy and the correspondingly preferential treatment given to the new industrial pool in southern France. Although we have not as yet been able to find the same state of affairs in the regions of Paris and Nord, we did nevertheless find in the analysis of the program formulation process that industrial associations tend to prefer alarm zones to protection zones. In protection zones the volume of emissions is limited in general, irrespective of the ambient air situation at a given time.

This tendency to use collective mechanisms to deal with what are local regulatory situations was first discovered in France. In a somewhat modified version such mechanisms could also be found in the collective bargaining processes by which emission quotas were set in other countries for the country as a whole or for given regions. A third, and again different, kind of collectivization of individual regulatory decisions not explicitly intended by the national program is the arbitrary setting of regulatory priorities by the regional committees for air quality control in the Italian province Emilia Romagna. Here, the standard procedure for new licenses for all industrial plants as specified in the law of 1972 was changed into an instrument of **selective** clean-up measures by dividing license applications into three groups. First of all, there were those applications that never received a formal response, thus leaving the relationship between agency and emitter up in the air.

Then there were applications to which the agency responded only with an acknowledgement of receipt, stating that the submitted documents were considered satisfactory. Finally, there was a small number of applications that were taken as an occasion to initiate clean-up measures for a specific branch or region. The individual licensing procedure as demanded by law thus only took place where an emitter found himself in a category of industry for which a collective decision had been made regarding appropriate regulatory actions.

In this way, the phenomenon of collective regulation, in addition to or instead of administrative actions dealing with individual cases, could be abstracted from the French context and fruitfully applied to the analysis of regulatory systems in other countries.

These four examples demonstrate that cross-national comparison may well be crucial for implementation studies in one national context. Cross-national comparison creates a sensitivity for various kinds of general patterns of interaction that cannot be fully replaced either by clever heuristics or by detailed familiarity with a single setting alone. In order to profit fully from the advantages of cross-national comparison it is, however, necessary to create a research organization that is based on the principle of informed cooperation between the central team and the experts from the individual national research teams.

THE CONSEQUENCES OF PROGRAM STRUCTURE

We have worked with a broad definition of the term program (Knoepfel and Weidner, 1982). We believe that our definition corresponds to the realities of program formulation insofar as various actors, especially economic interest groups as well as parliamentary bodies themselves, are quite aware of the different program elements on which decisions of relevance for their particular interests are made and which, when taken together, effectively shape the subsequent implementation of a given policy. From the perspective offered by this broad definition it would appear that the decisions on this set of program elements may indeed prestructure the implementation phase to a much greater extent than students of policy implementation have generally assumed.

Programs in the area of regulatory policy usually have as their core some set of performance standards that translate the general goals contained in laws or governmental programs into more specific guidelines for action. In the case of clean air policy, this program core consists of the ambient air quality standards. In order to be administratively feasible, these standards require an additional program element; i.e., a monitoring system and criteria for evaluating the data gathered, so that the actual quality of the air can be measured and compared with the standard. As in other areas of policy, the quality standard at the center of a given control program constitutes a general pattern of relative privilege or discrimination. The way in which this pattern is reflected in regulatory processes dealing with concrete cases (process-oriented administrative guidelines for action) can vary depending on the decisions made with regard to other elements of the control program. For this reason it is useful, when examining the interest bias of a given program, to distinguish the decisions on these additional dimensions of the program from the program core itself and to conceive of them as a group of elements constituting a first shell surrounding the core (**inner program shell**). By so doing, the analysis is able to note possible tensions that may exist between the performance standards oriented toward results and the action standards concerned with processes.

As is the case in many areas of regulatory policy the performance standards formulated in the program core require an organizational and instrumental foundation. We have designated the decision of these program elements as the **outer program shells.** Figure 10-1 shows the relationship between the various elements constituting the structure of a control program.

When the individual countries are compared in terms of the ways in which they define the control problem and the strategies used in dealing with it, the principal difference is found not in the control dimensions contained in a given program but rather in the extent to which the particular national program itself explicitly specifies which administrative level is to have jurisdiction for decisions on a given program element or to which these decisions have, in fact, been left to a subnational decision maker.

In air pollution control policy, as in other policy areas, the actual level at which controls are exercised often differs from those formally authorized to take such actions. This occcurs when local discretion is extended in practice as a result of specific local control demands. In particular, whenever explicit rules do not exist, administrative practices will emerge — usually at a lower level of jurisdiction — to fill the gaps left by the national program.

In almost every country examined we found an institutional division of labor that allocated responsibility for decisions with regard to the different control dimensions to the national, regional, and local levels. By classifying national program structures in terms of their patterns of allocation, it is possible to construct a useful

Figure 10-1

The Implementation Program Shells

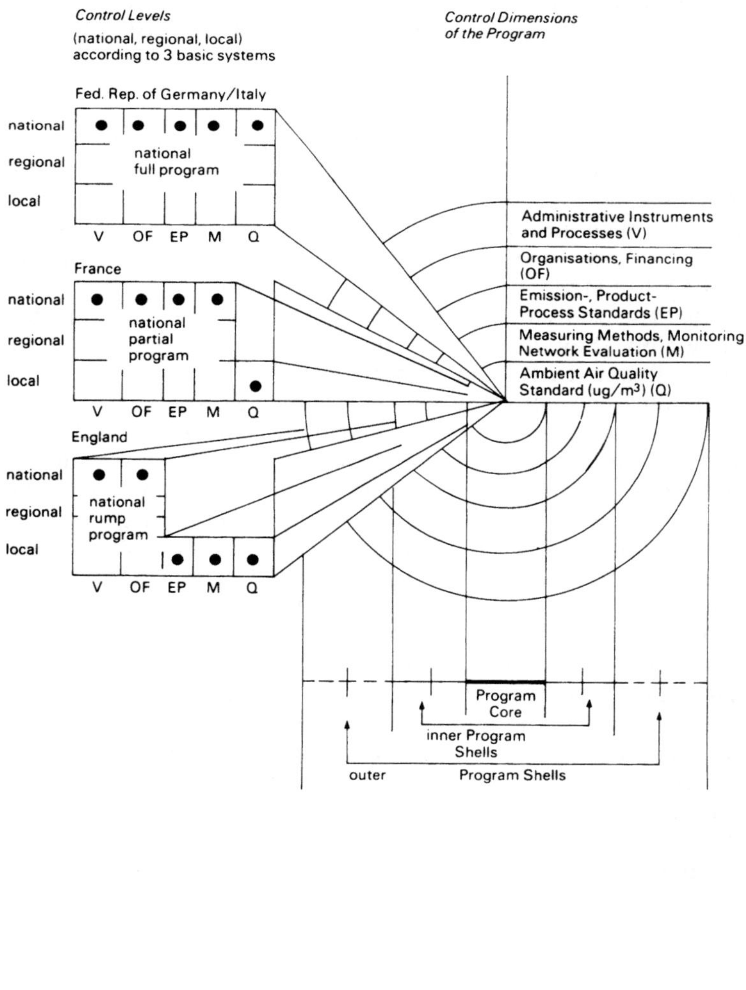

typology for comparing the different countries studied (see figure 10-1). Three general program structures and, with them, three general patterns of interest recognition can be distinguished: a **full national program**, where the decisions regarding practically all control dimensions are made at the national level; a **partial national program**, where the national level regulates only the inner and outer program shells; and a so-called **rump program**, where national decisions deal with the outer program shells only. In the following discussion some of the general points discussed above are illustrated by examples drawn from the data on Italy and the Federal Republic of Germany.

In both these countries, where decisions on quality standards are made at the central level in the national program, efforts of economic actors to advance their particular interests tend to be concentrated on decisions regarding the inner and outer program shells (for clean air policies of the FRG and Italy, see Knoepfel and Weidner, 1980). In situations where there is relatively wide public support for improvements in environmental quality, it is not possible for representatives of these economic interests directly to challenge demands for strict standards to protect citizen health. For this reason, the efforts of these groups are aimed not so much at the ambient air quality standards per se but more at those program elements surrounding this program core. In this way they attempt to undermine the program core by weakening the supporting enforcement structure. Thus we often find these interests avowing support for general quality objectives and publicly going along with the proposed quality standard while, at the same time, working behind the scene to lessen the impact of this standard by affecting the decisions on crucial supporting program elements.

This general strategy must be kept in mind when analyzing the extent to which different groups/actors are able to influence decisions on program elements and thus shape the implementation process in a manner more responsive to their interests. Evidence indicates that emitter organizations frequently use such shell strategies. Since they are often the only actors that are active both during program formulation and on the implementation front, they usually possess an effective system of information transfer by means of which they are able to judge the relevance of a decision on a particular program element for the subsequent implementation phase.

Therefore, actors wishing to weaken the actual impact of a given quality standard may resort to the following strategies with regard to decisions on the inner program shells:

Manipulation of the monitoring system. The value of an ambient air quality standard for enforcement practice can also be varied considerably by manipulating the type of measurement system employed, the size of the monitoring areas, the evaluative methods used, and the degree of publicity given to the measurement results. Thus, for example, enlarging the area for which the ambient air quality is monitored allows the measurement of more favorable results than where relatively small monitoring areas are used.

Percentile reduction. An ambient air quality standard in effect can be made less stringent by establishing a low percentile for which the average measured air quality value for the given time period is to be calculated. In this way, the number of peak values that do not have to be included in the calculation of the mean average value is increased, thereby effectively raising the frequency with which the standard can be surpassed.

In much the same vein, central decisions on the outer program shells, found especially in the full program type, frequently weaken the program core. To this end, strategies are often aimed at the following program elements:

Implementation structure. At the center of often quite heated debates regarding the appropriate organization of environmental enforcement is the question regarding the formal allocation of planning, approval, supervisory, and enforcement authority to local, regional, and national administrative agencies respectively. In the full program type, decisions on these matters are made at the central level. Not surprisingly, decisions regarding the administrative level to be responsible for a given function are often made with certain expectations as to which interests are likely to be advantaged or disadvantaged (Downing, 1979). In those cases where a particular actor feels it has better access at the national level, it will push to have the national administrative agency get jurisdiction. Likewise, those interests considering themselves particularly effective at the local or regional levels will push for some kind of decentralization of administratrive responsibilities. The critical reaction of different industrial groups to federal or decentralized solutions must be seen in terms of their evaluation of their relative strength at the national as opposed to the subnational level. Decentralized solutions; i.e., delegation to local enforcement officials of effective control over important program elements, are therefore frequently denounced as local protectionism. Thus in the FRG and Italy large industries see their interest in harmonizing and unifying the national markets (and even their competitive position in the international market) threatened by administrative arrangements that give strong powers for enforcement of environmental quality regulations to local officials. Given the fact that the effective implementation of air quality control programs requires sophisticated enforcement technologies (e.g., monitoring of production processes, measuring and analyzing of immission conditions), decisions regarding personnel and equipment to be allocated to the responsible administrative and technical agencies can become politically sensitive and controversial issues. This had been the case in Italy in particular.

Administrative instruments and procedures. In air pollution control policy the most significant control instruments have to do with the licensing procedures (along with the criteria for granting approval), the issuing of abatement orders, and the monitoring of compliance with license conditions. Consequently, formal administrative procedure, which continues to be an important factor determining the behavior of actors involved in enforcement activities, has significant consequences for the distribution of bargaining power (Knoepfel, 1979). This importance of administrative procedures both reflects and reinforces the significance of the legal training of a large proportion of enforcement officials and tends to lead to a high degree of routinization of implementation activities. In the Federal Republic of Germany, such formalization of the enforcement process, combined with the almost loop-hole-free system of legal protection, results in a relatively centralized control of the relevant dimensions of the process.

A more comprehensive study has demonstrated that by using such a broad concept of program it is possible to use an analysis of program structures in different countries to uncover the varying patterns of interest consideration they embody and to indicate the way in which these patterns operate to facilitate or obstruct subsequent implementation of the control program. Insofar as institutional patterns of privilege and discrimination are already incorporated in the program itself, the notion of implementation deficit as a shortfall caused by inadequacies of the implementation phase itself becomes quite relative. Viewed in the context of the decisions on program structure and the patterns of interests reflected therein, these deficits represent little more than the effects of the consciously or unconsciously built-in biases of the program shells on the program core which, in turn, is often falsely taken as the only (or most important) point of reference for evaluating implementation performance. In light of these considerations, implementation research should be able, by means of such an analysis of program structure, to suggest hypotheses as to what was to have been implemented in a given regulatory policy in the first place. It is often possible to answer this question only when, after analyzing the way in which a given program incorporates a pattern of interest recognition, the program structure is then examined with an eye to the way in which the interest bias of the different program elements are likely to affect program implementation. In this sense, implementation research will have to be extended to an integrated analysis of policy that joins both the implementation and program formulation processes.

MEASURABLE IMPLEMENTATION IMPACTS

Initially we had assumed that the choice of SO_2 control programs as the focus for an investigation of the implementation of air quality policy would offer almost ideal conditions for evaluating the impact of policy outputs on ambient air quality. Indeed the elaborate arrangements for monitoring ambient air quality with regard to the pollutant SO_2 — carried out at immense costs all over Europe — have in no small measure been justified in terms of their value as an effective instrument for evaluating the performance of air quality control programs. However, for most of the LIAs studied this assumption has in large part (with the exceptions noted below) proved to be false.

As it turned out, it has not been possible to find any clear correlation between trends in the volume of SO_2 emissions in the LIAs — which we conceived of as the indicator of the actual impact of implementation outputs on emitter behavior — and data on corresponding developments in ambient air quality (immissions). In part this lack of correlation is due to the generally problematic nature of the immission data themselves. At the same time, irrespective of the quality of the data, there are a number of considerations that can lead both politicians and administrators to question the validity of monitoring results whenever they show negative trends; i.e., deteriorating air quality. Thus, for example, in one year the severe winter will be made responsible for greater concentrations of SO_2, while in another year it will be the increased import of SO_2 immissions from other countries or regions, and in a third year unfavorable winds will be the root of all evil. It is also common practice to use interregional comparisons of differently generated data quite arbitrarily to document developments considered especially favorable and, just as quickly, to reject similar comparisons when the results put the city or region concerned in an unfavorable light. Despite intensive efforts, the European Communities have not succeeded in coming up with meaurement data that can be used for reliable cross-European comparisons of ambient air quality. Given the sophisticated debates on the reliability of measurement data, one might well speak of the kind of successful "rebellion of the means against the end" that Janicke (1979) has also noted in other areas of environmental policy. In any case, evaluation management and the endless discussions concerning the reliability of immission data seem to be the lowest common denominator achieved in European air quality control policies.

When the data on trends in SO_2 air quality for our LIAs are examined, a definite correlation exists between volume of emissions and developments in ambient air quality for only one point in time, namely, the marked decrease in both at the beginning of the seventies. Leaving aside for the moment variations in economic development found in the individual countries, these decreases were almost exclusively the result of national clean air measures aimed at the reduction of the sulfur content in light fuel oil (domestic heating) and heavy fuel oil (industrial combustion) in agglomeration areas (protection zones). Reductions in emissions and improvements in air quality at this time can also be attributed to other measures in the field of domestic heating, e.g., periodic controls of equipment and reduction in the number of emitting sources as a result of hooking up to municipal heating systems. It should be noted, however, that neither of these measures can be viewed as the results of regional implementation activities but are, rather, the direct result of national program decisions.

Additional reductions in the volume of SO_2 emissions that have occurred in the industrial sector were apparently too small to have significantly affected trends in the quality of ambient air in the localities examined. Reduction in the frequency of smog situations constitutes an exception to this. Here improvements correlate with a corresponding decrease in SO_2 emissions. On the other hand, the high stack policy pursued in some countries undoubtedly had long-term effects on immission trends but is directly reflected in the measured developments of ambient air quality in only a few of the LIAs studied (e.g., Creteil in France and Bologna in Italy). This minor impact of high stacks on local air quality trends can, in general, be explained by the low rate of industrialization and the relatively few new chimneys constructed during the 1970s.

The points discussed above provide sufficient evidence for the limited usefulness of air quality data as a means for evaluating the effects of control measures. Although the systematic monitoring of air quality had been sold politically with the argument that these measurements would provide reliable data for assessing the actual state of air quality and thus the performance of control programs, the only practical relevance these measurements seem to have had in the second half of the seventies has been to identify smog (alarm) situations. This, however, would not seem to justify the immense investments made in these monitoring systems since smog situations can be forecast as well — and more cheaply — on the basis of general meteorological data.

A second assumption originally made and subsequently put in doubt by the results of our research was to think that official data on aggregate emissions would provide a reliable basis for assessing the impact of clean air policy measures in the different LIAs. There are two main reasons why this is not the case. First of all, official emission inventories do not usually report data on actual emissions but rather present figures on emissions calculated on the basis of estimated or reported consumption of different types of fuel and the standard emission factors for different kinds of production processes. (This is true in the United States as well — see Downing and Kimball, chap. 13; Brady and Bower, chap. 2.) Secondly, and even more importantly, the assumption does not hold because it seems that environmental policy outputs directly influence emitter behavior only when the permits granted contain precise and explicit requirements concerning the sulfur content of the fuels used over and above what the national regulations required in this regard. However, interviews with industrial emitters in all LIAs indicate that this is more the exception than the rule. Normally, emitter behavior will be more decisively infuenced by such factors as the production situation of the company, relative price differences on the fuel market, and energy-saving measures undertaken by the firm on its own initiative, as well as by many other firm-specific considertions. In the field of SO_2 there is an inseparable relationship between production and emission volumes, and this is only marginally affected by environmental policy outputs.

Thus, contrary to the assumptions we had made (and that still enjoy widespread political acceptance), emission inventories proved in the end to be of limited use for assessing the impact of air quality control measures. Data on industrial emissions, collected for each LIA, are useful in this connection only when they cover a period in which the general regulations governing sulfur content in fuels were introduced or changed. From 1975 on, however, this was nowhere the case. As far as SO_2 emissions from individual plants are concerned, there is no evidence that there have been significant changes in the volumes emitted that could be attributed to the activities of agencies implementing air quality control programs. With regard to the field of domestic heating, the situation seems to be different. Here the regulations governing sulfur content of fuels have been the primary instrument of control policy. With regard to the implementation of these measures, the only activities involved are the inspection of the producers and distributors of heating fuels, the periodic control of heating plants, and the steps concerned with replacing individual sources with municipal heating plants. Such measures can indeed be viewed as impacts of air quality control programs and are reflected in the emission data (cf. the LIAs of Zurich, Basel-Land, Basel-Stadt, Turin, and Munich).

In summary, the following three points, which are crucial for research into the implementation of air quality control policy as well as for the critical evaluation of implementation performance, can be drawn from the initial analysis of project data:

1. Statements concerning the success or failure of SO_2 control measures that are based on official trend data should be treated with caution. It can generally be assumed that, especially in the industrial sector, there is no single-cause relationship between implementation activities and trends in emissions and ambient air quality.

2. There appears to be a definite correlation between administrative outputs and trends in air quality and — to a lesser extent — emission data only in those cases where there have been reductions in the sulfur content of fuels (for both industrial and domestic heating) or where controls of heating installations and source elimination are advanced as the reasons for the success or failure of control measures.

3. It is almost impossible to evaluate the regional implementation activites actually carried out with regard to the regulation of industrial sources where control dimensions other than changes in the sulfur content of fuels are used.

At this point the two reservations mentioned above should be recalled. A definite output-impact correlation exists only in cases of reduced producton activity during smog periods and when high stack policies are applied. In the latter case, however, the impact of the output is reflected only in the air quality data. It would seem, therefore, that SO_2 control measures are especially weak, in terms of measurable impacts, with regard to the regulation of industrial sources. For these emission activities, a definite relationship will be found only insofar as implementation authorities succeed in achieving drastic reductions in emissions by requiring flue gas desulfurization and/or fluid bed furnaces for major polluting industries. Throughout the seventies, and in all the LIAs studied, neither technology was considered to be best practicable means and thus implemented. In light of this fact, the strategy of reducing the sulfur content of fuels cannot be regarded as an achievement of clean air implementation activities. The relatively simple implementation of this control strategy is usually not carried out by local or regional agencies but takes place at the national level.

The almost complete absence of output-impact relationships in the area of SO_2 control policy is especially distressing when the financial aspects of these programs are considered. It is extremely doubtful that the often substantial investments in the construction of highly sophisticated monitoring networks during the seventies will prove to be as useful as originally expected in evaluating policy performance in this area.

The results of our study also seem to raise doubts about whether the equally costly institutional arrangements for air quality control activities in the industrial sector have been effective in light of the rather meager results achieved. In particular it is questionable whether the widespread practice of expanding already existing authorities responsible for the enforcement of trade regulations into more complex agencies incorporating the newer environmental policy tasks is justifiable. Contrary to our findings, it is assumed that it is possible to pursue air quality control policy and energy policy at the same time and through the same agency. The lack of an effective administrative (but also policy) link between these two causally interrelated policy areas is so widespread in practically all countries studied that one cannot help asking whether it is not due to some kind of deliberate coordination deficit. As things presently stand, energy policy can be pursued independently on the basis of its own premises with little thought to its impact on enviromental objectives. It is this cause-denying autism that inevitably makes air quality control policy both expensive and ineffective (see the corresponding chapters on energy policy in Knoepfel and Weidner, 1980).

THE INFLUENCE OF INSTITUTIONALIZED PUBLIC PARTICIPATION

At the start of the project it was assumed that the opening of the implementation processes to various forms of public participation would lead to strengthening of the ecological content of ambient air quality standards. Furthermore we assumed that as a consequence of the greater scope for participation by interested actors in the enforcement process, the number of conflicts over aspects of environmental policy would, on the whole, increase since it could be expected that the increased amount of information available would lead to a higher degree of mobilization of hitherto excluded elements of the public. If we take the number of suits brought before the administrative courts in the FRG against environmentally relevant development projects as an indicator of the level of conflict in connection with the implementation of environmental policy, then the latter hypothesis would seem to be supported for that country. On the other hand, we did not find any evidence supporting the expectation that greater public participation would improve the ecological quality content of permit decisions. The results of the implementation studies carried out in the other countries examined do not support either of the hypotheses advanced.

The output analysis meticulously carried out in our selected LIAs did not reveal any significant differences with regard to the environmental substance of the contents between those countries with a more open enforcement process (e.g., FRG, Belgium, France, and the Netherlands) and those with closed administrative procedures; i.e., those without institutionalized inclusion of members of the affected public (e.g., Italy, Switzerland, and the United Kingdom). In an overwhelmingly large proportion of cases in both categories of countries, the conditions stipulated in the permits finally granted did not differ from those on which agreement had been reached in the informal negotiations preceding the formal licensing procedure. In view of the small number of modified licensing decisions, it is difficult to distinguish the countries of one or the other category on the basis of the likelihood that the informal consensus reached on license conditions will be modified during the subsequent formal procedure. It does, however, seem that in countries with a more closed enforcement process the initiative for seeking stricter permit conditions is often taken by other agencies participating in the proceedings or by actors from the political sphere (e.g., in Italy, the local communities or members of the regional committees for air quality control; in the United Kingdom, local administrative authorities; and in Switzerland, the local communities).

Evidence from Switzerland the the United Kingdom suggests that compared to open systems, countries with closed enforcement processes are more likely to achieve a higher degree of compliance with the license conditions formally stipulated. The close cooperative relationships between the agency and emitter, which are not disturbed by public participation may, paradoxically, even lead to environmentally more favorable results in those cases where energy savings for the firm can be realized at the same time. In contrast to more open systems, such decisions, which are often combined with the introduction of complex technologies, can be carried out without great administrative costs.

When the countries with open enforcement processes are ranked with regard to the ecological quality of their outputs, the Netherlands clearly leads, while France ranks lowest. From this we conclude that the quality of the outputs depends more on the general level of environmental awareness found in a given LIA and less on the degree to which the permit process is formally open to public participation. This conclusion is reinforced when the closed system countries are compared in terms of output quality. Thus, for example, the low record of achievement of licensing decisions in Italy is due more to the low level of environmental consciousness in that country than to the closed nature of its adminstrative procedure. On the other hand, the relatively strict conditions contained in a typical license in Switzerland appear to be a function of the higher level of environmental sensitivity found there.

It is possible to produce a rough test of the validity of these general observations by comparing variations in the environmental quality of the regulatory outputs of those countries in which the formally available opportunities for public participation are actually taken advantage of. This has most clearly been the case in the Netherlands and the FRG. The relatively low levels of environmental consciousness in France and Belgium probably explain why persons and groups affected by emissions very seldom appear in the enforcement process. It is quite clear that among the countries with formally open enforcement systems, the Netherlands is also one of the most substantively open. Here modification of the agreement achieved in the negotiations preceding the formal licensing process are more frequent than is the case in the FRG, where, as may be concluded from the research undertaken by Mayntz et al. (1978), the opening up of procedure often serves more of an alibi function.

Such comparisons lead directly to questions regarding the basic function of an open or closed implementation process in the area of environmental policy. By providing increased access to previously excluded groups and interests, some observers had hoped to reduce the recourse to administrative courts by those not involved in permit decisions. However, the number of appeals on these decisions is much higher in the FRG than in the Netherlands. It would appear that the German system, which is open to third party participation, mainly serves the function of creating legitimacy for the regulatory outputs produced, while the substantively more open Dutch system is more appropriate for reconciling conflicting interest positions. At the same time, it would seem likely that as a result of the already relatively high level of environmental awareness in the Netherlands, participation in the licensing process would be less likely to lead to the mobilization of public interest and sensitivity with regard to the issues at hand. In Germany, on the other hand, conflicts often take on clear shape only in the course of confrontations during the licensing decisions. The greater willingness of the parties involved to turn to the courts in cases of conflict (especially the administrative courts) is probably a characteristic of the German political-administrative culture. For their part, the Dutch tend to be more oriented to political compromise. All in all, citizen participation in the Netherlands tends to have a high relevance for outputs and increases the conflict-resolving capacity of the enforcement process. In the formal, similarly designed arrangements found in Germany, the mobilization function of public participation appears to be more in the foreground.

The comparable licensing procedures of France and Belgium also tend to serve a more legitimizing function when one takes into account the political conditions found in these two countries. Here environmental consciousness is relatively low and correspondingly low is the number of citizen organizations active in the field of air pollution. Licensing procedures have been designed in such a way that implementation activities by agencies receive their legitimation from the silent consent of the persons affected, i.e., in the absence of objections. In much the same way these procedures protect investment decisions by industrial emitters against the risk of subsequent interventions by enforcement agencies by morally foreclosing later modifications of the original permit conditions as a consequence of policy changes (creation of well-earned pollution rights through the consent of the people affected). The research results so far from the LIAs in the three closed system countries (United Kingdom, Switzerland, and Italy) seem to suggest a basic difference between open and closed systems. The weakly developed legitimation functions in licensing procedures in closed system means that the licenses granted are more susceptible to interventions at a later point in time. Italian and British licenses are far less likely to be changed than are French, Belgian, or German licenses.

Due to the small number of licensing decisions in which conflict occurs in our LIAs, we are not able to make any statements about the importance of conflict for improving the ecological quality of permits. As has already been observed, our hypothesis that a positive relationship exists between conflict level and output quality may hold true for the Netherlands. If we also take administrative court suits into consideration, then the comparable cases from the FRG would support this hypothesis as well. The few cases involving conflict that can be found in the Belgian and French LIAs, however, seem to speak against this hypothesis. Indeed, in these instances the politicization of permit decisions as a result of conflict sometimes had a negative effect on the quality of the individual licensing decision in that it caused the emitters to become politically more active than they otherwise would have been. This, in turn, led to a more or less strong intervention by central state actors into the jurisdictions of the provinces responsible, who were not in a position to counter such pressures from above. However, it should be noted that in France and Belgium the reasons for such conflicts were not rooted in the existence and activities of citizen organizations but rather in the antagonistic relationship between the licensing agencies and the emitters during earlier phases of the permit process. In some cases the agency's actions in such conflict situations is even a welcome opportunity for the emitter — together with the national ministry of economic affairs — to make this case a national political issue.

NOTES

* The compartive study from which this chapter draws was funded jointly by the German Research Foundation and the Volkswagen Foundation. Parts of the third section have been previously published in Policy and Politics, vol. 10, n. 1, 1982. An extended version of this article will be published in Implementationsforschung, edited by Renate Mayntz (1983). The authors wish to thank Dagmer Kollande of IIES for translating major parts of the article.

1. The field research in the countries mentioned was conducted by Bruno Dente, Rudy Lewanski, Silvia Tozzi, and Sofia Mannozzi (Italy); Henrique de Magalhaes, Richard Darbera, and Corinne Larue (France); Volker Prittwitz, Helmut Schreiber, and Robert Bramer (FRG); Matthias Peters (Switzerland); Theo van der Tak, Kenneth Hanf, and Theo Toonen (Netherlands); Roger Kesteloot (Belgium); Michael Hill, and Patricia Garrard (U.K.).

REFERENCES

Bardach, Eugene, 1977. The Implementation Game: What Happens after a Bill Becomes a Law? (Cambridge, MA, London: MIT Press).

Borghorst, Hermann. 1978. Die wechselseitige Abhangigkeit von Bund und Kommunen in der Stadtsanierungspolitik der Vereinigten Staaten von Amerika (Berlin).

Downing, Paul B. 1979. "Implementing Pollution Laws: Observations from the American Experience," Zeitschrift fur Umweltpolitik, 4: 357-392 (December)

Janicke, Martin. 1979. Wie das Industriesystem von seinen Mibstanden profitiert (Darmstadt: Westdeutscher Verlag).

Knoepfel, Peter. 1977. Demokratisierung der Raumplanung (Berlin: Duncker and Humblot).

Knoepfel, Peter. 1979. Offentliches Recht und Vollzugsforschung (Bern: Paul Haupt Verlag).

Knoepfel, Peter. 1982. "Conceiving Comparative Policy Analysis. Conceptual Framework for a Comparative Analysis of the Implementation of SO_2 Air Quality Control Policies in Europe," Architecture et Comportement (special issue).

Knoepfel, Peter, and Helmut Weidner. 1980. Handbuch der SO_2

Luftreinhaltepolitik, 2 vols. (Berlin: Erich Schmidt Verlag).

Knoepfel, Peter, and Helmut Weidner. 1982. "Formulation and Implementation of Air Quality Control Programmes: Patterns of Interest Consideration," Policy and Politics, vol. 10, n. 1.

Knoepfel, Peter, and Helmut Weidner. Forthcoming. Luftreinhaltepolitik in Europa, vol. 1 and 2.

Knoepfel, Peter, Helmut Weidner, and Kenneth Hanf. 1980a. "The Implementation of SO_2 Control Policy in the European Community and Switzerland," American Bar Associaton (ed.), Air Pollution Control: National and International Perspectives (Washington D.C.).

Knoepfel, Peter, Helmut Weidner, and Kenneth Hanf. 1980b. "International Comparative Analysis of Program Formulation and Implementation in SO_2 Air Pollution Control Policies in the EC Countries and Switzerland: Analytical Framework and Research Guidelines for the National Research Teams," mimeographed (Berlin).

Krupnick, Alan J., and Winston Harrington. 1981. "Decision Rules Used in the Promulgation of Federal Regulations: The Case of EPA Effluent Discharge Standards,: in Implementing Pollution Laws: Intenational Comparisons, Paul B. Downing and Kenneth Hanf, ed. (Tallahassee: Florida State University).

Mayntz, Renate (ed.). 1980. Implementation Politscher Programme. Empirische Forschungsberichte (Konigstein/Taunus: Verlagsgruppe Athenaum, Hain, Scriptor, Hanstein).

Mayntz, Renate, H.-U Derlien, E. Bohne, B. Hesse, J. Hucke, and A. Muller. 1978. Vollzugsprobleme der Umweltpolitik (Materialien zur Umweltforschung, herausgegeben vom Rat von Sachverstandigen fur Umweltfragen). Stuttgart, etc.

Pressman, G.L. and A. Wildavsky. 1973. Implementation: How Great Expectations in Washington Are Dashed in Oakland (Berkeley, Los Angeles, London: University of California Press).

Sabatier, Paul A., and Daniel A. Mazmanian. 1982. "Policy Implementation," mimeographed 1980. Forthcoming in V. M. Deckar, ed., The Encyclopedia of Policy Studies.

11 MIXED IMPLEMENTATION INCENTIVE SYSTEMS FOR WATER QUALITY MANAGEMENT IN FRANCE, THE RUHR, AND THE UNITED STATES

Blair T. Bower

INTRODUCTION

Because no production or use activity transforms 100 percent of the inputs into desired products, services, or utility, some materials and energy will always remain for disposal into one or more of the environmental media. Those media represent common property resources with finite assimilative capacity. The general problem under all socioeconomic systems is to ensure that discharges to the environment will not result in unacceptable decreases in ambient environmental quality. The specific problem is to develop and apply implementation incentive systems that induce the activities to limit discharges to desired levels. Such systems can be comprised of one or more implementation incentives of one or more types; e.g., economic, regulatory, or judicial (see Russell and Bower, 1981; Bower et al., 1981). Virtually all systems are comprised of mixes of types of incentives. The purpose of this chapter is to describe the existing mixed implemetation incentive systems for water quality management in France, in the Genossenschaften areas of the Federal Republic of Germany, and in a sample of the many U.S. cities that levy sewer charges.

Characteristics of Implementation Incentive Systems

Before describing the systems, some explication of the characteristics of implementation incentive systems is necessary.

First, an implementation incentive system consists of:

1. **a set of implementation incentives,** e.g., rules or procedures that an activity must follow, a set of discharge limitations that must not be exceeded by a specified amount for a stated portion of the time, a set of subsidies related to specific investment or operating actions, or a set of charges related to inputs to the activity, to residuals discharges from the activity, or to some measure of performance;

2. **a system of measuring performance,** e.g., quantities of materials discharged, qualities and/or quantities of material

and/or energy inputs, quantity of residuals removed from discharge streams, or quality of product output;

3. **a system of on-site inspection** to determine if, for example, specified equipment is in place and operating, the system for measuring performance is in place and operating, and the analysis of the samples taken is accurate; and

4. **a set of sanctions** — fines, fees, withdrawal of operating permit, exclusion from government contracts, imprisonment — for failure to comply with the rules/procedures/standards or for failure to pay charges.

Whatever comprises the first element of an implementation incentive system, the other three elements are essential if the desired behavior is to be induced.

Second, there is no **pure** implementation incentive system. All existing systems have some mix of regulatory and economic, administrative, judicial, and publicity incentives. Point sources may have imposed on them two or more of: input standards; product standards; discharge standards; specifications with respect to technology of production; residuals modification equipment specifications by type and/or level of performance; grants for some portion of the construction cost of pollution control facilities; grants for some portion of the operation and maintenance costs of pollution control facilities; grants to cover some portion of investment in less polluting production technology; low interest rate loans to cover some portion of investment in pollution control facilities and/or less polluting production technology; rapid depreciation provisions and/or tax credits for installation of pollution control facilities; and technical assistance. Figure 11-1 illustrates possible loci of implementation incentives.

Nonpoint activities, such as agricultural and forest management operations, may face one or more of: a limit on annual soil loss for **each** acre of each type of soil; a limit on mean annual soil loss per acre for the **entire** agricultural activity; a charge on each ton of the total tons of soil lost from the area of an agricultural activity, e.g., suspended sediment (residual) discharged with no limitation on source, such as, specific soil types; required tillage/residue pratices and/or required installation of terraces/grassed waterways; public subsidy — state and/or federal — for terrace/grassed waterway construction; permitted deduction of soil and water cconservation expenditures from taxable income; rapid depreciation of investment in soil loss prevention facilities, such as terraces and grassed waterways; surcharges on prices of phosphorus containing fertilizers;

Figure 11-1

Loci of Possible Implementation Incentives for Water Quality Management

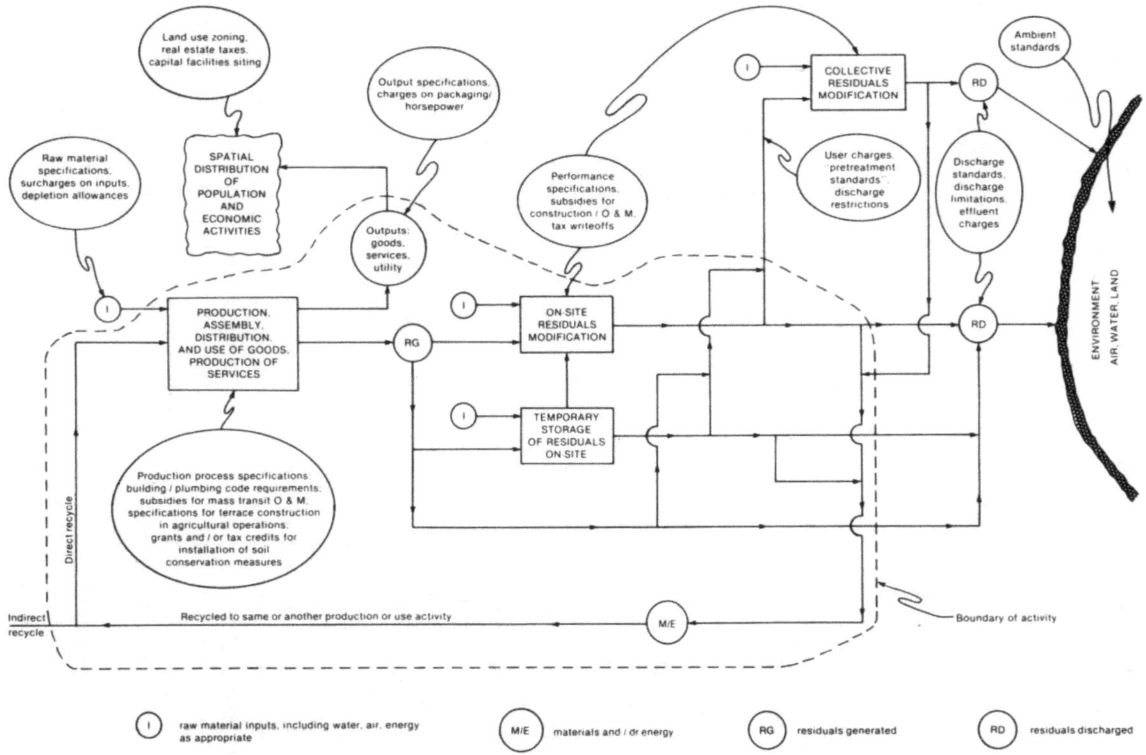

prohibition of use of particular pesticides; prohibition of operations on certain soils or slopes of soil-slope combinations; and technical assistance.

Third, implementation incentive systems are often driven by the objective of achieving specified ambient water quality standards, howsoever selected. A subordinate goal, as a means to that end, is to achieve some given level of discharge reduction from a given activity or from among several activities in a region.

Fourth, an implementation incentive system imposed on a given activity in relation to a given residual usually represents only one of several implementation incentive systems imposed on different liquid residuals, and others on gaseous and solid residuals, to which the activity responds. For some residuals, the same physical measure will reduce the discharge of more than one residual — e.g., BOD_5 and suspended solids — although not to the same extent. Often physical measures designed to reduce the discharge of a given residual may **increase** the generation of one or more other residuals. It is particularly important to recognize the joint cost and intermedia problems.

Fifth, some implementation incentives can be imposed at any of the levels of government. Further, the same type of implementation incentive can be imposed simultaneously by more than one level of government, for example, a federal effluent charge on suspended solids discharge into water courses combined with an additional state effluent charge in such discharges.

Sixth, many implementation incentives are not under the jurisdiction of environmental quality management agencies. Probably the clearest examples are tax policies such as those relating to depletion allowances, capital gains, severance, accelerated depreciation, and real estate.

Seventh, implementation incentives systems are imposed in relation to both **original** compliance and **continuing** compliance. The former refers to inducing the original installation of facilities or physical measures that are presumed to be able to meet or exceed the conditions specified in the discharge permit, whatever the basis for the permit and the means by which it was obtained. Continuing compliance refers to the activity's day-to-day meeting of the conditions specified the discharge permit. The same implementation incentive or implementation incentive system may not be effective with respect to **both** original compliance and continuing compliance.

Last, the response of an activity takes place in a dynamic context, both short-run and longer-run. Short-run relates to variability from day-to-day — and within a day — in the generation and discharge of residuals from the activity.[1] Longer-run relates to changes in factor input prices, technology, product characteristics, and types of raw materials. Short-run variations in residuals generation and discharge present major problems in devising implementation incentive systems that will achieve, **continuously**, ambient environmental quality standards.

WATER QUALITY MANAGEMENT IN FRANCE[2]

Implementation incentives imposed on individual dischargers to water bodies in France are comprised of (1) discharge standards and, in some cases, production process specifications incorporated in discharge permits; (2) grants to both public and private entities to cover some portion of capital costs of facilities to reduce discharges; (3) grants to both public and private entities to cover some portion of operation and maintenance costs of facilities to reduce discharges, where the amounts granted depend on how well the residuals modification facilties are operated; (4) loans at less than market rates of interest to cover some portion of capital investment in residuals modification facilities; (5) effluent charges on four different liquid residuals discharged; and (6) technical assistance to individual activities. The discharge standard/permit system applies to about four hundred types of activities, which are termed "classified establishments." These activities are divided into two categories, depending on the size and nature of the activity. The first is comprised of those activities that must only make a declaration to the Prefect and to the Service of Classified Establishments prior to starting or modifying operations, provided that the activity meets other regulations; e.g., sanitary regulations and departmental ambient water quality objectives. There are about five hundred thousand establishments in this category. The second is comprised of those activities that must apply for a permit prior to starting or modifying their activities. This involves: acceptance of stipulations of the measures to be taken to prevent or reduce disamenities; holding of a public inquiry; and preparation of an environmental impact statement. There are about fifty thousand establishments in this category.

The national Service of Classified Establishments (SCE) is responsible for defining, for each of these activities, the normal conditions for operation and for the discharge of residuals. The actual permit to the activity is granted by the Prefect, based on the conditions specified by the SCE and local/regional ambient water quality conditions and objectives. Discharges from **all** point sources to surface waters must meet certain minimum standards relating to temperature, color, and pH of effluent; impact on mortality of fish; and contents of floating objects. The SCE is responsible for inspecting the operations of activities for adherence to the permit conditions.

The various grants are made both from national and regional budgets and from the six river basin commissions. These commissions encompass the entire area of France and have the unique situation in France of being public establishments with a high degree of financial autonomy.

The primary formal functions of a basin agency are to levy charges on water users, to make grants and loans to cover part of the capital costs of sewage treatment plants of municipalities and industrial activities, to make grants — in the form of premiums and superpremiums — to municipalities and industrial activities to cover part of the operation and maintenance costs of sewage treatment plants, and to develop the multi-year program of spending by the agency. Informally, staffs of basin agencies provide technical advice to all types of dischargers.

It is important to emphasize that the basin agencies in France are not water quality management agencies in the full sense of the term "management," as are, for example, the river authorities in England and Wales and to a lesser degree, the Genossenschafte in the Federal Republic of Germany. The French river basin agencies cannot design, construct, or operate facilities; they cannot set discharge standards or ambient water quality standards; they do not give permits for withdrawals or discharges; they have no police or regulatory powers.[3] They are basically financial agencies, as their names imply; e.g., Agence Financiere de Bassin Seine-Normandie.

Financial Flows and Effluent Charges

To understand the operation of economic incentives in water quality management in France, it is necessary to understand the flows of money to finance sewage treatment plants and sewer systems. Essentially, only municipalities and industrial activities can build and operate treatment plants. With respect to municipal sewage treatment, capital costs of facilities are financed through: (1) loans and grants from the relevant basin agency; (2) the municipal budget; and (3) grants from regional and departmental budgets, which in turn come primarily from the national budget. Operation and maintenance (O&M) costs of municipal facilities are obtained from: (1) the sewage tax; (2) the premium; and (3) the superpremium, in cases where good efficiency of operation is achieved in the sewage treatment plant.

Effluent charges are levied by the basin agencies. The reason for the charges is to raise money to finance the multi-year programs of the basin agencies; to induce reductions in discharges is **not** the reason. These programs consist of helping municipalities and industrial activities finance their investments — by grants and subsidized loans — and their O&M costs — by subsidies — to reduce their discharges. In fact, neither the legal texts on which the charges are based nor the unit levels and structures of the charges have much to do with the concept of economic incentives.

The setting of the charges begins with estimates of the levels and spatial pattern of activities in the various coefficient zones of a basin over the five-year planning horizon and with the estimates of the generation and discharge of pollutants associated with these activities. Given the objectives defined by the basin agency, e.g., degree of treatment to be achieved and the amounts of financial aids to be provided, the cost to the agency over the five-year period is obtained. The assessment basis — in terms of estimated discharges — and the costs yield the levels of **unit** charges on the different pollutants. Then the consistency between the estimated effects of the multi-year action program, in terms of reductions in discharges, is tested against the initial assumptions concerning the assessment basis. Several multi-year action programs are developed and tested in this manner by the staff of the basin agency.

The basic rule is that there be an overall balance between revenues and expenses for each basin agency. Beyond that, there are two balances that must be respected. One is that there should be a balance between revenues and expenditures for each pollutant. In fact, one computaton is made for total suspended solids (TSS) and organic material (OM) jointly, then one each for toxics and salts, each of which has generally well identifiable specific costs of reduction. Separation between TSS and OM is partially arbitrary. The other balance is for the private sector on one side and for the public sector, i.e., municipalities, on the other.

Given these unit charges, the annual effluent charge for an activity other than a municipal one is computed according to the following formula:

TECHARGE (P) = VOL x KDIS (P) x KZONE x BASE (P)

where: TECHARGE = total **annual** effluent charge for pollutant P;

VOL = volume of production in physical units (grandeur caracteristique), implicitly per day;

KDIS (P) = specific coefficient (coefficient specific), i.e., the amount of pollutant P discharged per unit of volume of production as actually measured, or assigned from a table, assuming generation = discharge;

KZONE = zone coefficient (coefficient de zone), the magnitude of which depends on the location of the activity within the basin;

BASE (P) = base charge coefficient (coefficient de base) for pollutant P, for the given basin, francs per unit of pollutant P; and

VOL x KDIS (P) = amount of pollutant P discharged daily by the activity, also called the assessment basis (assiete de redevance).

The total annual effluent charge to be paid by the activity is the sum, for all relevant pollutants, of the charges for each of the pollutants. For municipalities the annual effluent charge is computed according to the following formula:

TECHARGE = NBIE x KSIZE x KZONE x BASE,

where: TECHARGE = total annual effluent charge for the municipality;

NBIE = number of inhabitant-equivalents discharging into the municipal sewage system;

KSIZE = city size coefficient, which reflects that the average pollutant generation per inhabitant-equivalent increases with city size;

KZONE = zone coefficient, the magnitude of which depends on the location of the municipality within the basin; and

BASE = base charge coefficient, francs per inhabitant-equivalent.

Two points with respect to the financial flows relating to municipal sewage treatment merit emphasis. One, households and other dischargers into municipal sewage systems pay the effluent charge via their water intake bills based on **assumed residuals generation**, not actual discharge. However, the operator of the sewage treatment plant receives a premium based on the difference between the inflow to and the actual discharge from the treatment plant.

Two, the effluent charge and the sewage tax are imposed on **water intake.** Hence, there is no incentive whatsoever to discharge less, for a **given** amount of water intake. In particular, the system is disadvantageous for an activity using municipal water for any uses from which it does not discharge into the sewage treatment plant, and advantageous for activities such as commercial laundries, which would not pay an additional amount for the discharge of chemicals.

WATER QUALITY MANAGEMENT IN THE RUHR

In the Ruhr area of the Federal Republic of Germany, as in France, water quality management involves two sets of agencies. One relates to the governments of general jurisdiction, specifically the Land (comparable to a state in the United States, to a canton in Switzerland) and the jurisdictions subordinate to it. The Land has primary responsibility for water quality management . The other set consists of the regional water quality management agencies, the Genossenschaften, established under special laws.

With respect to the former, three levels of administrative authority exist to execute the responsibilities of the Land. At the highest level are the ministers of the Land (state) ministries; e.g., Ministry of Nutrition, Agriculture, and Forestry. The second level is made up of five Regieurungsprasidien, which together cover the entire Land. Each of the Regierungsprasidien encompasses in its area all the categories of administrative responsibilities that are present in all ministries of the Land government. The third level is made up of Land agencies that have no broad — but only very specific — administrative authority and/or technical advisory functions. They are located in each Regierungsprasidium, covering the region of the Regierungsprasidium, and are overseen by the Regierungsprasidium in conducting their delegated responsibilities. Their real extension varies; it is, in general, larger than the area of a county. There is overlap among them with respect to areal jurisdiction, but every agency type covers the area of each Regierungsprasidium.

The implementation incentives imposed on activities are: discharge permits; grants to municipalities and water authorities to cover portions of the capital costs of discharge reduction facilities; loans at less than market rates of interest to public and private entities to cover portions of the capital costs of discharge reduction facilities; rapid depreciation provisions in tax laws; and effluent charges. Grants are made for the following types of facilities:

(1) mechanical-biological wastewater treatment; (2) stormwater treatment, including retention basins; (3) wastewater and stormwater pumping works; (4) sewer systems; and (5) pressurized pipelines. The discharge permits to individual dischargers are granted by various agencies of the Land. Facilities of the Genossenschaften do not receive permits as such, but the specific effluent conditions to be achieved by those facilities are reviewed, and must be approved, by the Regierungsprasidium. The Regierungsprasidium is also responsible for monitoring of discharges.

Effluent Charges

Effluent charges are imposed by each Genossenschaft in its area. The charges are based on the revenues necessary to cover most of the expenses of the association, such as operating its treatment plants, paying salaries and other administrative costs, and paying the interest on capital borrowed for investment in new treatment plants and related facilities. The anticipated expenditures in the forthcoming year are based on escalating the previous year's budget and five-year investment plan, which plan is reworked annually. (About 10 percent of the required revenue is obtained from miscellaneous sources.)

The unit charge is obtained by dividing the total revenues required by the number of damage suits associated with all the estimated discharges in the area. The number of damage units for any given activity is a function of: (1) the number of employees, (2) the nature of the production process, and (3) the amount of wastewater discharged into a facility of the Genossenschaft. Coefficients relating to the nature of the production process are based on samples of effluents from a number of dischargers in each activity category.

SEWER CHARGES IN THE UNITED STATEES

The mixed implementation incentive systems in water quality management in France and the Ruhr area of the Federal Republic of Germany have roughly comparable analogues in the sewer charge systems in many U.S. cities. The implementation incentives involved in these sewer charge systems include: effluent charges, i.e., charges on quantity and quality of discharges into the sewer system;[4] tax credits for capital investment; and rapid depreciation allowances on investments in pollution control facilities. Thus, these systems provide additional cases for analysis of responses to mixed implementation incentive systems.

At least 90 percent of U.S. cities with populations greater than fifty thousand have some form of sewer charges. The various charge systems were not designed explicitly to induce reductions in discharges from individual activities. Rather, the purposes of the charges are (1) to raise revenues — as in France and the Ruhr — to cover the costs of sewage treatment, including amortization of capital investment, operation and maintenance, and administration; and (2) to distribute these costs equitably among the users of the system. There are substantial variations among cities in what costs are to be covered by the charges. In some cities all costs associated with sewage collection and treatment are included; i.e., interceptor sewers, main laterals, sewage treatment, and sludge handling and disposal. In other cities one or another of these costs is covered by general revenues.

Table 11-1 shows the basic structure of sewer charge formulae. Unit costs to be used are derived in various ways, generally using costs in the previous year as a basis. However, to derive unit costs requires an allocation of system costs to the elements in any given sewer charge formula. Such allocations are more or less arbitrary; e.g., the asumption is made in Atlanta that the cost of treating a unit of BOD_5 equals the cost of treating a unit of TSS.

Pretreatment (discharge) standards typically cover: fats, oil, and grease; pH; temperature; explosives; radioactive materials; toxics; sulfides; phenols; and garbage and other solids that may obstruct sewers and treatment facilities. For some of these discharge is prohibited; for others a limit, in terms of concentration and/or total discharge, is specified.

RESPONSES TO MIXED IMPLEMENTATION INCENTIVE SYSTEMS

Given the nature of the mixed implementation incentive systems in water quality management, as described above, what can be said about the responses induced by these systems? Ideally, responses are best evaluated by obtaining empirical data on the behavior of individual plants. Rarely have such data been compiled. However, in the study in the United States (Urban Systems, 1979), 101 individual plants were visited to determine the responses to the mixed systems existing in five U.S cities in relation to combinations of pretreatment (discharge) standards and sewer charges. Types of plants visited included canning, production of chemicals, dairies and other food processing, meat packing, pulp and paper manufacturing, metal finishing, and commercial laundries.

In assessing responses, what must be emphasized is that

Table 11-1

Basic Structure of Sewer Charge Formulae

$$\$/ccf = V + A\,(C-C_o)\,TSS + A\,(B-B_o)\,BOD_5$$

where:

V	=	volume related charge ($/ccf)
TSS	=	TSS related charge ($/pound)
BOD_5	=	BOD_5 related charge ($/pound)*
C	=	actual TSS concentration (mg/1)
C_o	=	"normal" TSS concentration (mg/1)**
B	=	actual BOD_5 concentration (mg/1)
B_o	=	"normal" BOD_5 concentration (mg/1)**
A	=	conversion factor from mg/1 to lb/ccf = .006238

In Atlanta, the formula is:

$$\$/ccf = \$.88 + \$1.05 \times .006238 \times \ (C-250) + (B-250)$$

* COD in South San Francisco

** 250 mg/1 in Atlanta and Dallas; 0 elsewhere

Abbreviations:
TSS total suspended solids
BOD_5 five-day biochemical oxygen demand
ccf 100 cubic feet

Source: Urban Systems Research and Engineering, Inc., 1981.

multiple factors operate to affect the behavior of an individual plant. Included are: prices of factor inputs other than water, including energy and labor; capital availability; technical information available; regulations on discharges of gaseous and solid residuals; regulations concerning food safety; and regulations concerning worker safety. Attempting to isolate the effects of the implementation incentives relating to liquid residuals within this milieu is difficult. However, based on the 101 individual plant units, the following conclusions seem warranted.

1. Despite the fact that the sewer charges were low in all cases in relation to both total production costs of the activity and the cost of reducing discharges of liquid residuals by the activity, the charges did induce responses. These included better housekeeping, some changes in production processes, and some changes in by-product production. In a few cases significant innovation in production systems was induced.

2. The sewer charges induced more continuous adherence to the pretreatment (discharge) standards. The cumbersome nature of the regulatory system in imposing sanctions for each time the pretreatment standards are exceeded results in a relatively ineffective inducement for continuing compliance; whereas, receiving a bill each month reflecting actual behavior is a readily observable signal to plant management.

3. Responses in terms of discharge reduction beyond discharge standards are a function of the level of charges. As charges increase in proportion to total production costs, responses yielding greater reductions in discharges are induced.

4. Physical measures to reduce water intake, wastewater discharge, and energy use often reinforce one another.

5. Stringent regulations imposed on the discharge of toxics generally also result in reductions in discharges of BOD_5 and TSS.

6. Regulations directed toward air quality management, solid residuals management, food safety, and worker safety often lead to increased discharges; i.e. they exacerbate the problems of water quality management.

7. The availability of information is an important factor affecting responses. For plants producing the same product or products, significant differences in responses were found between single-plant firms and multi-plant firms. In general, a plant that was one unit of a multi-plant firm had more relevant information available than did single-plant firms.

Data comparable to those obtained for individual plants in the United States are not available for France or for the Genossenschaften area of the Federal Republic of Germany. However, investigations in France in connection with the previously cited report (Bower et al., 1981) suggest the following conclusions with respect to responses by individual activities in France to mixed implementation incentive systems.

1. The levels of effluent charges are low, relative both to total production costs and to the average annual costs — capital amortization plus operation and maintenance — of treatment by the individual activity. However, even with the relatively low levels of the charges, activities where it is cost effective to undertake some discharge reduction have found it profitable to do so.

2. Those industrial sectors where it is more cost effective to reduce discharges have been pushed, by both economic incentives and regulatory incentives imposed at the national level, to undertake reductions.

3. The river basin agencies, by means of their knowledge of individual dischargers and their criteria for grants, can allocate the available resources to subbasin areas having the more severe ambient water quality problems.

4. The regulatory side of water quality management and the economic incentives side have, in practice, turned out to be complementary. The regulatory side sets the framework in which, on the whole, the basin agencies operate in imposing economic incentives. The regulatory system has kept its importance and continues to be relevant for at least three reasons. First, some kind of licensing procedure is necessary in any case, even if only to check on the discharge of residuals that are necessarily forbidden by law, e.g., carcinogens. Second, experience has shown that industrialists in France are extremely reluctant to modify, even marginally, their production technology, even if the investment is paid back in one year, e.g., 100 percent return on capital. Such behavior has been observed in many cases in the Seine-Normandie Basin, for example, where an investment in a simple cooling water recycling system — which would have been paid back in less than two years — was not undertaken. There are individuals and managers for whom economic incentive has no real meaning. Third, in terms of actual behavior, the inducement for action appears to be a maximum when there is one stick — penalties and sanctions for disregarding standards — from inspectors of the SCE, and one carrot — technical advice, loans, and grants — from a basin agency.

Given the above, how can one assess, finally, the interplay of the regualtory incentives and effluent charge incentives for municipalities and individual private activities? For municipalities, the incentive effect of the regulatory system is fairly low because it is difficult, if not politically infeasible, to impose sanctions, e.g., send a mayor to jail. This means the economic incentive is crucial. Clearly, the system of grants of all kinds that reduce the capital costs of treatment plants to the municipalities provides a major economic incentive. Further, the superpremium paid for a given level of efficiency of discharge reduction is also relatively high for municipalities, which increases the economic incentive for reducing discharges. In fact, the system is set so that relatively little additional regulatory incentive is needed to push municipalities to take action to reduce discharges.

For private activities, the situation is quite different. For them, the regulatory incentive usually has real weight. Fines are actually levied, court actions are taken in many places, SCE inspections are made. All this reduces noticeably the margin of maneuver for dischargers. Nevertheless, these incentives have been insufficient in the past, as indicated by the fact that ambient water quality of French waters rapidly worsened in the 1960s. What was needed was some economic incentive, but also — and perhaps even more important than strict economic incentives — an independent interlocutor that could give technical advice on what actions the private activity could take and how to take them to achieve the discharge standards. The fact that this interlocutor — the basin agency — also makes grants to cover 30 percent of capital costs is a positive factor. Thus, what can be concluded is that the combined effect of regulations and economic incentives is to induce private activities to take substantial actions to reduce discharges.

Given the commonalities among the three sytems, one might hypothesize that the responses on the part of individual activities in the Genossenschaften area of the Federal Republic of Germany would be similar to those found in the U.S. cities and in France. However, pending data collection and analysis at an equivalent level of detail, that hypothesis must remain untested.

CONCLUDING COMMENT

Regardless of the mix of implementation incentive in any given situation, it must be recognized that responses by activities are a function of discharge reduction costs as the activity (discharger) sees them. Costs as a discharger sees them, and his response to implementation incentives, are not necessarily — and may in fact not likely be — equal to resource (social) costs.

The basic question then is: how effective are alternative implementation incentive systems in actually inducing dischargers to reduce discharges and maintain those reductions over time? The evidence cited above is suggestive. Mixed implementation incentive systems appear to be more effective in water quality management than any pure systems. But the optimal mix remains an elusive objective.

NOTES

1. In manufacturing activities at least six types of conditions occur that result in short-run variations in residuals generation and discharge: (1) start-up/shut-down of production processes; (2) clean-up operations; (3) upsets during production with no halt in production; (4) breakdowns such that production ceases; (5) accidental spills; and (6) variations during normal production operations. The reasons for the first five types of short-run variations in residuals generation are obvious. For the sixth type, some factors that result in less-than-daily and day-to-day variations in residuals generation and discharge are: (a) variations in operating conditions, e.g., operating a production unit beyond design capacity; (b) variations in the condition of operating equipment; and (c) daily and weekly variations in product mix.
2. Material in this and the next section is drawn primarily from Bower et al., 1981. Use is by permission of Resources for the Future, Washington, D.C.
3. Sewage treatment plants are constructed and operated by municipalities, industrial activities, and a few private water companies. Reservoirs are designed, constructed, and operated by regional and departmental agencies, by public and private water distribution companies, and by Electricite de France.
4. In the United States sewer charges are not termed effluent charges, even though they are imposed on effluents from activities. Sewer charges are categorized as user charges.

REFERENCES

Bower, Blair T., et al. 1981. Incentives in Water Quality Management in France and the Ruhr, Research Report R-24 (Washington, D.C.: Resources for the Future).

Russell, C. S., and B. T. Bower. 1981. "Effluent Charges and Other Implementation Incentives in Water Quality Managemet: An Overview" in Bower et al, 1981.

Urban Systems Research and Engineering Inc. 1979. "Responses to Local Sewer Charges and Surcharges," Final Report, Volume I, prepared for the Council on Environmental Quality.

12 COASTAL LAND USE REGULATION IN CALIFORNIA SEEN IN COMPARATIVE PERSPECTIVE

Paul Sabatier

INTRODUCTION

The chapter presents abundant evidence of the problems involved in applying central government policies in different local settings, of the discretion exercised by field level implementing officials, of the difficulties confronted in obtaining information on the activities of target firms; of the numerous uncertainties involved in enforcing permit decisions; and of the consequent need in most cases to negotiate mutually acceptable permit conditions.

The book is based on the premise that much can be gained from a comparative perspective, and I certainly agree. This chapter is comparative in at least three respects. First, while most of the chapter authors deal with air and water pollution control, this chapter examines a different policy area, namely, the regulation of coastal land use. Second, much of the chapter will compare decisions by different agencies operating under the same legal mandate but in different political environments. Third, while the chapter focuses on the activities of the California Coastal Commissions, it also briefly presents some tentative conclusions from an ongoing study of coastal land use management in Britain and France.

As we shall see, many of the difficulties confronting pollution control agencies in the United States and Europe were also faced by the California Coastal Commissions. Contrary to the apparent experience of some pollution control agencies, however, an analysis of the Commissions' permit review decisions indicates that these agencies were able to have a significant policy impact. They succeeded in altering the pattern of land use decisions concerning new coastal development that had previously been negotiated by a variety of private and public actors. In the absence of serious empirical inquiry it is impossible to ascertain the extent to which these differences in outcomes can be attributed to policy area (pollution control vs. land use) rather than the political and institutional setting in which the Coastal Commission found themselves. But I strongly suspect that the latter factors are preeminent.

The bulk of the chapter contains an analysis of permit decisions made by four of the California coastal agencies during the 1973-75 period. After some initial background material, it examines the extent of interregional differences in permit decisions and then presents a model to account for this variation. It also briefly examines some of the problems the Commissions faced in actually carrying out their permit decisions. The concluding section offers some tentative reasons for the relative effectiveness of the Coastal Commissions in altering the status quo ante. It also briefly reexamines some of the conclusions from the larger California study (Sabatier and Mazmanian, 1982) in the light of coastal management activities in Britain and France.

PERMIT REVIEW BY THE CALIFORNIA COASTAL COMMISSIONS: 1973–1975

Prior to the 1970s, government regulation of land use in California (or elsewhere in the United States and much of Europe) was largely in the hands of local authorities. Most local governments were, however, very reluctant to interfere significantly with market forces, particularly in rural areas and on the urban-rural fringe. This led to a number of perceived problems, including the destruction of over 60% of the state's coastal wetlands; the impairment of much of the magnificent scenery along the coast through second-home developments in rural areas; and restrictions on the constitutionally guaranteed access of the public to the coast, particularly in wealthy residential areas such as Malibu (just north of Los Angeles).

As a result, environmental groups and their allies tried to convince the state legislature to transfer some authority for the regulation of land use along the coast from local to state institutions. After repeated failures, these groups decided to bypass the legislature and go directly to the electorate by qualifying an initiative statute for the November 1972 ballot. It was approved by 55% of the voters, despite the well-financed opposition of the construction industry and unions, energy companies, and many local governments (Sabatier and Mazmanian, 1982; and see Healy et al., 1978; Rosenbaum, 1976; Popper, 1981).

The California Coastal Zone Conservation Act established six Regional Commissions whose memberships were equally divided between local elected officials and appointees of state officials (the governor, the assembly speaker, and the Senate Rules Committee), as well as a State Commission composed of a representative from each of the six regions and six appointees of state officials. The Coastal Commissions had the dual responsibility of (1) preparing a comprehensive coastal plan for presentation to the 1976 Legislature and (2) regulating all development in the interim from the seaward boundary of the state's jurisdiction to 1,000 yards (about one-half mile) landward of the mean high tide line. Unlike the ambiguous and conflicting policy mandates characteristic of most land use legislation, the Coastal Initiative placed a clear priority on protecting the beauty and the natural resources of the coastal zone, as well as public access to these resources.

This chapter examines permit review by the State Commission and three of six Regional Commissions — the North Coast, North Central, and South Coast — which we selected to provide diversity in background socio-economic characteristics (from the rural North Coast to the highly urbanized South Coast) and in electoral support for the Coastal Initiative (from 35% in the North Coast through 53% in the South Coast to 60% in the North Central; see the map in figure 12-1). Among the data bases utilized in this analysis are coded information from agency files on random samples and complete censuses of permit cases before the four commissions during 1973-75 period; responses from attitudinal questionnaires distributed to commissioners and commission staff in 1974, and interviews with commission officials and other actors. (For a more complete description of our methods, see Sabatier and Mazmanian, 1982.)

The Commissions' permit review process represents an excellent opportunity to examine the ability of a central government agency to alter the allocation of critical resources from what would have taken place in the normal system of control by the economic market and local governments. All permits reviewed by the Coastal Commission had previously been approved by local and, in some cases, other state agencies. Thus every condition imposed by the Commissions and every application denied represented a clear departure from what would have occurred under the antecedent (traditional) institutional arrangement.

Permit Decisions in Three Regions

During the 1973-76 period, any person, corporation, or state or local agency wishing to erect or alter any sort of structure, discharge any waste, change the intensity of land use in any fashion (e.g., a lot split), or engage in any dredging, filling, or other type of development was required to obtain a permit from the relevant Regional Commission. By this very broad definition, virtually any conceivable alteration of land use — e.g., repairing a highway culvert, cutting a tree, building a fence — constituted "development."

As part of his application, the applicant completed a form

Figure 12-1

The California Coast

describing the project's probable effects on habitat, water quality, public access, and a number of other topics. In addition to this information, the regional staff consulted with relevant agencies and made a site visit. The application then went to the Regional Commission for decision. About 75% involved such trivial impacts that they were put on the consent (or administrative) calendars and voted on en masse. The remainder were accorded a public hearing, in which presentations were made by the applicant, the regional staff, and anyone else who so desired. In most cases, the voting occurred at the same meeting. Applications involving dredging or filling or those affecting access, scenic views, water quality, or agricultural land required a two-third affirmative vote of the membership for approval.

This was normally the end of the process. About 4% of all Regional Commission decisions (12% of those on the public hearing calendars) were, however, appealed to the State Commission by the applicant and/or "any aggrieved party" (meaning anyone who had testified at the regional hearing). This very broad interpretation of legal standing provided ready access to opponents of development and, in fact, about two-thirds of all appeals were brought by environmental groups or neighborhood associations. In effect, the vast majority of controversial cases were ultimately decided by the State Commission. Since the appellate process involved de novo review, the general pattern of fact-finding, hearings, and voting procedures were repeated at this level.

About 24% of State Commission decisions (or about 1% of all applications) were subsequently appealed to the courts by the applicant or any other "aggrieved party". The courts — particularly at the appellate level — very seldom overturned the Commission's decisions, although appellants could sometimes use the process to negotiate a slightly more favorable settlement.

We can now examine the actual pattern of permit review decisions by the Regional and State Commissions during the 1973-75 period.

Table 12-1 indicates the distribution of decisions by three Regional Commissions on the 25% of all applications important or controversial enough to be accorded a public hearing during this period. At least two points are noteworthy. First, there was considerable variation in the stringency of decisions by the three Regional Commissions — a point to which we shall return in the next section. Second, these figures provide a first approximation of the difference the Coastal Commissions made in the pattern of new coastal development. For example, in the North Central Region, only 15% of cases were approved as submitted by the applicant and as previously approved by local authorities. Fully 50% were

Table 12-1

Permit Decisions of Regional Commissions on Hearing Calendar Items, 1973-1975

	Regional Commission			
	North Coast (n=273)	North Central (n=177)	South Coast[a] (n=1348)	
Commission Decision				
Approve as submitted by applicant	76 %	15 %		(56%)
Approve with minor conditions	11	35	79 %	(17%)
Approve with major conditions	8	34		(3%)
Deny	5	16	21	(24%)
	100 %	100 %	100 %	

[a]Unfortunately, the coding of the complete **census** of South Coast permits (n=1,348) did not distinguish among types of approval. Thus the figures from a separate analysis of a random **sample** of 100 hearing calendar permits during roughly the same period are provided in parenthesis.

subjected either to major changes in the project or to outright denial. The figures for major changes/denials were, on the other hand, considerably lower in the other two regions: 13% in the North Coast and about 25% in the South Coast.

But this is only a preliminary estimate of the Commissions' impact, for it neglects the role of appeals to the State Commission. Thus table 12-2 indicates the decisions of, first, the Regional Commission and, then, the State Commission on a random sample of all appeals during the 1973-75 period.

As can be seen, the appellate process had a very significant impact in the North Coast Region. Whereas 40% of these cases had been approved as submitted by the Regional Commission, only 7% were eventually approved in that form by the State Commission. By the same token, the state increased the rate of denials from 17% to 47%. Note that the appeals process also resulted in a somewhat more stringent pattern of decisions in the South Coast Region, but had virtually no effect in the North Central. In short, precisely as intended by the proponents of the Coastal Initiative, the appeals process served to "correct" the decisions of the more lenient Regional Commissions and thus to standardize somewhat the stringency of development review along the coast. The key to this success was twofold: (1) the presence of environmental groups and other actors in every region able to monitor the Regional Commissions and initiate appeals to the State, and (2) a State Commission with a substantial majority of members strongly committed to the policies of the 1972 Coastal Conservation Act (see Sabatier, 1977).

In fact, if one assumes that the vast majority of important or controversial cases were eventually appealed to the State Commission, then the last column of table 12-2 provides one of the best overall indicators of the changes that the Coastal Commissions made in the pattern of major land use decisions along the coast. Only 13% of this subset of critical applications were approved as submitted by the applicant and as previously approved by local governments and other state agencies; 43% were approved only after additional, and often very substantial, modifications; while another 44% were denied outright. Thus in 87% of these cases the Coastal Commissions altered the permit decisions of the institutions traditionally charged with development review.

Explaining Interregional Variation

Tables 12-1 and 12-2 clearly document one of the most salient features of regulatory policy-making — namely, that agencies operating under precisely the same legal mandate can nevertheless

Table 12-2

Regional and State Commission Decisions on a Random Sample of Permits Appealed to the State Commission, 1973-1975

	Regional Commission			
	North Coast (n=30)	North Central (n=26)	South Coast (n=43)	Combined Total of All Six Regions[a] (n=166)
PART A: Regional Commission Decision				
Approve as submitted	40 %	0 %	33 %	31 %
Approve with conditions	43	73	28	36
Deny	17	27	39	33
	100 %	100 %	100 %	100 %
PART B: State Commission Decision[b]				
Approve as submitted	7 %	0 %	12 %	13 %
Approve with conditions	47	69	42	43
Deny	47	31	46	44
	101 %	100 %	100 %	100 %

Note: Following are the 95% confidence intervals (p=.5) for each of the three regions: North Coast (±.09), North Central (±.09), South Coast (±.13), Total (±.07).

[a] This includes the remaining three regions that are not otherwise discussed in this chapter.

[b] This is a combined index of those cases where the state simply reaffirmed the Regional Commission decision and those where it altered that decision.

come to quite different patterns of decisions. The design of our coastal study permits us to examine the process by which such variation came about.

Figure 12-2 presents a model of the factors affecting permit decisions. It assumes that the needs and resources of different regions affect public and elite opinion, the basic policy orientation of commissioners and their staff, the participation of outsiders (nonapplicants) in the permit hearing, and thus the eventual decisions of the Regional Commissions. But the attitudes of agency officials are also influenced by their legal mandate, while their decisions in individual cases are affected by the perceived impacts of each case.

Table 12-3 presents data on most of the variables in the model for the North Coast, North Central, and South Coast regions:

1. **Community Needs and Resources.** The first three indicators (population, per capita income, and median education) have all been found to be modestly related to public support for environmental protection and land use controls (Springer and Costantini, 1974; Coke and Brown, 1976; Buttel and Flinn, 1978). Conversely, unemployment should be inversely related to such support. The last two indicators (county population per mile of coast and per capita park/forest land) probe different aspects of the need for coastal recreational opportunities and thus public support for controls of nonrecreational coastal development: the greater the population per mile of coast, the greater the demand for the coast as a scenic and recreational resource; conversely, the greater the existing per capita land available within the region for recreational purposes, the less the demand for coastal recreational opportunities.

2. **Public Opinion.** Regional vote on Prop 20 (the Coastal Initiative) provides a straightforward measure of public support for coastal protection. While it would have been desirable to include subsequent indicators of public opinion during the 1973-75 period, none were available on a regional basis.

3. **Basic Policy Orientation of Commissioners and Staff.** Reported here are (a) the percentage of each group who supported Prop 20 in retrospect and (b) their scores on an Environmental Protection Scale (with a maximum of +3 and a minimum of -3) derived from responses to a survey questionnaire (see Mazmanian and Sabatier, 1980).

Figure 12-2

Causal Model of Factors Affecting Permit Decisions

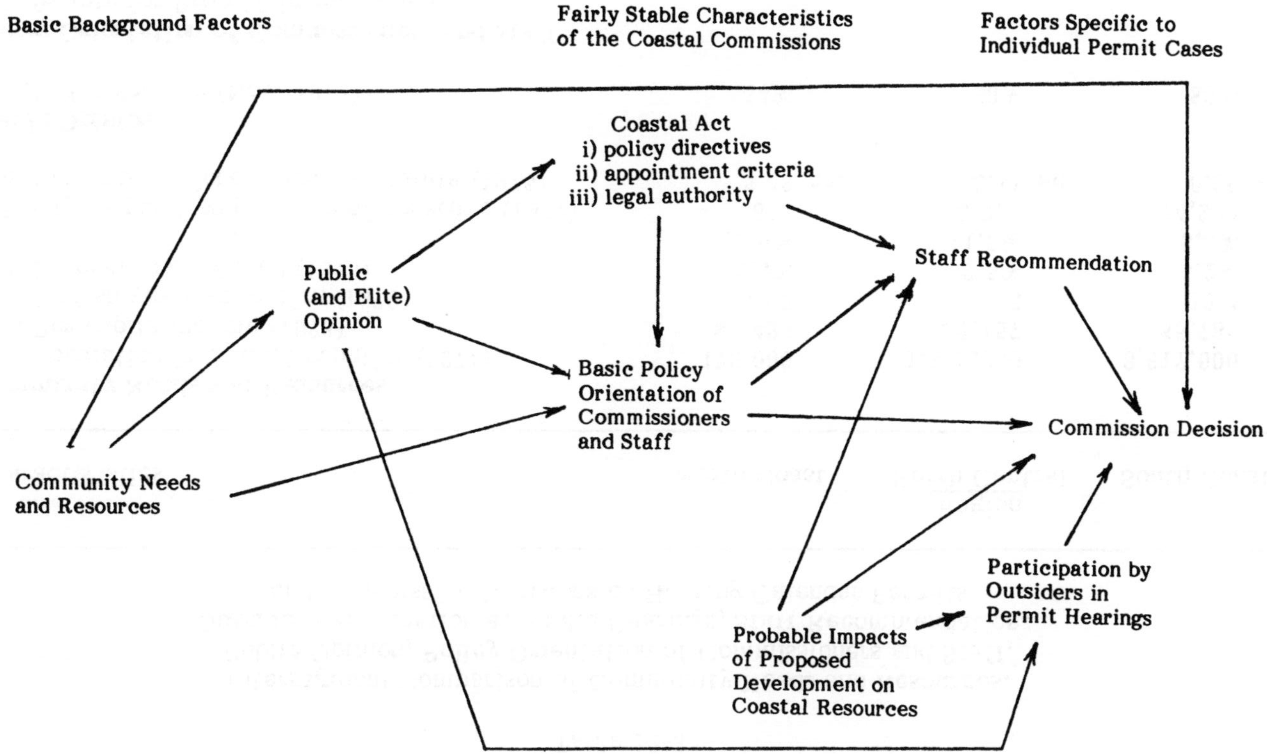

Table 12-3

Interregional Comparison of Community Needs and Resources, Public Opinion, Policy Orientation of Commissioners and Staff, Outsider Participation at Public Hearings, Staff Recommendations, and Commission Decisions on Hearing Calendar Permits

Characteristics	Region: North Coast	North Central	South Coast
Community Needs and Resources			
1. Population in coastal counties (1974)	176,000	1,132,000	8,617,000
2. Per capita income (1973)	$4,423	$7,157	$5,782
3. Median years education (1970)	12.2	12.5	12.4
4. Percent unemployed (1973)	9.0%	7.5%	6.2%
(1975)	15.0%	11.5%	9.3%
5. Cty. population per mile of coastline (1974)	613	8,028	74,284
6. Public park, forest land per capita (1975)	7.48 ac.	0.11 ac.	0.09 ac.
Public Opinion			
Vote for Prop 20 (Nov. 1972)	34%	60%	53%
Policy Orientation of Commissioners and Staff			
1. % vote for Prop 20 in retrospect			
a. Commissioners	36%	100%	56%
b. Staff	91%	100%	100%

2. Environmental Protection Scale			
a. Commissioners	-.80	.19	-.36
b. Staff	.26	.10	.46
Outsider Participation at Public Hearings			
% permits with opposition	34.6%	42.0%	30.7%
Staff Recommendation			
On hearing calendar items, 1973-75			
Approve as submitted	72%	15%	41%
Approve with minor conditions	12%	37%	28%
Approve with major conditions	10%	31%	8%
Deny	6%	16%	22%
Commission Decision			
On hearing calendar items, 1973-75			
Approve as submitted	76%	15%	56%
Approve with minor conditions	11%	35%	17%
Approve with major conditions	8%	34%	3%
Deny	5%	16%	24%

Source: Sabatier and Mazmanian, 1982, ch. 4.

4. **Outsider Participation at Public Hearings.** Here we use the percentage of hearing calendar permits on which there was opposition expressed, as what we are really interested in was the continued participation of the constituency that had originally supported Prop 20.

5. **Staff Recommendations.** Reported here are the staff recommendations on all hearing calendar items in the 1973-75 period on a 4-point scale, from 1 = approve as submitted by applicant, to 4 = deny.

6. **Commission Decision.** This too involves all hearing calendar permits during the 1973-75 period reported on the same 4-point scale.

In fact, the only variables in our model for which indicators are not provided in table 12-3 are, first, the policy directives and the legal authority provided by the 1972 Coastal Initiative and, second, the probable impacts of development. The former is omitted because the statute was constant across all three regions and thus incapable of explaining interregional variation in permit decisions, while the latter is not included because of the lack of feasible empirical indicators.

The model assumes that community needs and resources are the driving force behind the entire permit process. In addition to their indirect effects (via, e.g., public and elite opinion), local needs and resources presumably have some direct effect as commissioners respond to perceived needs unmediated by any of the intervening variables. On the basis of this reasoning, one would clearly expect the **least** stringent permit review in the North Coast Region. It had the lowest population, per capita income, and educational levels of any of the three regions; the highest unemployment levels; and the least need for coastal recreational opportunities. This prediction is certainly confirmed by the data on permit decisions, as the North Coast had by far the highest percentage of outright approvals and the lowest percentage of denials. Moreover, the data confirm the model's predictions concerning several of the intervening variables. For example, the North Coast had by far the least support among the general public and regional commissioners for coastal protection of any of the three regions. On the other hand, agency staff in this region were as supportive of the Coastal Act as their colleagues in the other two regions. Nevertheless, the data presented here and elsewhere suggest that staff recommendations on permit items were less a function of staff members' beliefs concerning the desirability of environmental protection than their perceptions concerning community needs and resources and the prodevelopment policy orientation of their bosses on the commission. Finally, the extent of outsider opposition to permit approval at the public hearings was quite comparable to that of the other two regions — despite the low level of support for coastal protection among the public as a whole. This is, in fact, a tribute to the role of environmental groups (particularly the Sierra Club) in maintaining an effective presence in a rather hostile political environment.

Turning now to the other two regions in our study, an examination of community needs and resources would lead one to expect slightly more stringent commission decisions in the South Coast than in the North Central, mainly on the grounds of a lower unemployment rate and a much higher ratio of population per mile of coast. This was not, however, the case, as the North Central had a much lower percentage of permits approved as submitted (although also a slightly lower pecentage of denials). The link between community needs and commission decisions was similarly reversed throughout the intervening variables. It was the North Central rather than the South Coast that had the greater degree of public and especially commissioner support for coastal protection, as well as the higher percentage of permits with opposition. The explanation for this mild reversal in rank between the two regions probably lies in the fairly long history of support for land use restrictions in the San Francisco Bay Area, as well as significantly greater economic consequences of restricting coastal development in the South Coast. Although the **percentage** of county population in the permit area was very similar in the two regions (4-5%), the **number** of people — and the amount of construction activity — within the coastal permit area was much greater in heavily populated Los Angeles and Orange Counties than in the North Central, where coastal portions of two of the three counties were sparsely populated. As a result, the construction industry — to say nothing of the concentrations of economic power associated with the ports of Long Beach and Los Angeles and the commercial complex of Marina del Rey — had a much greater stake in the South Coast than their counterparts in the North Central and therefore much greater incentive to influence the vote on Prop 20, the appointments to the regional commissions, and the voting behavior of regional commissioners.

In short, our model predicted the large differences between the North Coast and the other two regions. It also worked fairly well in explaining differences between the North Central and South Coast regions — at least after incorporating into the discussion some indication of the extent of economic activity subject to regulation by the Commissions.

From Permit Decision to Intended Impact

Many of the chapters in this book have emphasized the difficulties of going from permit decisions to intended impacts. First, there are problems of enforcement, i.e., of securing target group compliance with the permit. Since the target population — whether polluters or land developers — often have substantial financial (and other) incentives to avoid compliance, the regulatory agency must (a) be able to detect noncompliance; (b) have a credible array of sanctions at its disposal; and (c) be reasonably certain that the prosecuting attorneys and the courts will have the resources and the desire to impose those sanctions.

With one notable exception — to be discussed shortly — noncompliance with permit decisions does not appear to have been a major problem for the Coastal Commissions during the 1973-75 period. There were a few cases of people building without permits or of violating permit conditions, but these were relatively minor. The reasons were threefold: first, noncompliance was almost sure to be detected. The coastal permit zone was rather narrow (about one-half mile in width) and the vast majority of it was visible from the coastal highway or other roads. The regional commission staff were continuously driving those roads in the course of doing site visits; and their surveillance efforts were supplemented by local environmental groups. Even in areas such as water pollution control where detection was more difficult, the Commissions' efforts were actively supported by regional staff of the state fish and game department, the state water quality control boards, and, in most cases, by the local public health departments. Second, the 1972 Coastal Act provided an adequate range of sanctions: fines up to $10,000 and $500 for each day the violation continued. Third, the Commissions had the active support of very competent lawyers in the Attorney General's Office and, as already indicated, almost never lost a case in the appellate courts. But prosecution was not costless: the attorneys' time was limited, and a few trial court judges demonstrated very little concern with enforcing the Coastal Act. As a result, violators had a little negotiating leverage, and there were instances when the Commissions decided it was simply not worth the effort to prosecute violations. On the whole, however, these were minor exceptions to the general pattern of substantial compliance.

The lone major exception involved the failure of many permit applicants legally to record deed restrictions granting public easements through their property from the coastal road to the beach. The Commissions did not become aware of the extent of noncompliance until the late 1970s. No staff had been charged with ascertaining that the conditions were, in fact, being met, nor had environmental groups ever thought to check the deeds in the County Recorder's Office. Once that problem became known, the Commissions were able to develop procedures to prevent its reoccurrence, but some of the early permit conditions may have been lost because of the normal five-year statute of limitations.

The public access program also serves as an excellent example of the second set of difficulties in moving from permit decision to intended impact. Even if target group compliance is perfect, the program will not have its desired outcome unless implementing officials know **how** to achieve that impact and are given sufficient legal and financial resources to do so. For example, the Coastal Commissions could require applicants only to provide an easement. Except in the case of large developers, they could not realistically require applicants to pay for the physical improvements and the liability insurance required before that easement could actually be opened to the public. Likewise, they could deny a permit as a means of keeping it open for park use. But nothing could happen until some public agency had the funds to acquire the land and to manage it. In short, it became clear by 1975 that a purely regulatory approach was insufficient to increase public access to the coast. Thus the 1975 Coastal Plan prepared by the Comissions recommended that the legislature provide funds (via a bond issue) for the acquisition of coastal parks and that a new agency (the Coastal Conservancy) be created to provide some of the missing management functions. While the legislature generally accepted these recommendations, the process of actually opening a park or easement requires the cooperation of a number of autonomous actors (largely state and local parks departments) that has not always been forthcoming — particularly in the period of budgetary restraint following the passage of Proposition 13 in 1978.

It should be noted, however, that the problems afflicting the access program have been much less serious with respect to the Commissions' two other principal objectives: to protect wetlands and the scenic beauty of the coast. But they do serve as a poignant reminder of what Pressman and Wildavsky (1973: ch. 5) have termed "the complexity of joint action".

THE COMMISSIONS' EXPERIENCE IN COMPARATIVE PERSPECTIVE

When one views the experience of the California Coastal Commissions from the perspective of programs in other policy areas and/or political systems, at least three sets of implications seem to emerge.

First, the permit review experience of the Commissions echoes many of the themes mentioned by other contributors when dealing with pollution control programs in somewhat different legal and political settings: (1) the presence of substantial interlocal variation in permit decisions; (2) problems with enforcement and with securing the cooperation of autonomous actors to achieve program objectives; (3) the need to supplement the traditional regulatory approach with a variety of financial incentives (e.g., subsidies) and more flexible management tools; and (4) the problems posed to any regulatory program by a deteriorating economic environment, at which time cost considerations become a more politically important factor.

Second, and in contrast to the conclusions reached in some of the chapters, the Coastal Commissions managed to have a discernible effect on the pattern of new development along the coast during this period. To cite only a few examples: They denied an application for a large hotel on the shores of Humboldt Bay north of Eureka that had previously been approved by local governments. The Commissions cut the permissible build-out rate by about 50% and imposed numerous access restrictions at the Sea Ranch, a large second-home subdivision north of San Francisco approved by county authorities in the mid-1960s. And they made some progress in opening Malibu, a twenty-five mile stretch of beachfront homes north of Los Angeles, to public access.

A number of factors appear critical in understanding the relative effectiveness of the Commissions. (1) The Coastal Initiative did a good job of "structuring" the implementation process by providing relatively clear policy directives, by creating a process in which the State Comission would ultimately make most of the critical decisions, and by encouraging public participation. (2) The creation of new agencies after an intense political campaign resulted in the self-recruitment of staff and, to a lesser extent, commissioners who were strongly committed to achieving the Act's objectives. (3) The environmental groups and their allies who had sponsored the Initiative generally did a superb job of monitoring its implementation during the 1973-76 period.

Third, the importance of central legal controls, supportive professional staff at the local level, and an active local constituency have generally been confirmed by an ongoing study of coastal zone management in Britain and France (Sabatier, 1983). There are, however, interesting nuances. For example, one is struck by the remarkable homogeneity of local land use decisions throughout England on many policy issues, particularly restrictions on housing in the countryside. This is in contrast to the substantial variation in policy decisions one finds in California and France and exists irrespective of interlocal variaton in relevant socio-economic conditions. The key to understanding this anomaly appears to reside in the remarkably strong and uniform ideology of professional planners throughout England on this issue, although central directives and constituency support have also been important. Likewise, the framers of the 1972 California Coastal Initiative assumed that support for environmental protection would be stronger among state appointees than among local elected officials and that local government dependence on property tax revenues was an important factor in their generally prodevelopment orientation (Adams, 1973). While the former premise appears to be true in France also, the insignificant role of property taxes in French local finance cannot provide the causal explanation. Instead, the crucial factor seems to be the very small size of most French communes which makes it very difficult for local elected officials to refuse their neighbors' applications for development permits; in addition, the paternal role of French mayors seems to create enormous incentives for them to build some projects for which they will be remembered.

Finally, the English and French cases confirm the conclusion eventually reached by California authorities that effective land use management requires not only police power controls but also authority to acquire and manage land. The latter is critical to guarantee (on a permanent basis) protectionist objectives in selected areas, particularly when cost-bearers are strongly opposed to the restrictions placed on their use of property and thus risk raising the level of tension in the political system to unacceptable levels. But the apparently greater willingness of English property owners to acknowledge a community interest in their use of land means that greater reliance can be placed on informal negotiations to resolve the conflicts created by public access and wildlife protection, while French and American authorities must rely more on governmental purchase.

NOTE

This chapter is based upon research supported by the National Science Foundation under Grant No. ENV77-20077. Any opinions, findings, and conclusions expressed in this report are those of the author and do not necessarily reflect the views of the National Science Foundation.

REFERENCES

Adams, Janet. 1973. "Proposition 20 — A Citizen's Campaign," Syracuse Law Review, 24 (Summer): 1025.

Buttel, Frederick and William Flinn. 1978. "The Politics of Environmental Concern," Environment and Behavior, 10 (March).

Coke, James and Steven Brown. 1976. "Public Attitudes about Land Use Policy and and Their Impact on State Policy-Makers," Publius, 6 (Winter).

Healy, Robert et al. 1978. Protecting the Golden Shore (Washington, D.C.: Conservation Foundation).

Mazmanian, Daniel and Paul Sabatier. 1980. "A Multivariate Model of Public Policy-Makers," American Journal of Political Science, 24 (August).

Popper, Frank. 1981. The Politics of Land Use Reform (Madison, University of Wisconsin Press).

Pressman, Jeffrey and Aaron Wildavsky. 1973. Implementation (Berkeley: University of California Press).

Rosenbaum, Nelson. 1976. Land Use and the Legislatures (Washington, D.C.: Urban Institute).

Sabatier, Paul. 1977. "State Review of Local Land Use Decisions," Coastal Zone Management Journal, 3.

Sabatier, Paul. 1983. Coastal Land Use Management in Britain and France (Bonn: Institute for European Environmental Policy).

Sabatier, Paul and Daniel Mazmanian. 1982. Can Regulation Work? The Implementation of the 1972 California Coastal Initiative (New York: Plenum).

Springer, J. Fred and Edmond Costantini. 1974. "Public Opinion and the Environment" in Stuart Nagel, ed., Environmental Politics (New York: Praeger): pp 203-208.

IV
ENFORCEMENT

13

ENFORCING POLLUTION CONTROL LAWS IN THE UNITED STATES

Paul B. Downing and James N. Kimball

INTRODUCTION

The enforcement of pollution control laws is an important component of the implementation process. Much has been written about the implementation of pollution control laws in the United States, but there has been relatively little attention to the issues of enforcement. In this chapter we gather together the existing literature on enforcement of pollution laws, supplement it with a case study of water pollution control equipment, and interpret the findings in terms of the economics faced by the firm and the control agency.

A REVIEW OF THE LITERATURE

Major concern for enforcement among economists can be found in the property rights literature. Demsetz (1964) argues that different assignments of property rights will generate different enforcement costs. Crocker (1971) conducted an empirical study of how the redefinition of property rights changed what he calls the information, contractual, and policing costs of an air pollution problem so that a bargaining solution could be reached. Many other authors recognize the importance of enforcement costs (Furubotn and Pejovich, 1972). However, few studies have attempted to analyze the effect of enforcement alternatives on the level of regulated activity.

In a study of air pollution enforcement, Downing and Watson (1974) show that regulatory enforcement employs a set of policy parameters and that a cost minimizing firm will react to these parameters in determining the desired level of emissions. They suggest that the agency has options on how it defines violations, how it detects possible violations, and how it applies monetary penalties to provide an incentive for the firm to comply. They conclude that even under the most ideal circumstances, including certainty in penalties for violations, a firm will be in violation of the announced standard as much as 70% of the time and never be cited for a violation. It is highly unlikely in practice that the ideal assumptions of this study would hold. Thus, one is left to wonder what policies are actually employed in the field and how the firm reacts to them.

Fortunately, literature exists on actual enforcement practice in U.S. pollution control agencies that can provide us with clues. In order to supplement this literature we have conducted a case study of the enforcement practice for the Virginia State Water Control Board (SWCB). Our approach will be to summarize the major points discussed in the literature and review actual experience as it parallels the case study.

The Enforcement Process

The enforcement process can be divided into three basic steps. First, the required actions are determined. This process usually revolves around setting an emission standard. Second, the control agency conducts information gathering to determine if a firm is in compliance with the required standard. This is the process of detecting violations. Third, the control agency takes remedial action to correct detected violations, which includes obtaining conviction and levying fines. We will explore the policy choices revealed in the literature in the context of these steps.

Setting a Standard

While pollution control laws nominally require that emission standards be set by the control gency, in fact the standard to be met is subject to negotiation between the agency and the firm. In a study of water pollution enforcement in eight states, the Environmental Law Institute (ELI, 1975) concludes that the enforcement process emphasizes voluntary compliance, by which is meant obtaining control without imposing penalties. The first step in the process is bargaining with the firm on the level of control and/or the date by which the required control must be installed. ELI also concludes that " . . . considerations of technical and economic feasibility continue to play an important role in the choice of appropriate enforcement remedies." The ELI report implies that this bargaining outcome is subject to political pressures that reduce the effectiveness of enforcement. Joskow and Noll (1981) point out that the interaction of the control agency and the firm presents the opportunity for strategic behavior of both parties. The strategic behavior of the firm is more highly detailed in the Cole and Sommers study (1981) prepared for the U.S. Small Business Administration. This empirical study attempts to quantify the cost of compliance for small versus larger firms. The authors point out, however, that the cost to the firm for regulatory compliance is dependent upon the enforcement strategy adopted by the control agency.

In a review of air pollution enforcement in seven states, the U.S. General Accounting Office (1973) also concluded that heavy reliance was placed on voluntary compliance. This study lists long delays in obtaining compliance, citing numerous examples from various states. In many states there was no organized system for identifying potential emitters.

The bargaining process may take two forms. One alternative is to challenge the level of control required. Here, the control agency is faced with plant engineers who argue that the level of control desired is not technically feasible. If the agency does not bargain, the firm has two choices. One is to challenge the standard in court. Almost all 1977 federal water pollution emission standards were challenged in court.

The other alternative is to seek delay in complying with the required standard. Delay may be accomplished through a variance procedure that grants the source temporary permission to emit above the standards in exchange for the promise to try to meet the standard (Baitos, 1973). Often variances are granted repeatedly as in the case of the Los Angeles Pollution Control District (Willick and Windle, 1973).

Delay in compliance may be accomplished in another way. Under a permit system, the permit states the date by which control must be achieved. However, the permit can be modified to extend the date of compliance. The ELI (1975) study shows that such extensions are very common, often being granted repeatedly to the same source in exchange for a promise to do better. An inspector for the Maryland Bureau of Air Quality and Noise Control suggested that each lawyer a firm brings to a conference with Bureau personnel on permit requirements is worth an additional year's delay in compliance. Current data on rates of compliance with federal water pollution control permits are very high, in part because firms who have been granted delays or variances are listed as being in compliance even though they have not completed construction of all required equipment.

Bargaining in the South Central Region of the Virginia State Water Control Board (SWCB) has taken a similar form (Kimball, 1979). Starting in 1973 National Pollution Discharge Elimination System (NPDES) permits were issued by the SWCB in response to the 1972 Federal Water Pollution Control Act. These permits set temporary emission standards to be met at the time the permit was issued or shortly thereafter. They also set permanent standards to be met in mid-1977. Of the companies surveyed, 83% stated that they had negotiated their permit limits with the SWCB. With a very few exceptions, the interim limit sought by the firm was the limit granted on the permit. Twenty of the twenty-six firms (76%)

received an interim limit that was above or within the average daily or maximum daily limit on their permit request. Nine firms (34%) received a limit on at least one of their parameters that was above what they requested on their application. Eleven firms (42%) received parameter limits that were between average and maximum daily limits set forth on their permits. The limits set forth in the firm's application represent what they were currently discharging. Therefore, over three-quarters of the firms did not have to make any basic modifications to be in compliance. In other words, over 75% of the surveyed firms were already in compliance with their permit limits when the permit was issued. Further, considerable padding takes place. If we assure that the firm does not account for future growth potential, the average biochemical oxygen demand (BOD) limit received on the permit is 2.91 times the average monthly discharge. The total suspended solids (TSS) limit, using the same argument, is 97% larger than the amount discharged.

In summary, a large amount of evidence from the literature, supported by our case study, suggests that both the level of control and the date by which controls are to be effective are subject to bargaining. When bargaining occurs many factors play a part. A state may be reluctant to push a firm too hard for fear that the firm will move to another state (Hines, 1966). Other studies show that industrial dischargers are given very preferential treatment (Coggins, 1972). This preferential treatment by the control agency coincides with the analysis of Hirschey and Pappas (1981) on managerial incentive structures. They show clearly that the incentive toward profit maximization by industrial managers is diminished with inclusion of regulatory policy. After discussing this matter with control agency personnel in Maryland and Virginia, we concluded that they are receptive to, or constrained by, the economic consequences of their control actions.

Detecting Violations

Once a standard has been agreed upon, the source installs the required equipment. Control agency personnel keep track of the due date and receive reports on progress from the source. At the due date, the agency will determine by inspection or other communication whether a source has complied. In some cases, particularly with large sources, some proof of effectiveness of devices may be required. When devices are tested it can be the case that the parameters of the test may cause the agency to accept a device as effective even though it does not meet the standards (Watson and Downing, 1976).

Once a device is installed and certified, it is necessary for the control agency to determine that it is operated effectively. This is done in two ways. The control agency periodically inspects each source to determine compliance. Various studies of the frequency of inspection show that it is highly variable among control programs and among individual sources within a program. The most frequent inspection in the literature is attributed to the Los Angeles County Air Pollution Control District, which inspects each major source once every month (Willick and Windle, 1973). On the other hand, water treatment inspections in North Carolina are conducted sporadically and many facilities have not been inspected for years (Schoenbaum, 1972). The reason given for this infrequent inspection is inadequate staffing. In a study of New York City, the Air Resources Department was quoted as saying, "There are probably 60,000 violations a day, and we catch only about 600 a month" (Schachter, 1974).

In S.C. Virginia inspections are infrequent. According to NPDES regulations, major industries are to be inspected at least twice a year. Minor industries are to be inspected at least once a year. Our survey indicates that major firms have been inspected, on average, less than once a year during the 1976-1977 period. Seven major firms (58%) reported inspections of once a year or less. Three (25%) reported that they were inspected two to four times per year. Finally, two out of twelve reported that they had never been inspected by the SWCB. The staff suggested that there is neither time nor personnel available to conduct the required inspections.

The experience in water pollution control in Virginia is typical. Average frequency of inspections is less than one per year. Inspections are conducted during normal working hours and are almost always preannounced. Permission to enter the plants is obtained from the firm's water pollution control officer. Obtaining permission to enter is a central part of the voluntary compliance scheme, but it also ensures that each inspection is expected. As stated by a staff member, only one inspection (to his knowledge) was conducted during nonworking hours. Incidentally, during that inspection the SWCB personnel did not gain access to the property because they were stopped by plant guards (Interview, 1976). Most important, however, was a staff member's statement that inspection or monitoring by the SWCB almost never occurs unless they have reason to believe a severe violation has developed. In other words, unless a serious violation is reported to the SWCB by the firm itself or by some other source, the specialists will not inspect the facility.

Even when inspections are conducted it appears that only major violations will be detected. As long as the control equipment appears to be operating effectively, the inspector will pass it. He may take a sample of the plant's effluent if it seems that the operation is suspect. However, the inspectors are limited in the number of samples they can send to the state laboratory for analysis. Furthermore, the accuracy of the tests, typically plus or minus 25% or more, and the variability of effluent quality over short periods of time make this sampling procedure highly inaccurate. It is treated merely as indicative of a potential problem.

The principal method of detection of violations comes from the firm's self-monitoring reports. This is true both nationally (Tunderman, 1976) and for our surveyed firms (Maus, 1976; Bailey, 1976). Firms are required by their permit to report any violation and to notify the control agency within five days as to the reason for the violation, extent of damage, and steps taken to correct the problem. Failure to do so constitutes a violation of the permit. They are also required to monitor their emissions (usually daily in S.C. Virginia) and report their results monthly to the agency.

In summary, we find that the typical agency does not inspect frequently. Furthermore, those inspections that do occur are usually preannounced. Thus we find that the probability of being found in violation is virtually zero. There are two exceptions to this conclusion. One would be cases where a third party reports a violation. They constitute a major source of reports of violations in air pollution (Schachter, 1974; Connecticut, 1975). The other case occurs when a source self-reports a violation. Our case study did indicate that many violations were reported by the regulated companies.

Conviction

Not every violation, whether detected by the control agency or reported by the firm, results in court action. Typically, the control agency initiates action through various informal means such as telephone calls and letters. If these efforts do not generate compliance, more formal actions may be taken. The source may be called into the agency's offices for a conference. Next, a notice of violation may be issued. If there is still no corrective action, court action may be recommended. It is, in fact, very rare that a court case is instituted and even more rare that it is not vacated before the court hands down a decision. It is extremely rare that a source is found guilty and fined.

This administrative process is very cumbersome and time consuming. A study of air compliance in Connecticut (1975) provides an example. Of 4,000 premises inspected between 1971 and 1974, 1,469 or 37% were found not in compliance. After notices of violation were issued, 323 or 8% of the total number of inspections did not comply quickly. In these cases compliance orders were issued. One hundred seventy-one or 4% of those inspected failed to meet compliance order deadlines. Twenty-seven of these had delays of over fifteen months. Those with long delays were either very large or very small sources.

Other agencies have similar results. For example, the Minnesota Pollution Control Agency " . . . disposes of all but a handful of violations informally through the 'twilight zone' process of seeking voluntary compliance and negotiating stipulations" (Anonymous, 1972). Texas water pollution control agencies try never to use legal sanctions in obtaining compliance (Jacks, 1970). In the most recent and comprehensive study of water pollution enforcement, the ELI (1975) concluded in part:

(1) Pollution control agencies, particularly at the state level, continue to emphasize informal cooperation — as opposed to issuing warnings, orders, etc. — in their dealings with dischargers.

(2) Enforcement is most often a graduated process. Government responses vary with the gravity of the violation and the degree of pressure necessary to bring about compliance.

(3) Past violations will usually be forgiven if compliance is in the offing.

(4) Considerations of technical and economic feasibility continue to play an important role in the choice of appropriate enforcement remedies.

(5) Dischargers will often be given repeated opportunities to comply before serious enforcement actions are taken.

(6) Negotiation continues to play an important role in enforcement.

Again referring to the Connecticut (1975) study, only 22% of those sources that were issued a notice of violation were also issued a compliance order. Of these compliance orders, only 4% were referred to the attorney general. Of these cases, 19% were settled out of court, 6% were lost by the control agency, 56% remained undecided at the end of the study period, and 19% resulted in court issued injunctions. No fines or other penalties were levied. Long delays and indecision in the courts appear elsewhere in the literature. In New York City by the end of 1970 there were 9,310 outstanding cases out of a total of 12,699 cases brought to court. Of the 3,309 resolved cases, 325 were dismissed, 282 withdrawn, and 2,702 convicted (Schachter, 1974).

Ten of the thirteen plants in S.C. Virginia who self-reported violations were in violation of biochemical oxygen demand (BOD) and/or total suspended solids (TSS) interim permit levels during the eighteen-month period covered. In only one case was there an enforcement action taken. In several instances permits were revised to convert violations into compliance.

Fines

Economists hypothesized that increasing money fines will increase the cost of noncompliance and thus stimulate the firm to comply. In our sample of firms on S.C. Virginia, only one out of twenty-six plants was ever fined, and that was for violation of our enforcement order. Given these results, it appears difficult to suggest that fines play any significant role in enforcement within the South Central region. (This result also appears reasonable for violations of OSHA standards as noted by Kimball and Marlow, 1981.)

A second factor that would seem to undermine the effectiveness of fines is the court's ability to set a very low dollar amount even given a successful verdict. The ELI (1975) report is full of such case examples. The average fine in New York City was $35. There are a few exceptions in the literature. In one case in Illinois a fine of $149,000 was levied, but the Pollution Control Board later settled for $50,000 (Currie).

Control Agency's Prosecution Effort

This variable can be defined as the ability of the control agency to win a successful verdict against a discharger in a court of law. Although very few cases actually go to court, there are several major obstacles that tend to reduce the probability of gaining a successful verdict.

Resource limitations is probably the largest factor working against successful court cases. Extensive documentation is required for any judicial action, and the responsibility for attainment of that data falls upon the regional staff. According to Mr. Charles Maus (1976), his office does not have the time or manpower to gather data on all the dischargers who have violated their permits. This is particularly true for municipal dischargers. The court usually requires a week's (24 hours a day) survey of the effluent discharge from an emitter before it will render a judgement.

Data problems form another resource constraint. Courts often require extensive amounts of new data in addition to that already obtained by the control agency. Therefore, a great deal of time is utilized by the control agency to review and survey existing data and compile new data.

Lack of cooperation between state agencies often frustrates court action. In Virginia, prosecution is handled by the Commonwealth Attorney's Office. This office might require a large amount of data just to review a case and subsequently decide not to file for a judgement. A case's referral to the Commonwealth Attorney's Office is no guarantee of action.

WHY FIRMS CONTROL

In theory it is possible to set and enforce an effluent standard for an individual source that produces the efficient level of emissions; that level for which social marginal benefits equal marginal control costs. What would cause the firm to comply with that effluent standard? The economic theory answer to this question is that the firm will look at its costs of controlling emissions and compare them to the costs of not controlling its emissions or not controlling them as much. Two conditions are necessary in order that the firm meet the standard. At the control level specified in the standard, it has to be the case that the marginal cost of control is less than the expected penalty (Downing and Watson, 1974). In addition, it is necessary that the corner solution of no control not generate a greater net benefit to the firm than control. In other words, it is possible that being a scofflaw is a lower cost option for the firm.

The information presented above suggests that the firm's marginal cost of controlling is well above any marginal penalties it might expect for being in violation. What we observe is firms that control to some level less than the initial proposed standard (and even less than their agreed upon standard) but certainly more than the scofflaw alternative. This implies that the marginal penalty is perceived as being positive and/or that the costs of not controlling at all exceed the benefits. In this section we explore these cost and benefit issues and develop possible explanations for observed firm behavior. These explanations are in the form of reduced control expenditures, entry restrictions for unregulated firms, risk reduction and enhanced corporate image.

Cost Subsidies

The costs of the control equipment a firm installs can be reduced through the use of several explicit and implicit cost sharing mechanisms. The net effect can be a reduction of over 50% in out-of-pocket costs of control.

Pollution control bonds (PCB) have become a very significant funding source for capital expenditure projects. Sales of PCBs have risen from approximately $88 million in 1971 to almost $3.0 billion in 1974 (Wall Street Journal, July 8, 1973, p. 24). In 1973, Pollution Control Bonds raised more than $1.8 billion for private firms or approximately 8% of total corporate long-term borrowing. Under Section 103(c)(4) of the Tax Code, substantially all of the proceeds of a pollution control bond issuance must be used for the qualifying pollution-control facility (Fox, 1976). Proposed Regulations Section 1.103-8 defines "substantially all" to mean 90% or more of the proceeds of an issue after deducting amounts used to pay issuance expenses. Interest on the bonds that qualify is exempt from federal income taxes. This allows them to be sold at lower interest rates than ordinary, taxable, corporate bonds. The amount of interest savings to a firm requiring a $1 million investment could be as high as $300,000.

PCBs are not the only way major corporations can reduce the cost of compliance. One of the significant cost items often overlooked is the federal income tax. This cost category is very important when dealing with pollution control capital equipment because of the various possibilities for savings. One tax provision that could have special tax saving appeal for corporations is Section 169 of the Internal Revenue Code (Interview, 1977). Section 169 allows rapid amortization over sixty months for qualified pollution control facilities in place of the normal depreciation deduction.

Combining pollution control revenue bonds with the investment tax credits and the standard rapid depreciation provisions of the federal income tax system can reduce the financial burden of pollution control capital by over 50% (Kimball, 1979). Operation and maintenance expenditures are written off as an expense, thus reducing tax liability. Furthermore, the firm's state taxes are reduced by many of these provisions. The net effect is a substantial reduction in out-of-pocket control costs.

Gains from Being Regulated

There is evidence to suggest that firms will have an interest in being regulated by government if that regulation provides them with some protection from entry by potential competitors (Orr, 1974;

Joskow and Noll, 1981). Pollution regulations increase the cost of entry for new firms thereby providing some short-term monopoly gains to existing firms. This gain is only temporary in nature, however, because soon after they are inaugurated they become fully capitalized (Buchanan and Tullock, 1975). It would appear reasonable then that firms lobby for laws that will generate these transitional gains. The effectiveness of this lobbying effort would be improved by an acknowledgement that the firms are in compliance with existing regulations. In fact, the argument presented by Dupont in urging a modifiction of the stringent 1983 federal water pollution control requirements followed these lines. They argued that industry was spending large sums of money to control, was for the most part in compliance, and had done enough. It was time municipalities caught up (Conference Board, 1976).

Reducing Interaction with Government

Another possible reason for compliance is risk aversion. Many studies suggest that firms are risk averse in various investment decisions. This charateristic may explain why firms are complying even though it does not appear to be in their self-interest.

A firm may perceive that noncompliance will generate an adverse response from the control agency and/or the legislature. Having been found in violation once, a firm may then find that the control agency monitors them much more closely. Also, the control agency may be more reluctant to compromise on future compliance dates and levels of control. This implies that the expected penalty for the first violation includes the additional cost of raising the frequency of inspections and the probability of future standards and penalties. The firms have correctly surmised that appearing to be in voluntary compliance can effectively reduce government scrutiny.

Corporate Image

In a study of corporate managers, Ostland (1977) found that efforts to be socially responsible in order to maintain or improve the corporate image were considered to be "very important." Furthermore, these managers rated pollution control as second only to equal opportunity as a corporate social priority. The reason for this importance may be the educational level and political awareness of the corporate managers in the study. They are of higher income and education than the average and thus are more likely to be heavy users of environmentally sensitive activities such as outdoor sports. Also, the executives of corporations have a certain amount of discretion in deciding on corporate expenditures. If being socially responsible on the environment generates personal gain for the executive with little or no effect on visible profit for the firm, he may use his discretionary funds in this way.

WHY AGENCIES BARGAIN

Agency personnel find themselves in a difficult position. On the one hand they have public demands and political pressures to control emissions and improve the environment. On the other hand, they are faced with important resource and political constraints that prevent them from fully achieving the goals set out in the laws they implement. Furthermore, they face a set of incentives that may lead them to pursue goals other than those stated in the law. This combination of forces gives the agency the incentive to bargain. The inevitable flexibility in interpreting laws and rules combined with the high cost to others of obtaining information about agency actions provide the room needed to bargain with the sources. The end result is control at a lower level than the law states.

The arguments for bargaining made by agency personnel are of two types. The first type is the technical uncertainty argument. Control technology is not perfected. Often, specific situations cause a particular control process or device to behave differently than expected. This leads to uncertainty about the application of the technology and, consequently, room for bargaining. The second type of argument for bargaining is the perception by agency personnel that if they are "reasonable" in their demands they can maintain a good working relationship with a firm. This will lead to more timely control than might be the case if they follow the letter of the law. Agencies believe that court cases are not as effective as bargaining because they tend to polarize the issue thus causing significant delay. Furthermore, agency personnel cannot be certain that a court case will lead to a clear-cut mandate for control. Often the result has been a court decision saying that the firm and agency need to work out a compromise. In such cases all that is gained by the agency is some additional leverage in its bargaining. At the same time it has used up scarce resources that could have been employed to generate greater control elsewhere.

We are not arguing that bargaining is necessarily efficient. Nevertheless, it has the potential of moving control decisions toward a more desired level and it may do so at lower cost than a strict adherence to the letter of the law.

CONCLUSION

We believe that the literature supports a consistent argument for the compliance actions of firms as being the least costly alternative. They have reduced the cost of compliance through various means. They have reduced the stringency of the standard. They have created a circumstance wherein the penalty for being in violation is zero so long as they convince the agency that they are making "good faith efforts" to comply. Thus they have expended some resources to ensure that enforcement costs are indeed small. Evidence also has been presented that establishes a minimum impact on firm profits through various favorable tax and bond provisions. In addition, the case study supports the notion that these actions extend to a very localized region.

It has also been recognized that the benefits of complying minimally are larger than it would at first appear. There may be transitional gains to being regulated because of the increased cost of entry. Compliance may reduce the costs imposed on the firm by other regulatory agencies. And compliance may forestall the passage of more costly pollution control laws. Thus, when the firm compares the benefits of compliance to the costs, it finds that the benefits outweigh the costs.

REFERENCES

Anonymous. 1972. "Note: The Minnesota Pollution Control Agency — A Study in State Administrative Law," Minnesota Law Review 56: 1033 (June).

Bailey, Richard. 1976. From interview with Mr. Bailey, Director, Bureau of Enforcement, Virginia State Water Control Board, August 17.

Baitos, J.C. 1973. "The Limits of the Law: Functional Failures of the Air Pollution Variance Board," University of Colorado Law Review 44: 513-551.

Buchanan, James M. and Gordon Tullock. 1975. "Polluters, Profits and Political Response: Direct Control vs. Texas," American Economic Review 65: 139-147 (March).

Coggins, George C. 1972. "Regulation of Air and Water Quality in Kansas: A Critical Look at Legislative Ambiguity and Administrative Discretion," Kansas Law Review 21.

Cole, R.J. and P. Sommers. 1981. Complying with Government Requirements: The Costs to Small and Larger Businesses, Final Report for U.S. Small Business Administration, Battelle Human Affairs Research Center (Grant No. SB-1A-0004-01-0).

Conference Board. 1976. The Conference Board Record 13: 54-57 (April).

Connecticut. 1975. Department of Environmental Protection, State of Connecticut, Economic Law Enforcement (September).

Crocker, Thomas P. 1971. "Externalities, Property Rights, and Transaction Costs: An Empirical Model," Journal of Law and Economics 14: 451-464 (October).

Currie, D. "Enforcement Under the Illinois Pollution Law," Northwestern Law Review 70: 389-485.

Demsetz, Harold. 1964. "The Exchange and Enforcement of Property Rights," Journal of Law and Economics 7: 11-26 (October).

Downing, Paul B. and William D. Watson, Jr. 1974. "The Economics of Enforcing Air Pollution Controls," Journal of Environmental Economics and Management 1: 219-236 (November).

Environmental Law Institute. 1975. Enforcement of Federal and State Water Pollution Controls, Report to the National Commission on Water Quality (Washington, DC: ELI).

Fox, Lawrence H. 1976. "IRS Issues Long-Awaited Proposed Regulations under Section 103(c)(4)(f)," The Journal of Corporate Taxation, vol. 2 (Winter).

Furubotn, Eirik and Svetozar Pejovich. 1972. "Property Rights and Economic Theory: A Survey of the Recent Literature," Journal of Economic Literature 10: 1137-1162 (December).

Hines, N. William. 1966. "Not Any Drop to Drink: Public Regulation of Water Quality, Part I: State Pollution Control Programs," Iowa Law Review 52: 186-235.

Hirschey, M. and Pappas, J.L. 1981. "Regulatory and Life Cycle Influences on Managerial Incentives," Southern Economic Journal 48 (2).

Interview with Virginia State Water Control Board Staff, September 7, 1976.

Interview by telephone with Charles Burtner, Director of the Division of Industrial Development, Richmond, Virginia, September 21, 1977.

Jacks, W.T. 1970. "Local and Regional Water Pollution Control in Texas," Texas Law Review 48: 1287-1383 (November).

Joskow, P.L. and R.G. Noll. 1981. "Regulation in Theory and Practice: An Overview," in G. Fromm, ed., Studies in Public Regulation (MIT Press).

Kimball, J.N. 1979. The Economic Effect of Water Effluent Regulation and Enforcement upon Firm Behavior, Unpublished Ph.D. dissertation, Virginia Polytechnic Institute and State University, Blacksburg.

Kimball, J.N. and M.L. Marlow. 1981. "Issues in Administrative Enforcement: The Special Case of Virginia," Virginia Social Science Journal, vol. 16, no. 1 (April).

Maus, Charles. 1976. Interview with Mr. Manus, Regional Director, Virginia State Water Control Board, August 23.

Orr, Dale. 1974. "An Index of Entry Barriers and Its Application to the Structure Performance Relationship," Journal of Industrial Economics, vol. 23, no. 1 (September).

Ostland, Byman F. 1977. "Attitudes of Managers toward Corporate Social Responsibility," California Management Review, vol. 19, no. 38 (Summer).

Schachter, E. 1974. Enforcing Air Pollution Controls (New York: Praeger).

Schoenbaum, T. 1972. "The Efficiency of Federal and State Control of Water Pollution in Interstate Streams," Arizona Law Review 14.

Tunderman, D. 1976. Memorandum to Mr. Tunderman, Executive Office of the President, Council on Environmental Quality.

U.S. General Accounting Office. 1973. Assessment of Federal and State Enforcement Efforts to Control Air Pollution from Stationary Sources, Report to the Congress, Washington, DC.

Watson, William D., Jr., and Paul B. Downing. 1976. "Enforcement of Environmental Standards and the Central Limit Theorem," Journal of American Statistical Association 71: 567-573.

Willick, D. and T. Windle. 1973. "Rule Enforcement by the Los Angeles County Air Pollution Control District," Ecology Law Quarterly 3: 507-534.

14 THE IMPLEMENTATION OF AIR POLLUTION CONTROL IN GERMAN INDUSTRY

Arieh A. Ullmann

INTRODUCTION

In recent years an increasing number of studies has been published analyzing the process of formulation and/or implementation of government policies (Mayntz, 1980). The reason for this growing interest in the result of political programs can be attributed to the limited success of political reforms developed during the 1960s in many industrialized countries. The case of Germany's environmental policy — which as an explicit policy dates back to the declaration of the federal government in 1969 (Federal Government, 1969) — is a good example of this. In the first Report on the Environment of the Council of Advisors on the Environment, the term "enforcement deficit" was used for the first time to describe the unsatisfactory effect of environmental policies (Rat von Sachverstaendigen, 1974: p. 180). In the second report published in 1978 the findings of a project initiated by the Council were summarized which described and explained the obstacles encountered in the implementation of environmental regulations from the enforcement agencies' viewpoint (Rat von Sachverstaendigen, 1978: p. 472.; Mayntz et al., 1978).

The purpose of the study reported here was twofold, namely to:

(1) investigate the reasons for this "enforcement deficit" in the industrial sector in a coordinated effort with Mayntz et al. (1978) focusing on the firms affected by the regulations;

(2) contribute to the development of a behavioral theory of corporate regulation at the micro-micro level (Leibenstein, 1979). At this level, the business/government interface has up until recently been neglected.[1]

The goal of this chapter is to explore what the companies' strategies are when confronted with air pollution regulations.

The data given here are based on a study of a randomized sample of 412 German firms from five highly polluting industries (iron and steel, chemical, nonferrous metals, pulp and paper, stone, and clay and glass) using industry and firm size as stratification criteria. The interviews with top or middle management were carried out in late 1977 and covered the firms' experiences with the Federal Immission Control Law from 1974 to 1977 (Ullmann, 1982). Based on the number of employees in the companies interviewed, the sample represents an average of 19% of the industries included in the study.

THE FEDERAL IMMISSION CONTROL LAW

The Law for the Protection from Harmful Environmental Effects Due to Air Pollution, Noise, Vibration and Similar Processes (Federal Immission Control Law - FICL), which replaced the regulations of the Industrial Code as well as various laws issued by the Laender (the equivalent of states and provinces) became, effective on April 1, 1974. At that time it was claimed to be one of the most stringent laws on environmental protection in Europe. As indicated by its title, the law covers various emissions and is applicable to the construction and operation of both stationary and mobile sources. In order to prevent harmful impacts on man and nature, the law specifies air pollution abatement requirements for fixed installations, vehicles, materials, products, and fuels. This chapter is concerned only with the legislation relating to stationary sources.

Similar to the approach in the United States, standards are set at national and local levels. The main feature of the FICL is a permit granting process without which the construction and operation of approximately 100 types of industrial plants are not permitted. However, not only new developments of plants are subject to approval, but also large-scale alterations of existing ones. The permit specifies the quality and quantity of emissions as well as the measures for pollution control using the Best Available Control Technology approach (BACT).[2] A further condition for obtaining a permit is set by regional ambient air quality standards that may not be exceeded by the additional effect of the new or altered plant. Finally, with the help of injunctions the responsible authority can initiate additional pollution abatement measures even after a plant has started operation in order to implement more advanced antipollution technologies in cases where the protection of the neighborhood or the general public is not ensured. An injunction is, however, not permitted if (1) it is economically unjustifiable as proven by the emitter, or (2) if compliance is technically impossible based on BACT. It should be pointed out that such ex post directives are not issued only in those cases where the operator of a plant himself is responsible for noncompliance with the conditions laid down by the law, but also whenever the ambient air quality has deteriorated because of reasons outside the operator's range of influence.

The institutional framework of implementation of the FICL is not specified in the law itself, since this does not lie within the authority of the federal government. At the Laender level a highly varied and fragmented implementation structure can be found involving the ministerial level for planning and programming functions and occasionally a middle level authority in charge of granting permits and supervising implementation. The lower level is charged with enforcing regulation. In Northrhine-Westphalia technical and administrative enforcement responsibilities are concentrated in one single agency, in all the other Laender, the two tasks lie with separate authorities, which can cause problems of coordination.[3] The process of obtaining a permit is linked with similar processes concerning building codes, etc., which forces various agencies to cooperate (Hucke, 1978; Mayntz, 1978). Special legal devices are available to the agency in order to safeguard the environment and ensure compliance with the law, such as the monitoring and reporting of emissions by the operator, continuous monitoring of emissions and ambient quality by the agency, inspections, subsidies, injunctions, fines, penal sanctions, orders to stop production temporarily, or, ultimately, the closing of the process or plant, i.e., revocation of the permit.

The FICL enables citizens and citizen interest groups (CIG) as well as other authorities to participate in the management of air quality and, particularly, in the permit-granting process, since access to a firm's application for a permit as well as to some of the related documents is guaranteed in order to allow for objections. In addition, private claims are settled on the basis of the Civil Code according to the right to the neighborhood.

Thus, the requirements of the FICL outline the general framework for the contacts between the firm as the emitter on the one side and the authorities responsible for the implementation of the law on the other side. The law specifies the instances when contacts between the firm and enforcement agencies occur (control of emissions, pollution abatement measures in existing plants, permit for enlargement or construction of new plants). Depending on the institutional setup in the Laender, the agencies a firm must deal with in those instances vary greatly. In addition, other actors such as citizens or CIGs and, as indicated by the results, industry associations as well as other agencies can influence the interaction between the firm and the agency. Also, situational variables such as existing air quality, business cycle, the local economic situation, etc. may play an important role (see figure 14-1).

EMPIRICAL EVIDENCE

General Aspects

For the period investigated (1974-1977) the overwhelming majority of firms (357=86.9%) reported activities relevant for interaction processes with enforcement agencies. In particular, 76.9% of the companies reduced the emission level of their equipment, 57.5% expanded their facilities, and 14.3% built new facilities at new sites. Of these 357 companies, 63.0% (225) reported that air pollution was a problem, because either pollution abatement measures were taken in order to reduce discharges or air pollution was an issue during the permit-granting process. Given the requirements by the law, the number of firms with an air pollution problem is (1) the highest in the iron and steel industry (65.7% of the total sample) and the lowest in the pulp and paper industry (27.3%) and (2) size specific with a share of 47.5% in the lowest bracket (50-199 employees) and 76.0% in the firms with 1,000 or more employees. Of this subset of companies with air pollution problems, 71.1% (160) reported very intensive interactions with enforcement agencies. Several findings suggest that these activities involve bargaining processes whereby each opponent's behavior is dictated by his and his counterpart's interests, resources, and actions (Young, 1975). For instance, if compared with the rest of the sample negotiating firms these firms:

not only had more frequent contacts with the responsible authorities, but also interacted frequently on an informal level (73.0% of the negotiating firms compared to 39.0% of the rest),

report more conflicts with enforcement agencies (34.5% vs. 16.5%), but consider the atmosphere of these negotiations in no way less constructive and friendly,

more often make mention of a particular understanding on the agencies' side for the company's situation (74.3% vs. 62.4%),and

were more frequently coordinating their strategies toward the enforcement agency with other firms (68.1% vs. 52.2%) and/or industry associations (63.4% vs. 37.2%), respectively.

This very general pattern of relationships, attitudes, and behavior becomes more detailed when the various issues at stake in the negotiation process are analyzed.

Special Issues

As indicated in the outline of the FICL, the injunction backed by various sanctions is the main instrument used to foster reductions of discharges in existing facilities. Mayntz et al. report, however, that in 1975 informal agreements between enforcement agencies and firms were much more common than injunctions (58.9 informal agreements vs. 10.2 injunctions per agency; Mayntz et al., 1978: 401; Hucke, 1978: 112). There is no evidence that the situation has changed since then. The obvious arguments for a firm to counter requirements for pollution abatement measures are either to point out the cost involved and to demonstrate the negative impact on competition and employment and/or to challenge the technical feasibility of the measures put forward by the agency. Either one or both objections were raised by 61.4% of the 208 firms that had to curb the emissions of their facilities. It goes without saying that economic costs and technical sophistication are very often closely connected so that a high correlation can be found between the two lines of argument. Still, a few interesting observations should be mentioned:

The share of firms not raising any objections to the agencies' proposals is twice as high among smaller firms with less than 500 employees than in their larger counterparts with 500 and more employees (44.1% vs. 22.0%).

Objections claiming the economic unjustifiability are more frequently raised by smaller firms (14.5% vs. 6.0%).

The percentage of firms raising objections with regard to both aspects is significantly higher among large firms (50.0% vs. 22.8%).

Table 14-1

Corporate Objections Concerning Economic Justifiability and/or Technical Feasibility of Agency Demands (Percentage of Firms)

	Firm Size	
	Small (up to 499 employees)	Large (over 500 employees)
Economic justifiability	14.5	6.0
Technical feasibility	25.7	22.0
Both	15.8	50.0
No objections	44.1	22.0

Significance: .0005

These percentages change insignificantly when weighted with the average number of annual agency contacts reported by the firms. Thus, the agencies' efforts toward a most cost effective allocation of their resources resulting in more frequent controls of the big polluters explains only a small part of the differences. The findings summarized in table 14-1 can be interpreted in various ways. First, they could indicate a higher degree of technical complexity of the pollution abatement problems in large firms. Second, they suggest a higher propensity to negotiate among larger firms based on their power as significant employers and taxpayers, availability of financial resources and technological know-how. Third, the findings could indicate that the agencies are using a different yardstick for large corporations, thereby concentrating their resources on the biggest emitters. Fourth, the data could reflect a statistical phenomenon, because, given a fixed probability of corporate objections, their likelihood increases with the number of installations in a firm. Due to the methodology used, it was not possible to determine the relative importance of the four interpretations, although the fourth one can be rejected intuitively.

The most frequent mode of conflict resolution was the granting of delays for compliance followed by the implementation of other, less costly and/or less stringent measures. A third way of solving the conflict was to initiate further investigations that, in a way, is synonymous with granting delays. With regard to the economic justifiability of the pollution abatement measures requested, only 2.7% of the firms involved ultimately failed to obtain concessions compared to 33.0% with regard to the technical feasibility. The data reveal that bigger firms more often mentioned concessions than did smaller ones, with regard to both economic and technical matters. In addition, firms belonging to industries that in the past have experienced high pollution prevention and avoidance costs reported significantly more concessions concerning economic matters (see table 14-2).

Table 14-2

Number of Compromises Reported per Firm
Concerning Economic Justifiability and Technical Feasibility

Firm size	Economic	Technical
50-199 employees	1.1	0.7
200-499	1.1	0.8
500-999	1.2	1.0
1,000 or more	1.5	1.5
Significance:	.05	.005

Very similar results were obtained concerning the enlargement of existing facilities. Of the 85 companies with air pollution problems, 55.3% questioned the technical feasibility of the agency's requirements, predominantly large firms of the iron and steel and chemical industries. The most important way to resolve the conflict was to grant delays for compliance followed by the implementation of less stringent measures. Just as before, the share of large firms reporting concessions is significantly higher. It is interesting to note that 27.1% of the firms reported that the agency demanded that existing facilities must be improved before a permit for the additional installation would be granted. Such a combination is legally possible only if the plans laid down in the application also affect other installations. Otherwise, pollution abatement measures concerning other installations must be initiated with an injunction. The results indicate, however, that the strategy to link a permit with improvements regarding other installations (junctim strategy) is widespread, particularly with larger firms (smallest firms: 15.8%, largest firms: 54.5%). On the one hand, this reflects the weak bargaining position of the agency vis-a-vis large corporations when pollution abatement measures should be implemented. Therefore, the agency takes advantage of its relatively favorable position when a firm seeks to obtain a permit for enlargement in order to exploit advantageous market conditions. On the other hand, the higher frequency among large firms perhaps also implies a conscious strategy on the firms' side, i.e., to delay improvements in order to have a quid pro quo available when they need a permit. For statistical reasons, such a situation occurs more frequently among bigger firms with more sources. Also, it is probably easier for large firms to resist the agency's pressure for improvements.[4]

In those 14 firms where air pollution problems were involved in the construction of new plants, the same pattern of conflict resolution can be found. Delays for compliance and the implementation of less stringent measures were the most frequently mentioned ways to reach an agreement over technical or economic issues.

Figure 14-1 suggests that other actors influence the negotiations between the emitter and the agency. On the corporate side, these include other firms, and industry associations as well as other agencies primarily concerned with economic aspects (regional and economic development); on the agency's side, primarily individual citizens and CIGs. An analysis of the ties with other firms and industry associations reveals that the share of firms cooperating with other firms and/or industry associations regarding efforts to counter or lower the demands of enforcement agencies does not correlate with the prevalence of a particular cause of interaction such as injunctions. Differences can only be found when distinguishing between firms with and without negotiations. This could imply that contacts with other firms and/or industry associations are not solely initiated in order to strengthen one's position in a particular case, but maintained habitually, particularly among large firms where the likelihood of negotiations with enforcement agencies is high. For obvious reasons interviews with corporate representatives are not the most suitable method to investigate whether firms have tried to influence the bargaining process by appealing to other agencies. However, the fact that the share of companies explicitly mentioning one or several agencies with a special understanding for the company's situation is somewhat larger among the negotiating firms compared with the rest, can serve as evidence for this hypothesis.

Figure 14-1

MODEL OF IMPLEMENTATION

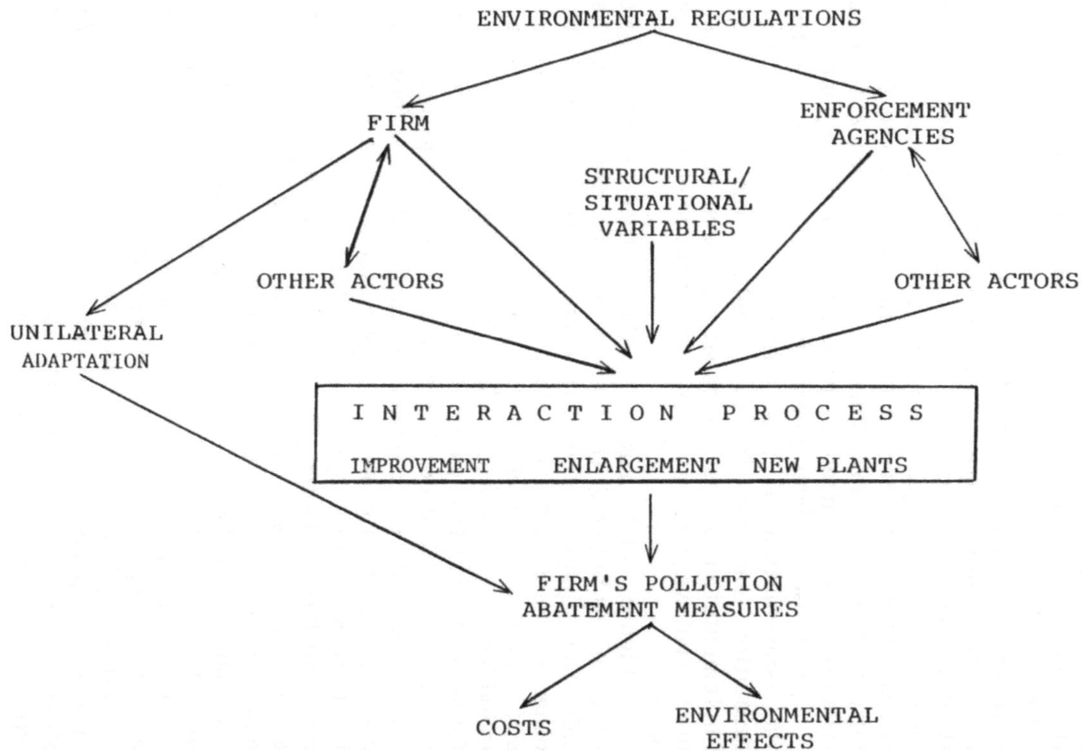

Table 14-3

Special Understanding of Agency for Firm's Situation Mentioned (Percentage of Firms)

	With	Without	Significance
Bargaining over improvement	75.0	66.7	.05
Bargaining over enlargement	86.4	61.4	.05
Bargaining over new plants	74.3	62.4	.05
Overall	74.3	62.4	.05

Citizen activities related to the enforcement of air pollution regulations are perceived to be considerably less important than those of enforcement agencies. Still, the relevance of citizens' observations is highlighted by the fact that one out of four firms reported that citizens' complaints were the cause of agency inspections. Furthermore, it can be assumed that citizen actions were also at least partially responsible in those instances where the reason for inspections was unknown to the firm. However, direct negotiations between polluters and citizens or CIGs outside the interaction structure determined by the law occurred very rarely. Thus, citizens can be considered as an additional source of information for the agencies (Mayntz et al., 1978: p. 301).

The results reported here coincide with those found by Mayntz and her collaborators in their survey of enforcement agencies. Particularly, the data concerning the mode of conflict resolution show a similar picture and enhance the credibility of the firms' responses.

This is not to say that the conflicting interests of the two principal actors do not influence their responses. For instance, whereas agency representatives consider the firms' willingness to reduce discharge as low to medium, two out of three firms emphasize that the measures taken were initiated on their own initiative.

CONCLUSION

Coping with Short-Term Uncertainty

Implementation of environmental regulations occurs in a highly fragmented field. The law has to be implemented in many different industries, sometimes displaying a high degree of internal variety; encompasses many types of polluting technologies and processes; has been confronted with an unfavorable economic environment with varying impacts on the individual firm; and refers to different ambient situations. The FICL and related decrees attempt to reduce this variety by stating regional ambient air quality standards; minimum discharge levels for a number of pollutants providing guidance when determining BACT; formulas for computing stack heights; and air quality management plans in some of the highly polluted areas.

Nevertheless, a certain degree of vagueness exemplified in terms such as BACT, economic justifiability, and technological feasibility is unavoidable. For the agency, this suggests a case-by-case determination of the pollution abatement measures to be adopted by the regulatee

From the firm's perspective, the uncertainty inherent in this situation can imply a threat or an opportunity given the agency's discretion in interpreting the law. The firms' behavior regarding the implementation of the environmental regulations can be subsumed under two grand strategies, i.e., (1) uncertainty reduction and (2) uncertainty exploitation.[5]

Uncertainty Reduction

In order to reduce the uncertainty the firm is faced with, the firm attempts to achieve a tentative agreement with the agency about the measures to be taken on an informal basis before an official application is submitted (Mayntz et al., 1978: p. 318) or on a routine type basis (Mayntz et al., 1978: p. 147). In addition, informal negotiations occur simultaneously with the formal negotiation process to achieve a concensus thus shortcutting, facilitating, or even replacing the cumbersome formal process (Doerries, 1978: p. 147).

A second substrategy attempts to change the nature of the emission and ambient air quality standards in the Technical Instruction Air by granting them the status of a law. As a consequence, enforcement agencies would be obliged to adopt those standards and would not be allowed to request more stringent standards based on a dynamic interpretation of BACT (Arbeitskreis fuer Umweltrecht, 1978).

Uncertainty Exploitation

The fact that the agency has the task of applying general guidelines stated in the law to individual situations implies that the firm has the chance to influence the agency's decision making process.

As a first substrategy, the firm can explicitly concentrate on the vague terms used in the law in order to arrive at a favorable interpretation of those terms. Given the different resource endowment among large and small firms, it is not surprising that the former concentrate on technical aspects whereas the latter stress economic limitations.

A second corporate substrategy attempts to activate the potential conflicts of interest inherent in a structure where several agencies with different objectives have to cooperate (Mayntz et al., 1978: p. 281). The objective is to form quasi-coalitions with other agencies with complementary objectives in order to increase the pressure on the enforcement agency to adopt "reasonable" standards.

As a third sub-strategy horizontal cooperation with other firms and/or trade associations attempts to align the firms' stand vis-a-vis the agencies and to take advantage of any precedent set by an agency's favorable decision somewhere in the country. This strategy is an outgrowth of intrafirm networks developed in large multi-plant firms.

Coping with Strategic Uncertainty

The term "enforcement deficit" entails a negative connotation that is questionable. Failure to achieve certain objectives stated by politicians years before implementation occurs and effects can be evaluated may compensate for mistakes in the policy formation process or account for significant changes in the economy or the public mood, respectively (Mayntz et al., 1977). In order to evaluate an enforcement deficit the context and tradeoffs in a dynamic sense have to be considered. From this perspective, the bargaining processes described above allow for additional short-term flexibility beyond what is included in the law.

The lack of flexibility provided by the FICL, however, constrains the firm in a way not intended by the law-maker. The existing legal framework to control air pollution focuses on two levels. On the macro-level, regional ambient air quality standards were established to prevent negative impacts on public health and welfare. At the micro-level emission standards based on BACT intend to minimize air pollution of various sources. The fact that the two constraints are not linked in any way reveals that the law-maker presupposed that discharge minimization from a limited number of sources at the micro-level would ensure that the threshold at the macro-level will not be reached. Implicitly, it is assumed that air is still a free good that can be provided at nil cost. What are the consequences if this assumption has to be dropped, as seems to be the case in some highly industrialized regions of Germany? (For the following see Rohde, 1979.) The problem becomes particularly acute when a company important to the economy located in an area with air pollution levels approaching the threshold level intends to expand its facilities and thereby emissions. Since it is crucial for the accomplishment of the project that enough air reserves exist for certain regulated pollutants, the company asks the enforcement agency to set aside the necessary reserves for the pollutants in question. However, such a planned management of our air resources is currently impossible. First, by compliance with Section 4 FICL an emitter is entitled to a permit. The agency has no right to withhold a permit from any emitter because it has set aside air reserves for another source. Thus, air management is currently based on a "first come, first served" basis. Second, the instrument provided by the law-maker for planning purposes, the provisional permit according to Section 9 FICL, is also impractical. This permit (1) is only valid for four years — which is much less than the span of time required for the planning and execution of large projects, and (2) can only be granted when detailed information concerning the technologies used and the products manufactured is submitted — which again is virtually impossible in cases of long-term projects within rapidly changing markets and technologies. Thus, a rational management of an air basin is rendered impossible by the case-by-case approach adopted by the FICL.

The empirical evidence of widespread bargaining between agencies and sources has initiated initiatives to instill some flexibility in the law. In particular, a so-called restoration clause is being discussed. According to this clause, a permit can be granted for a facility even if air quality levels are thereby exceeded, provided that the submitter of the proposal replaces other facilities in order to offset the emissions caused by the new one. In other words, attempts are being made to legalize the junctim strategy described above. The "restoration clause" is very similar to the bubble policy initiated by EPA in December 1979. Given the number of facilities in each firm, smaller companies are at a competitive disadvantage because they generally have fewer means to offset additional emissions. It should be noted, however, that the degree of flexibility introduced by the restoration clause is very limited because tradeoffs are only possible between the facilities of one and

Table 14-4

Main Strategies Used in Bargaining with Emitters as Reported by Regulatory Agencies Related to Air Pollution Control
(1 = never used, 5 = very frequently used)

Strategy	Mean Score
Delay of compliance granted regarding improvement of existing plants	3.8
License granted onlywhen in addition old plant is improved (junctim strategy)	3.5
Renunciation of fine in exchange for antipollution measures	3.1
Less stringent emission standards	2.9
Delays permitted for compliance of new or enlarged plants	2.6
Less stringent standards for new plant in exchange for improvement of old one	2.5
Firm's compliance rewarded with bonus in other areas of agency's responsibility	2.0
Firm's compliance rewarded with bonus of another agency	1.6

the same company. Considerably more flexibility could be achieved when allowing for tradeoffs between all sources in an air basin. Such an approach would be very similar to the emission reduction banking and trading system currently introduced in the United States.

The data presented here are, of course, only a first step toward a more detailed picture of corporate strategies vis-a-vis the enforcement of environmental regulations. Therefore, the strategies presented above should be considered as conjectures based on incomplete data. For further investigations, a case analysis approach researching specific instances is commendable, although the practical difficulties in obtaining information should not be neglected. After all, it is not in the interest of the major actors to reveal the inner mechanism of regulatory enforcement.

Given all the empirical evidence and taking the various political undercurrents into consideration, it may very well be that Germany's environmental policy will considerably change its regulatory approaches in its second decade. An increasing readiness can be assumed to replace the traditional regulatory approach by economically more efficient instruments.

NOTES

1. The increasing interest is reflected in the creation of a Social Issues in Management Division within the Academy of Management.
2. For a number of pollutants, standards are specified in the Technical Instruction Air (TA Luft) which, however, reflect only the level of technological development of 1974 when the instruction was issued. Since the Technical Instruction Air does not have the status of a law, the enforcement agency is free to set more stringent standards if necessary and technologically feasible.
3. In contrast to the United States it is not customary in Germany to create specialized agencies to fulfill new tasks. Rather, the range of responsibilities of existing ones is enlarged. For an overview of the different approaches, see Mueller/Vogelsang (1979).
4. An illustrative example can be found in Winter (1975), where a firm was able to resist requirements for pollution abatement measures regarding water pollution for 20 years.
5. Strategies aiming at similar objectives are commonly employed in the process of public policy formulation. It can be assumed that a rational pattern of corporate intervention in public policy

formulation and implementation exists and that it depends on a large number of variables such as type of regulation, regulatory mechanism, number and characteristics of the regulators, as well as other stakeholders, distribution of regulatory costs and benefits, etc. Ultimately, studies of enforcement processes should be linked with similar efforts focusing on the formulation of regulations.

REFERENCES

Arbeitskreis fuer Umweltrecht. 1978. Umweltrecht mildern? Imissions-schutz und Standortvorsorge, Anhoerung des Arbeitskreises fuer Umweltrecht, Beitraege zur Umweltgestaltung A 64 (Berlin: Erich Schmidt).

Doerries, H. 1978. "Wozu eigentlich eine neue Umweltpolitik?" in Wirtschaftsdienst, no. 3: pp. 145-148.

Federal Government. 1969. Regierungserklaerung vom 26 (Oktober).

Federal Immission Control Law (FICL). 1974. Gesetz zum Schutz vor schaedlichen Umwelteinwirkungen durch Luftverunreinigungen, Geraeusche, Erschuetterungen und aehnliche Vorgaenge (Bundes - Immissionschutzgesetz - BImSchG) vom 15. Maerz 1974 i.d.F. vom 22. April 1977 (BGBl. I, S. 667) translated in Steiger, H. and O. Kimminich, 1976: The Law and Practice Relating to Pollution Control in the Federal Republic of Germany (London: Graham and Trotman).

Hucke, J. 1978. "Bargaining in Regulative Policy Implementation: The Case of Air and Water Pollution Control," Environmental Policy and Law 4: pp. 109-115.

Leibenstein, H. 1979. "A Branch of Economics is Missing: Micro-Micro Level," Journal of Economic Literature 17: pp. 477-502.

Mayntz, R. (ed.) 1980. Implementation politischer Programme (Koenigstein/Ts.: Anton Hain).

Mayntz, R., H.-U. Derlien, E. Bohne, B. Hesse, J. Hucke, A. Mueller. 1978. Vollzugsprobleme der Umweltpolitik. Empirische Untersuchung der Implementation von Gesetzen im Bereich der Luftreinhaltung und des Gewaesserschutzes, Materialien zur Umweltforschung, Ran von Sachverstaendigen fuer Umweltfragen, ed., (Wiesbaden: Kohlhammer).

Mueller, J. and I. Vogelsang. 1979. Staatliche Regulierung. Regulated Industries in den USA und Gemeinwohlbindung in wettbewerblichen Ausnahmebereichen in der Bundesrepublik (Baden-Baden: Nomos).

Rat von Sachverstaendigen fuer Umweltfragen. 1974. Umweltgutachten 1974, Bundestags-Drucksache 7/2802, Bonn.

____. 1978. Umweltgutachten 1978, Bundestags-Drucksache 8/1938, Bonn.

Ullmann, A. A. 1982. Industrie und Umweltschutz. Die Implementation von Umweltschutzgesetzen in der deutschen Industrie Unternehmen (Frankfurt/M., New York: Campus).

Winter, G. 1975. Das Vollzugsdefizit im Wasserrecht, Beitraege zur Umweltgestaltung A 42 (Berlin: Erich Schmidt).

Young, O. R. 1975. "Strategic Interaction and Bargaining," in Young, O. R., ed., Bargaining: Formal Theories of Negotiation (Urbana: University of Illinois Press): 23-37.

THE ENFORCEMENT OF WATER POLLUTION CONTROLS IN THE UNITED KINGDOM

15

Genevra Richardson

POLICING POLLUTION: THE ENFORCEMENT PROCESS

When governments intervene to control the generation of "pollution" by industrial enterprises they frequently do so by means of legislatively imposed standards backed by negative sanctions. According to orthodox economic theory, in order most effectively to encourage a socially efficient level of pollution such standards should keep to a minimum the costs of abating the interference and the costs imposed by the interference on others, while the sanctions for noncompliance should establish a penalty whose expected value exceeds the costs of compliance (see Burrows, 1979). While both the assumption underlying this simply stated model and the problems raised by it have been the subject of much debate and analysis at the theoretical level, the actual process whereby the controls are implemented has attracted less attention in the literature. In this chapter, however, the findings of some empirical research into the enforcement of certain legislative standards are presented in the hope that examination of the practice of control will increase our understanding of the process of regulation itself.

The implementation of the legal controls relating to the discharge of trade effluents into sewers provides the subject matter for the research. In England and Wales the formal responsibility for the application of such control rests with the ten Regional Water Authorities (RWAs). During the period late 1976 to early 1978 the author visited the trade effluent sections of two such Authorities with a view to gaining some understanding of the working perspectives of those involved in the daily task of trade effluent control. This chapter presents a summary of some of the study's findings. A full account of the research was published in 1982 (see Richardson et al, 1982).[1]

THE LEGISLATIVE STRUCTURE

In England and Wales effluent from trade premises may only be discharged into public sewers with the consent of the RWA. Such consent may be granted unconditionally or subject to conditions relating to such factors as duration of the discharge, its quality, rate, quantity, and composition. To discharge without consent or in breach of consent conditions amounts to a criminal offense for which liability is strict (for the legislative structure see Public Health Draining of Trade Premises Act of 1937 and Public Health Act of 1931). The power to prosecute for the offense, however, is in effect restricted to the RWAs. In contrast, therefore, to the provision of a general standard in the legislation itself the scheme provided for the control of trade effluent vests the RWAs with responsibility for both the formal definition of lawful conduct and the enforcement of that standard.

Elsewhere I have argued that the legislative scheme outlined above can be seen as an attempt to achieve a compromise between two approaches to administrative decision making: precise rules versus broad discretion, certainly versus flexibility (see Richardson and Ogus, 1979; Richardson et al., 1982). Arguably the trade effluent legislation combines the advantages of both approaches. First it provides a degree of certainty and accountability. The formal definition of unlawful conduct is precisely stated in the form of a conditional consent and may be challenged by the trader. It also provides for a considerable degree of flexibility insofar as the RWA may formally subject each trader to individually tailored conditions. In theory at least, this provision for flexibility in the formal definition of the conditions, when decisions are still visible and open to challenge, obviates the need for discretion in their application or enforcement and may be contrasted with schemes involving the implementation of a general legislative standard, where individualization must occur, if at all, at the less visible enforcement stage. As reported elsewhere, however, the actual implementation of the controls does not accord with this theoretical model (Richardson and Ogus, 1979). Individualization does not take place at formal definition but is retained instead until the actual enforcement of the consent conditions. In this chapter I shall accordingly concentrate on the enforcement process and the factors that appeared to influence the officer's behavior in that context.

THE ENFORCEMENT PROCESS

Enforcement Stimuli

The factors that served to stimulate the enforcement process fell into two broad categories: the technical breach of consent limits and the presence of actual or threatened harm. The presence of a technical breach was typically discovered in the course of routine sampling of the trader's premises and in some areas the rate of formal noncompliance thus discovered amounted to over 30%. However, most officers regarded the sampling process as insufficiently rigorous to provide truly representative samples and were accordingly reluctant to attribute much significance to the technical breaches it identified. Further, in cases where the officers were dissatisfied with the consent conditions imposed by the Authority and regarded them as underresearched or arbitrary they were disinclined to insist on strict compliance. Technical noncompliance was attributed to the irrational nature of the conditions rather than the culpable behavior of the traders.

In contrast to the officers' reaction to technical breach, the presence of any threatened or actual harm to the fabric of the sewage treatment system would almost invariably lead to enforcement action. In the officers' view the controls should be designed to achieve an acceptable quality of sewage and any noncompliance that threatened that objective should be taken seriously. The striking difference in attitude toward technical breach on the one hand and the threat of harm on the other indicates that the officers viewed the enforcement of the law primarily as a means of preventing harm rather than an end in itself (see Bittner, 1967).

The Cooperative Approach

Once initiated, the enforcement process was directed toward the elimination of all "unacceptable" noncompliance, and its character was strongly influenced by the causes attributed to such noncompliance. Thus, the officers argued that a policy of confrontation and strict law enforcement would be inappropriate since the most common causes of noncompliance were the practical and economic difficulties confronting traders, their ignorance and "bad housekeeping." Instead, a cooperative approach was required, which would give the officers the opportunity to act as expert advisers making reasonable demands. Of course a small minority of traders were regarded as "rogues" or "cowboys," the so-called amoral calculators for whom noncompliance is a deliberate act (see Kagan, 1979). In their case cooperation was not necessarily regarded as the most appropriate response and a more severe approach was occasionally adopted.

The cooperative approach was characterized by a process of gradual persuasion. The officers had first to present their demands as reasonable and themselves as treatment experts ready to give advice. Having once established a satisfactory relationship with the trader the officer was in a position to help him to solve his treatment problems. Indeed the business of problem solving comprised a very significant portion of the officers' working routine. Only if this tactic failed would the enforcement strategy become more assertive. If an officer felt that a firm was either moving too slowly or was attempting to avoid compliance altogether he would increase both his visits to the firm and the number of samples taken. This device carried with it an implied and unspecified threat that would become both more explicit and more specific as noncompliance continued, and might eventually culminate in the taking of a "legal sample." Such samples were the necessary precursors to prosecution and had to be taken in a statutorily prescribed manner (Public Health Act 1937, s. 10). In practice they were used either as control devices in their own right or were taken in specific preparation for prosecution. In either event they were rare and in one of the Authorities (Southern) visited none had been taken since 1974.

If legal samples were rare, prosecutions were even more so. While none had been brought in Southern for breach of trade effluent conditions between the years 1974-77, only 48 were brought in Northern Authority and almost 90% of that total emanated from one division. The officers' reaction to the marked variation in the incidence of prosecution indicated, through the significance attributed to differences in the severity of the problems encountered across divisions, that prosecution was commonly regarded as the last resort in the face of intractable difficulties. Further, with reference to their attitudes to specific cases, it became evident that the officers tended to view prosecution chiefly in terms of deterrence, whether special or general, rather than with reference to the imposition of just deserts: the criminal sanction was accorded a preventive rather than a retributive role.[2]

THE INFLUENCES

This section is concerned with the extent to which the presence of discretion at the enforcement stage shapes the nature of the controls. Four major sources of influence affecting the exercise of this discretion can be identified: the trader and his effluent, the Authority and third parties, the Authority and the individual officer, and individual inclinations. This chapter will deal with the first of the four to the virtual exclusion of the other three.

The Trader and His Effluent

A far-reaching and significant influence over the whole enforcement process was exercised by the character of the trader and his effluent. For ease of analysis it has been possible to identify three main sources of this influence: the impact of the effluent, the position of the trader and the intentions of the trader. With reference to more general theoretical issues, these sources of influence relate essentially to damage costs, abatement costs, and the question of liability.

Impact of the Effluent

The first and frequently the most significant influence on the officers' behavior was the impact of the discharge that they assessed in relation to the formal objectives of trade effluent control: namely, the protection of the works and sewers, the maintenance of sludge quality, the state of the receiving watercourse and the environment generally, and the safety of personnel.

The Protection of the Works and Sewers. A concern with the safety of the works and sewers was expressed by the vast majority of officers. In the first place, if a persistent breach of consent had no apparent impact on the system, eventual compliance with the formal limit would not necessarily be sought and an informal relaxation might take place. Indeed, it was common practice in some divisions to allow a permanent degree of noncompliance from traders discharging to works that could cope with the additional load.

More frequently, however, some adverse impact was perceived and, at the level of rhetoric at least, eventual compliance was sought with the formal limits. In these circumstances the degree of adverse impact perceived affected the assiduity with which compliance was pursued. The position in one particularly large and heavily industrialized division will illustrate the general point. The division was subdivided in two for administrative purposes, but certain features were common throughout. Most of the works discharged into nonsupply rivers and both sections experienced high rates of formal noncompliance. The main enforcement activity, however, was concentrated in the western section where the works were small, old and overloaded, and a concerted effort was required to protect them. The policy in this instance was coordinated and official, but policies of similar nature appeared to exist in most areas although typically their evolution was less formal. Individual officers would concentrate their efforts where they perceived the greatest potential harm. In this way they both achieved greater personal satisfaction from the job and helped to reinforce the impression that only essential demands were made upon the traders.

In certain circumstances the nature of the substance

discharged was itself sufficient to affect the method of enforcement. Some substances were automatically regarded as potentially more dangerous than others and more likely to harm the system. In this context the distinction between toxic effluents on the one hand and those that the system was designed to treat on the other was of considerable significance. While excuses and prevarication were often regarded with tolerance when treatable effluents were involved, the limits on toxic discharges were enforced more assiduously.

Sludge Quality. A desire to protect or improve sludge was extremely strong in some areas, with the result that the enforcement policy adopted in any one case could be significantly influenced by any perceived threat to its quality. In order to dispose of sludge to agricultural land the metal content had to comply with guidelines issued by the Ministry of Agriculture, Fisheries and Food, and thus the presence of metals in sludge was the source of most problems in this context.

The information on which the officers based their judgments concerning impact on sludge quality was commonly fairly formal in nature. In some areas special surveys were designed to estimate the impact of individual discharges, but in any event sludge quality was regularly monitored at the sewage works. Indeed, in the case of one prosecution brought against a copper discharger, data gathered at the sewage works provided the first indication of any problem. The concern thus generated was further compounded by the fear of public opinion, and the problem was taken so seriously that many man-hours and much expensive television monitoring equipment were employed in order to obtain enough evidence for a prosecution.

Safety of Personnel. As might be expected, the officers would never tolerate a discharge that could endanger the safety of personnel. A number expressed this attitude in very strong terms, and even those officers most inclined to leniency said they would act firmly against any discharge that could endanger life, whatever the cost.

Watercourse and Environment in General. This final category of harm is very closely connected to the first, especially insofar as it related to a concern with the quality of the watercourse. If a discharge significantly damages the works and renders them less capable of treating effluent, the receiving watercourse will suffer.

Yet, although all the officers agreed that their choice of enforcement technique was affected by a desire to protect the works, only a minority expressed a similar concern for the watercourse and the environment generally, and very few mentioned the need to ensure that the sewage works themselves complied with their consents.

The influence of an adverse impact on the environment was often connected with a desire to protect the Authority's image. A discharge that had a significant and visible impact on the environment or watercourse commonly generated comment from members of the public. In such cases prosecutions were occasionally brought against traders whose "accidental" discharge had had, or had threatened to have, a significant impact on the environment.

Just as the presence of impact on the environment might give rise to stricter enforcement, so the perceived absence of such an impact occasionally encouraged a relaxation in the required level of compliance or a greater leniency in the enforcement process. The first point is well illustrated by the case of a remote farming community. The local works was badly overloaded by gross solids and unsettled farm waste, and it was thought that some of the farmers were hosing waste from their yards straight into the sewers, in breach of their consents. The officer involved initially determined to find the culprits and undertook a number of early morning "raids." Before long, however, he relented. The final effluent from the works was undeniably foul, but it discharged directly into a hole in the ground and had no apparent impact on the environment. The "offenders" were accordingly left in peace to breach their formal consents as they pleased. The case also provides an illustration of the officer's own concept of substantive reasonableness and the extent to which it influenced his enforcement behavior. There was, by chance, one farm in the community that was not connected to the sewers. It had its own septic tank, which happened to drain into a corner of a field hardly ten yards from the tiny local works, with the result that its effluent and that from the works discharged at roughly the same point. In the absence of adverse impact the officer felt it would be both unreasonable and unfair to insist on strict control vis a vis the connected farms while the unconnected farmer discharged as he wished. It was the desire to be reasonable and fair, the officer explained, that led him finally to adopt the lenient policy.

It would appear from the above account that the officers were influenced by the perceived damage costs of the discharges. The possibility of both damage to sewage works, sewers and sludge quality, and injury to personnel were particularly influential, while damage to the environment in general was less frequently mentioned. It is possible that this distinction reflects both the priorities of the Authority and the nature of the information available concerning the various forms of damage. The officers had ready access to data on sludge quality, for example, while data concerning wider environmental damage were seldom referred to.

The Position of the Trader

The influence of the factors in this category typically became significant only after due consideration had been given to the impact of the discharge. If the latter were negligible the perceived position of the trader might be most influential, whereas its influence would diminish as the impact of the discharge increased. Thus abatement costs were typically awarded less priority than damage costs. The various aspects of the trader's position that appeared to be of most significance in relation to enforcement strategy can be broadly divided into financial and technical difficulties, the social utility of the firm's activity, and the length of time it had been located on the current site.

Technical and Financial Difficulties. In cases where only very low damage costs, if any, were perceived the difficulties faced by the trader occasionally encouraged the officers to allow a permanent, albeit informal, relaxation of the required level of compliance. The issue was frequently raised in connection with small traders. In the majority of cases, however, a more significant adverse impact was perceived and the officers aimed for eventual compliance with the formal limits. In these cases the financial and technical difficulties confronting the trader typically served only to extend the time allowed for the eventual achievement of formal compliance.

Some explanation of the distinction adopted between technical and financial difficulties is required. It might be argued that it is a distinction without a difference: almost all effluents can be treated and the essential difficulty is to devise treatment at a "reasonable" cost. In objective terms that argument is unexceptional, but we are concerned here with the officers' construction of the issues, and in that context the distinction is significant and helps to throw light on the officers' general attitude toward abatement costs. The officers' reactions to the difficulties confronting traders varied. A few professed to ignore a trader's difficulties and to adopt an unrelenting policy of strict enforcement. They relied on the basic argument that their job was to protect the system and it was up to the dischargers to meet the limits as best they could: the traders' abatement costs were no concern of theirs. Significantly perhaps, nearly all justified this position by arguments relating to financial rather than technical difficulties, a classification that might suggest that the officers found it easier to discount a difficulty if it were characterized as financial rather than technical. They were expected to deal with technical problems, whereas constraints of a purely financial nature were outside their competence and could not constitute an adequate justification for leniency. This reluctance to consider financial difficulties was quite common among the officers, and even those who were prepared to attach slightly more significance to a trader's difficulties tended to label as technical those which for the stricter group would have been financial. Thus, most officers identified those difficulties of which they were prepared to take account as either technical or financial but amenable to a technical solution. The majority of them adopted an approach that closely resembled that endorsed officially by the Authority. They expressly described the issue in terms of "reasonableness." If the trader was confronting real difficulties and the impact of this noncompliance was acceptable at least in the short term, it would be unreasonable to ignore his problems and demand immediate compliance with the formal limits.

A few officers were prepared to admit to being influenced by the traders' financial problems alone and justified their attitude in terms of fairness. One officer went even further and argued that if it was unfair to demand compliance from the financially insecure, it was quite fair to do so in the case of the rich. Finally, there was a tiny minority of officers who adopted a most permissive line. The issue for them centered around the price that society was prepared to pay for clean rivers, and in their estimate that price was not high. Costly treatment measures were only justified, they believed, when the impact of noncompliance was severe. Unlike the fairness rationale presented in support of the lenient yet more moderate attitude described above, here the justification was expressed in very clear social efficiency terms involving an unusually broad approach in which consideration was given to the abatement costs imposed on society at large.

The above account should give some indication of the influence of abatement costs. In the first place, an officer's reaction to a plea for leniency might be affected by his classification of the problems facing the trader: financial or technical. In the case of the latter, the officers were more inclined to be lenient; the solution of effluent treatment problems was their job. In these cases many officers were prepared to weigh the costs to the trader against the likely damage costs, at least in the short term. Some were prepared to indulge in this exercise even where the problems were regarded as purely financial: but they constituted a very small minority. Few officers, however, seemed prepared to make comparisons between traders. An individual's abatement costs might be weighed against the likely damage caused by his effluent, but the balance of these costs was seldom compared between traders and the only exception encountered seemed to be based on ability to pay rather than on actual costs. The overall impression given was that the officers were primarily concerned with each trader as a unit, and their assessment of what demands it was substantively reasonable to make of that unit depended in part on whether the trader's problems were in any sense technical. If they were, they could legitimately be taken into account.

Social Utility. At the beginning of this section, the social utility of a firm's activities was mentioned as a potentially influential factor. The evidence of its influence in practice, however, was meagre. The clearest example occurred in relation to a waste oil reclamation plant. It was persistently noncompliant and the management seemed resolutely opposed to spending any money on effluent treatment. The local officer tried every device from problem solving to legal samples, but he was disinclined to recommend the ultimate device of prosecution because he believed that the firm fulfilled a useful social function by recycling waste oil. A few officers used a similar argument when they expressed a disinclination to act through a fear of causing redundancies. Whatever their personal preferences, however, most officers believed that their job was to protect the sewerage system and that it was not therefore appropriate for them to consider the social consequences that might flow from the pursuit of that aim: their notion of abatement costs was typically confined to those imposed directly on the trader.

Length of Time in Current Location. One officer's attitude to the complaints of newcomers to his rural area is illustrative here. The "pollution" caused by farm waste, the officer argued, did not exist until the suburban dwellers moved into the country and discovered it. The farms were there first and, in his view, if the incomers objected they should move back into the towns. This attitude perhaps indicates some realization of the reciprocal nature of pollution, and the leniency shown to the first-comer might be objectively justifiable in terms of social efficiency (for further discussion see Richardson et al., 1982: ch. 3), but the officers themselves justified their approach solely in terms of fairness. It was unfair and consequently unjustifiable to penalize the original user merely because additional conflicting users had moved in.

The appropriate identification of unlawfulness in relation to environmental offenses involves, in theory, highly complex issues. In practice, the truly significant identification occurs informally at the enforcement stage. It is now possible to draw some tentative conclusions about this process of informal definition in the context of trade effluent control. In the first place, the officers were clearly concerned with the substantive justifications for the controls and typically sought such justification in either economic considerations or unqualified fairness. On the one hand, they undoubtedly had a notion of balancing the benefits of the controls against their costs. While, on the other, certain alternatives, such as the similar treatment of long established traders and newcomers, were regarded as so blatantly unfair as to render irrelevant any economic balancing exercise. Secondly, when indulging in balancing the officers used estimates of damage and abatement costs derived from data of varying degrees of adequacy. Whatever the data base, however, the officers' notions of damage and abatement tended to be narrow. Damage costs were often confined to impact on the sewers and works, while abatement costs typically related to the individual trader alone; few comparisons between traders were made and little attention was paid to the wider social costs of abatement.

Intentions of the Trader

The degree of intent attributed to the act of an individual is extremely significant in the context of the formal law. Traditionally some form of mens rea, be it intent, knowledge, or recklessness, must be present before the commission of a criminal offense can be established (Law Commission, 1978). There does exist, however, a category of offense where the notion of mens rea is virtually abandoned and many regulatory offenses including the breach of trade effluent controls fall within this category. The proliferation of these offenses of strict liability, as they are called, has led to a heated debate fueled by the belief, held by some, that criminal liability should not be imposed in the absence of culpability (see Packer, 1968; Kadish, 1963; Ball and Friedman, 1965; Geis and Edelhertz, 1973). Whatever the state of the theoretical debate, however, during the enforcement process itself the details of the formal law were seldom considered and prosecutions were numerically insignificant. Nonetheless, a number of studies have documented the not inconsiderable influence of the intentions and attitudes of the regulated on the enforcement behavior of the regulators and in this respect the behavior of the trade effluent officers was no exception (see Carson, 1970; Kagan, 1979). The intention and attitude of the trader were extremely influential on a number of different levels.

Carson has described how the factory inspectors mitigate the severity and apparent inflexibility of the criminal law by incorporating an element of "moral fault." In the context of trade effluent control, where the liability imposed by law is even stricter, there was clear evidence of a similar tendency.[3] In the first place, the officers' understanding of the traders' intentions was crucial to the diagnosis of the causes of noncompliance: the relationship between those perceived causes and the method of enforcement has already been stressed. Secondly, the pervasive attitude toward law enforcement as a means of achieving the appropriate level of effluent quality rather than as an end in itself did not encourage the adoption of an aggressive enforcement policy where the trader's intentions were seen to be "good." Thirdly, the Authority's image would suffer if it was seen to be bullying a well-intentioned firm. Finally, to the extent that a "just deserts" approach was adopted, the traders' intentions were relevant to the calculation of his culpability. Strict enforcement, and particularly prosecution, were regarded as inappropriate in the face of good intentions on the part of the trader.

General Issues. The process of assessing the traders' intentions was widely regarded by the officers as a most important aspect of their job but one which presented enormous problems. As one officer explained, the main difficulty lay in the fact that all the traders said they would act while only a very few did so, leaving the officers with the unenviable task of distinguishing the genuine statements of intent from the mendacious. It was a task that demanded particular skills and expertise that the officers felt could only be acquired through experience. While most officers stressed the need to become acquainted with a trader before any assessment of his intentions could be made, it was also recognized that although a close relationship with the trader was essential in some respects, it could lead to difficulties. The judgements of individual officers could be very subjective and there was danger of bias. However, it was felt that such a price was worth paying and the dangers could be reduced with sufficient liaison and supervision.

Undeniably, the personal view of the individual officer as to the character and intentions of the trader played a significant role, and many senior officers referred to the importance attached to the local officers' impressions. Nevertheless, it was not the only evidence available. The past history of the firm was regarded as an important indicator and a poor formal compliance record, a reputation for a lack of cooperation or a previous involvement in incidents all served to establish the discharger as a "problem firm." By way of contrast, any positive actions that demonstrated a desire to cooperate on the part of the trader were accorded great significance. In each case, the factors interacted in various ways, and in this context the distinction between persistent offenders and "one-off" incidents was particularly significant.

Persistent Offenders. Typically in the case of persistent offenders, the officers were able to build up their assessments over a period of time. In order to do this, they used the firm's past history, its apparent attitude, and its actions. The cases of two firms visited by the same officer, John, on the same morning will provide interesting examples. Both were platers, both had bad compliance records, and both had received warning letters informing them of their noncompliance and its possible legal consequences. John regarded both as persistently noncompliant and probably lacking the will to comply, but in his view the second, D Co., was the more intransigent. It needed "a bomb under it," he explained, and he began his interview with the director by explaining that the next instance of noncompliance would lead to a legal sample. In that event, however, the interview ended with a promise from John to take no further action for two months to enable D Co. to have time to experiment with new treatment techniques. By contrast, the interview with the first firm, C Co., was concluded with a stiff warning from John that further samples would be taken soon.

The two cases provide a clear contrast. John had no preconceived notion of C Co.'s attitude, but he left the interview with the conviction that they were determined not to "waste" money on compliance. The individual in charge had rejected both John's diagnosis of the problem and his suggested cure and had given no impression of concern. John was not, therefore, prepared to show him any leniency and resorted to implied threats of legal action, which he clearly intended to carry out if the need arose. By contrast, he had a prior impression of D Co.'s attitude and had entered the meeting intending to "come on strong" and "wave the big stick." But their apparent concern and willingness to accept his advice had caused him to change his tactics. He was impressed by their attitude, he later explained, and he himslef contrasted it with C Co.'s. He was even prepared to accept D Co.'s claims to financial hardship although they offered no concrete evidence. Thus, C Co.

was seen as an amoral calculator and treated accordingly while D Co.'s noncompliance was attributed to lack of expertise.

While the influence of the trader's attitude and oral undertakings often served to counteract the impression given by his formal compliance history, such an effect could not be sustained indefinitely. The presence or absence of visible steps toward the promised improvements generally provided more definitive evidence, and the absence of remedial action over a prolonged period of time could counteract any mere professions of good intent. The length of time that might elapse before disillusion set in would vary from case to case depending on, among other factors, the relationship between the trader and the officer, the impact of the noncompliant discharge, and the intervention of third parties from either within or without the Authority.

"One-offs." Many of the principles discussed above in relation to persistent offenders were equally applicable to "one-off" incidents. The intention of the trader was again crucial but the emphasis differed slightly. The intervention of third parties was more common in relation to one-offs, and this phenomenon tended to exert its own particular pressures. Thus, the desire to be seen to be effective occasionally inclined the Authority toward a stricter enforcement policy in the case of visible "accidents." Indeed, the possibility of prosecution was referred to more frequently in relation to one-offs than to persistent offenders, especially in those divisions where prosecutions were rare. This contemplation of legal action coupled with the element of publicity, it is suggested, made the officers attach even greater significance to the intention of the trader. In the first place it was considered counterproductive to react too strictly to a genuine accident for the fear that the traders might be deterred from reporting such incidents in the future. And secondly, most officers were firmly of the opinion that the prosecution of genuine accidents would lay the Authority open to criticism, and a few also believed that such action was morally inappropriate.

In any one case the enforcement policy adopted would in part depend on the extent to which the offending discharge was seen as accidental, deliberate, or negligent. Again, reliance would be placed on the history of the firm and the attitude of the trader. The existence of certain evidence might, however, controvert any initial assumptions. The fact that the discharge consisted of raw materials, for example, was regarded as evidence of its accidental nature, whereas a discharge of waste material was more likely to be deliberate. Similarly, the regular occurrence of "accidents" on

Friday evenings and immediately prior to holidays was regarded with considerable suspicion.

One large "accidental" discharge may be used to illustrate the interplay of these various factors and their eventual effect on enforcement behavior. The incident involved a large caustic discharge that had a significant effect on the local works and its final effluent. The discharge occurred over the Christmas holiday period. The firm had a long history of highly caustic discharges and had failed to report the present incident. Nevertheless, the local officer was prepared to regard it as an accident or, in any event, to treat it as such. His attitude, he explained, was largely influenced by the firm's action following the incident. They had started to build the settlement tanks that were necessary to solve their problem; they had already spent over 90,000 pounds and in view of this he was prepared to drop all ideas of prosecution. It was not clear, however, whether the officer regarded the action taken by the firm as evidence of the accidental nature of the discharge, or whether he was prepared to be lenient because he perceived the presence of remorse, or whether he merely felt that strict action on his part was unnecessary in the light of the firm's subsequent cooperation. Remedial activity by the "guilty" firm was certainly regarded by a number of officers, for one reason or another, as a sign for leniency.

The above discussion concerned the distinction between accidental and deliberate spillages, and it appears that a strict enforcement strategy was considered appropriate for the latter but not for the former. However, there was a third intermediate category: the negligent discharge. "Accidents" were often attributed to the "negligence" of the trader, but "negligence" in this context covered a broad spectrum of behavior and the method of enforcement adopted depended on the degree of negligence perceived. Negligence in the form of mild incompetence gave rise to a problem solving approach; gross lack of foresight, on the other hand, was dealt with severely and could result in a prosecution. One officer illustrated the distinction: "If a waste tank merely splits, then fair enough. But if it's rotten and full of holes you come down on them like a ton of bricks." One of the most influential factors from the officers' point of view appeared to be the presence or absence of a previous warning. If a trader had been warned of a potential danger and had done nothing to guard against it, he would be dealt with severely if the danger subsequently materialized. The refusal to accept sound advice was regarded as tantamount to the deliberate assumption of risk. The "negligent" trader in this context was thus perceived as an amoral calculator and dealt with accordingly.

Many officers remarked that operator fault was an excuse frequently offered by the traders following a spillage. The amount of credibility attaching to such an excuse would depend again on the apparent attitude of the trader and the degree to which his account matched the visible evidence. The significance attributed to the excuse, assuming it to be credible however, would vary from officer to officer. Some felt that the excuse failed entirely to absolve the trader from responsibility: incompetence or carelessness on the part of the work force was precisely the type of contingency against which the trader should guard. Others adopted a more lenient approach, arguing that it was unreasonable to expect continual supervision of the work force.

In the course of the debate surrounding strict liability, several attempts have been made to provide theoretical justifications for its imposition in certain circumstances by reference alternatively to a utilitarian, preventive approach to the criminal sanction and to a just deserts approach (see Richardson et al., 1982). The above account should give some impression of how strict liability offenses are interpreted in practice. I have argued that in general the officers regarded the enforcement of the law as a resource rather than as an end in itself and that, in particular, the attitudes toward prosecution indicated a concern with prevention rather than with the imposition of just deserts. More specifically, their concern with the intentions of the trader could prima facie be said to reflect either. It is possible now to be more specific about the practical interpretation of intent. In the context of the continuing process of persuasion that surrounds the persistent offender, it would seem that the officers' emphasis on intention was largely instrumental. There was no need to adopt stricter enforcement tactics where the trader displayed good intentions and vice versa. When prosecution was in issue, however, a slightly different emphasis was apparent. Prosecutions were typically brought to achieve either special or general deterrence and in relation to both, especially the former, the notion of intent was relevant. However, particularly in relation to "accidental" spillages, it was evident that whatever the instrumental necessity for intent, prosecutions were only considered morally appropriate where the trader was in some degree culpable. In practice the officers were avoiding many of the theoretical difficulties associated with strict liability. On the question of negligence, for example, the officers considered it appropriate to prosecute only where the damage was reasonably foreseeable and avoidable. Such a degree of intent arguably would not be essential to justify a prosecution in purely utilitarian terms. It is hard to contend from this, however, that the officers' **primary** concern was with the imposition of just deserts. Such might possibly have been the case in instances of deliberate "dumping" where the officers were genuinely outraged. But the practice, in cases where the genuinely accidental nature of the spillage was in grave doubt, of abandoning the idea of prosecution because improvements were underway indicates that just deserts alone would not be regarded as sufficient reason for prosecution where the aims of special deterrence were being achieved through other means.

NOTES

1. The research was undertaken under the auspices of the Centre for Socio-Legal Studies, Oxford.
2. This debate is currently attracting much attention in relation to penal policy. For a statement of the just deserts approach see, particularly, von Hirsch, 1976, and Bottoms and Preston, 1980, for a useful critical discussion.
3. The statutory provision studied by Carson, Factories Act 1961, s. 16(1), contained a defense of "due diligence" in certain circumstances and can, in that respect, be contrasted with Public Health (Drainage of Trade Premises) Act 1937, s. 2(5).

REFERENCES

Ball and Friedman. 1965. "The Use of Criminal Sanctions in the Enforcement of Economic Legislation: A Sociological View," 17 Stanford Law Review 197.

Bittner. 1967. "The Police on Skid-Row: A Study of Peace-keeping," 32 American Sociological Review 699.

Bittner. 1967. "Police Discretion in Emergency Apprehension of Mentally Ill Persons," 14 Social Problems 278.

Bottoms and Preston (eds.). 1980. The Coming Penal Crisis.

Burrows. 1979. Economic Theory of Pollution Control.

Carson. 1970. "Some Sociological Aspects of Strict Liability and the Enforcement of Factory Legislation," 33 MLR 396.

Geis and Edelhertz. 1973. "Criminal Law and Consumer Fraud: A Sociological View," 11 American Criminal Law Review 989.

Kadish. 1963. "Some Observations on the Use of Criminal Sanctions in Enforcing Economic Regulations," 30 University of Chicago Law Review 432.

Kagan. 1979. "The Criminology of the Corporation and Regulatory Enforcement Strategies," presented at the Symposium on Organizational Factors in the Implementation of Law, University of Oldenburg.

Law Commission No. 89. 1978. Report on the Mental Element in Crime.
Packer. 1968. The Limits of the Criminal Sanction.
Public Health (Drainage of Trade Premises) Act 1937.
Public Health Act 1961.
Richardson et al. 1982. Policing Pollution: A Study of Regulation and Enforcement (Oxford University Press).
Richardson and Ogus. 1979. "The Regulatory Approach to Environmental Control," 2 Urban Law and Policy 337.
von Hirsch. 1976. Doing Justice: The Choice of Punishments.

V
MODELING THE ENVIRONMENTAL POLICY PROCESS

INSTITUTIONAL CHOICES AND SOCIAL REGULATION: THE CASE OF ENVIRONMENTAL AND OCCUPATIONAL HEALTH STANDARDS

16

Giandomenico Majone

A MODEL OF INSTITUTIONAL CHOICE

Recent developments in environmental and occupational health policies in the United States are conspicuous for a certain paradoxical quality of the outcomes. Consider the following:

The advocates of an expanded federal role in these areas (public-interest groups, organized labor, some political entrepreneurs, and segments of the federal bureaucracy) have succeeded in bringing about major shifts in statutory authority from state and local agencies to the federal level. Yet the fruits of their victory have proved to be disappointing. Federal agencies have been forced to assume a greater share of the political and financial costs of implementation than was originally envisioned. In one case — the Clean Air Act of 1977 — decision-making power was returned to the states where it had been prior to the passage of the 1970 Act. The earlier act was " . . . killed by the self-interest which had shaped its creation" (Downing and Brady, 1979). Despite logically cogent arguments that effluent charges and other penalty taxes (e.g., on occupational hazards) are both more effective and more efficient than standards and direct regulation, environmental, safety, and health legislation continues to rely almost exclusively on the "inferior" traditional approaches.

Federal standards, though now legally enforceable as demanded by unions, environmentalists, and other public-interest groups, have been few in number and weakened, moreover, by feasibility requirements and lack of adequate scientific support.

The most significant long-term effect of toxic substance and other health standards should be to channel growth away from industries and materials that are hazardous to health and toward safer methods of production. Instead, under the pressure of feasibility requirements and inflationary impact statements, there is a growing tendency for standards to merely codify existing technical and economic conditions. Despite initial hopes of great methodological progress in standard setting - a hope based on the superior financial and scientific resources of the federal government — the derivation of standards still remains an art rather than a science. In fact, since regulatory agencies rely on informal procedures in combining scientific evidence with economic and other considerations, the logic of the standard-setting process has become, if anything, even more opaque.

In this chapter, it will be argued that such seemingly paradoxical results can be explained by a simple conceptual model in which policy actors are not assumed to take the institutional framework as given, but to pursue their self-interest also by devoting resources toward obtaining favorable institutional changes.

According to this model, to understand a particular process of institutional choice — the passage and implementation of an environmental law or the setting of occupational health standards, for example — one should focus attention on the following key variables: (a) the set of policy actors; (b) the resources available to them both to pursue their goals directly and to modify the institutional constraints that determine the level of achievement of those goals; (c) the amount and quality of information (skills, expertise) available to the different actors; and (d) background factors, including societal values, ideologies, and cognitive paradigms.

In a simplified version of the model, which still resembles the traditional model of rational choice, one would assume that policy actors act independently or in monolithic coalitions, like the consumers and the firms of neoclassical economic theory; that they have a single, homogeneous resource — money; that information is imperfect and unequally distributed among the different actors, but is not subject to manipulation; and that all background factors are taken as given. Under these assumptions, marginal analysis leads directly to the conclusion that each actor will allocate his scarce resources in such a way that the expected marginal return of the last unit of resource spent on influencing institutions in any particular policy area will be roughly equal to the benefit of the last unit of resource spent on any other type of influence, and of the marginal investment on any good (Goldberg, 1974).

As the above assumptions are relaxed, more complex patterns of group behavior can be incorporated in the model. Consider first the assumption that interest groups act as a single individual in pursuit of their goals. In fact, we know that collective action always confronts the free rider problem. Consider union goals like safer working conditions. Safety represents a public good that benefits all employees, regardless of union membership. Similarly, a better environment benefits everyone living in a given area independent of their direct contribution to environmentalist causes. In this way, actual or potential group members have incentives to be free riders. If the amount of resources available to a group depends significantly on its ability to induce or coerce its members to contribute to the common goal, the group leadership will try to obtain rules facilitating joint action on certain issues. For example, unions may attempt to obtain legislation making safety and health issues mandatory subjects for collective bargaining. The possibility of class-action suits against polluters, or against employers in the field of occupational health, facilitates collective action by reducing the cost of using the courts to enforce claims. An important institutional change, like the passage of the Occupational Health and Safety Act in the United States, may even create opportunities around which new forms of collective action can be organized.

Consider now the nature of the resources available to the policy actors. In the policy arena many resources other than money (e.g., votes, political influence, expertise, and information) are important; moreover, these resources are unequally distributed among the different actors. Less widely appreciated is the fact that the comparative advantage that various types of resources give to their owners depends on institutional factors. Any given institutional framework tends to favor some resources over others. For example, environmental and occupational health regulation affects the nature of property rights, reducing the power of private capital relative to political influence. Rule changes can create as well as favor resources. Financial support for public participation in regulatory proceedings, or membership in advisory committees and administative bodies, are both illustrations. Policy actors accordingly will attempt to achieve institutional changes that either give them new resources or increase the value of those they already have.

The information available to the policy actors is both incomplete and unevenly distributed. As N. A. Ashford (1976) writes,

> Inequality of access — for example, between management and labor or between large firms and small ones — creates incentives for special interests to withhold or distort potentially damaging (or beneficial) information. Differential access converts information into a bargaining advantage for the more knowledgeable party, and compounds the difficulties of public and private decision-makers who must evaluate the merits of a bewildering variety of conflicting claims. Thus the phenomenon of differential access to information transforms the purely scientific and technical realm of information generation, dissemination and utilization, to the "political" arena.

It follows that policy actors also have incentives to invest resources in restructuring the institutional channels through which information is collected, evaluated, and disseminated. For example, the ability to influence the institutional setting or the composition of research bodies and advisory boards may significantly affect the kind of data that are collected and the ways in which they are evaluated. In some cases, even the choice of rules of evidence becomes crucially important. Thus in the case of toxicologic or epidemiological evidence relevant to standard setting, strict criteria of scientific proof imply that fewer exposure limits can be determined while, at the same time, making legal challenges easier. For this reason, advocates and opponents of regulation tend to support different rules of evidence.

As Victor Goldberg has suggested, the self-interest model of instituional choice can be extended to include efforts to alter cognitive paradigms and cultural values. Health regulation again provides many examples. Thus, whether or not safe thresholds for carcinogens and other toxic substances exist is not a question that can be definitely settled on the basis of available scientific knowledge. In fact, it is doubtful that the issue will ever be settled because, in the last analysis, the answer depends on one's views concerning the degree to which the defense mechanisms of the body can be safely drawn upon to offset insults from toxic agents. According to what is probably the prevailing opinion among American and European toxicologists, no threat to health exists so long as the exposure does not induce a disturbance capable of overloading the normal protective mechanisms of the body. However, some scientists maintain that a potential for ill health exists as soon as the organism undergoes the first detectable change from its normal state.

Neither position can be dismissed as being either unreasonable or contrary to established biological laws. But the practical implications for acceptable levels of exposure are vastly different in the two cases. Individuals and groups favoring the adoption of very strict health standards support the view that no safe levels of exposure exist (and generally also a health-only approach to standard setting). Those concerned with the costs of regulation understandably stress the adaptability and resilience of the human organism. The step from scientific and policy disagreements to general philosophical opposition can be surprisingly short. Thus, a well-known American toxocologist, opposed to a no-threshold approach to standard setting, argues that to keep concentrations of environmental agents below one's level of perception may produce . .

> a creature (that) would have a Faustian life span but (one that) could receive no new knowledge, an existence barely removed from that of the amoeba in its ability to experience the world around it. . . It seems that man is destined to fail and challenge, to perceive and appreciate his world, but at the cost of mortality. Otherwise, what an immortality, what a life! (Dinman, 1972)

Since very concrete regulatory decisions may depend on basic philosophical attitudes, it is not surprising that policy actors allocate resources toward altering societal values and beliefs. The cultural milieu is thus not simply a constraint, but a target of political action (Goldberg, 1974).

SOME EMPIRICAL EVIDENCE: THE OSH ACT OF 1970

In this section the history and key features of the Occupational Health and Safety Act (OSH Act) will be briefly reviewed. In the next section these developments will be interpreted in the light of our model of institutional choice.

The OSH Act, passed by the U.S. Congress in 1970, is the first comprehensive attempt by the federal government to assure safe and healthful conditions for American workers. Prior to the passage of the Act, the federal government's involvement in the regulation of occupational health and safety was limited to certain industries (e.g., mining, construction, and maritime) and certain business with federal contracts; the primary regulation of industry was at the state level. As in the case of much recent environmental regulation, congressional action was in response to widespread claims of ineffectiveness of state enforcement and to the lack of uniform safety and health standards.

The administrative agency responsible for administering the provisions of the Act is the Occupational Safety and Health Administration (OSHA), located within the Department of Labor. OSHA is required to set occupational safety and health standards and to conduct inspections at workplaces to ensure compliance with the standards and with the general-duty obligation of employers in all cases not covered by specific standards.

Two more agencies have been established under the OSH Act: the Occupational Safety and Health Review Commission, a quasi-judicial review board that rules upon all challenged enforcement actions of OSHA; and the National Institute for Occupational Safety and Health (NIOSH), a research body located within the Department of Health and Human Services. NIOSH is responsible for developing occupational safety and health standards and recommending them to OSHA; for conducting research in occupational health and safety; for training personnel to enforce the Act; and for conducting risk evaluations. The agency is specifically required to publish a list of all known toxic substances and the concentrations at which these substances exhibit toxic effects.

OSHA may promulgate a standard on its own initiative, in response to the petitions of employees or employers, or in response to the recommendations of NIOSH. It is interesting to note that from about 1940 to the passage of the OSH Act, private organizations such as the American Conference of Governmental Industrial Hygienists (ACGIH) played the major role in the development of occupational health standards in the United States and, indirectly, also in West Europe. The ACGIH's Threshold Limit Values (TLV) Committee, made up of nationally recognized toxicologists, industrial hygienists, and other experts not employed by private industry, has published lists of maximum acceptable concentrations (MAC) for hundreds of toxic substances. Though the occupational standards derived by the ACGIH were presented only as voluntary guidelines for industry, their influence on the development of industrial hygiene in the United States and abroad has been enormous. As one toxicologist writes:

> For nearly thirty-five years the ACGIH provided the leadership and council necessary to improve working conditions in the United States and many foreign countries. In fact, many western countries have adopted, almost in toto, the recommendations of the ACGIH. In 1971 OSHA promulgated the recommended TLVs of the ACGIH into law in the United States. (Calabrese, 1978)

This is not to say that the methodology used by the ACGIH was wholly satisfactory. The recommended standards depended to a certain extent on professional judgement and confidential data, while documentation was often inadequate (although the situation had been improving, in this and other respects, since 1962). According to some experts, as late as 1968 24 percent of all TLVs published by the ACGIH were based on analogy (Ashford, 1976). Many occupational health professionals hoped that the OSH Act would be of decisive help in improvng standard-setting methodology, as well as providing the first opportunity to develop uniform and legally enforceable national standards.

State regulation, however, was the main target of the critics, especially labor unions and public-interest groups. Lack of sufficiently trained personnel and research facilities, bureaucratic inefficiency, capture by business interests, and reliance on simple warnings, rather than first-instance citations, in case of violations of occupational safety and health standards were the most frequently mentioned failures of state regulation prior to the passing of the OSH Act. Mandatory standards, an informed and strong enforcement force, and a greater emphasis on occupational disease were seen to be necessary components of a sincere federal effort to reduce industrial accidents and disease. The embodiment of this effort was the Occupational Safety and Health Act of 1970.

The issue of state participation loomed large in the first years after the passage of the Act. In 1972, the President's Report on Occupational Safety and Health had argued that "the purpose of the act is not to eliminate state (occupational) and health programs but to include the States as major participants in the implementaton of the Act as clearly stated in the 'Congressional Findings and Purposes'" (Ashford, 1976). In fact, Section 18(b) of the Act states:

> Any State which, at any time, desires to assume responsibility for development and enforcement therein of occupational safety and health standards relating to occupational safety or health issues with respect to which a Federal standard has been promulgated under Section 6 shall submit a State plan for the development of such standards and their enforcement.

Sections 32(a), (b), (f), and (g) provide that the federal government may pay up to 90 percent of the cost of developing state plans, and up to 50 percent of the cost of administering them.

The conditions that a state plan must satisfy in order to be approved by the secretary of labor are listed in considerable detail in Section 18(c). One of the most significant conditions is that state standards "are or will be at least as effective in providing safe and healthful employment" as the federal standards. Also, state agencies are required to supply any information required by OSHA. Under Section 18(f), the secretary of labor must make a continuing evaluation of the state plan, retaining the right to withdraw approval for cause after affording a state adequate notice and an opportunity for a hearing.

By mid-1975 all states but five had submitted plans for consideration, and twenty-two state plans had been approved. It has been suggested that such a widespread submission of state plans may have been stimulated by industry's opposition to the Act and by

President Nixon's "New Federalism." Organized labor feared a new state takeover. As AFL-CIO President George Meany wrote in 1974,

> Unless the regressive process can be stopped, every American worker covered by this Act will witness a return to the situation which caused the Act to be passed in the first place — a fragmentized, weak-kneed and wavering decentralized system, impossible to police, becoming progressively more impotent as big and small business pick it to pieces at the state level. (Ashford, 1976)

As will be argued in the next section, it is doubtful that this was a correct analysis of the situation. After passage of the Act, the structure of the incentives of the major actors had changed. Industry, in particular, no longer needed to concentrate resources on gaining influence at the state level. OSH Act contained a number of provisions that could be skillfully used to slow down federal action. In fact, if state control of occupational health matters were so important to industry, how can we explain that four major industrial states (New Jersey, New York, Illinois, and Wisconsin) had withdrawn plans previously underway in the first six months of 1975, and that five other states (including Georgia and Pennsylvania) had done the same prior to 1975? It seems more reasonable to suppose that the 50 percent funding provided by the Act did not seem sufficient to the states to compensate for the technical and political difficulties of implementing mandatory occupational health standards.

The OSH Act has been characterized by George C. Guenther, former assistant secretary of labor for occupational safety and health, as "essentially a labor standards law . . . its heart is the development and enforcement of safety and health standards" (Ashford, 1976). Consequently, an analysis of the Act is, to a large extent, an analysis of the role of standards as tools of occupational health policy. In a policy context, the two key questions are: (a) who should set and implement the standards? and (b) how should the standards be set?

On the first issue there had been considerable debate in Congress prior to passage of the Act. In House and Senate bills introduced in August 1969 and again in September 1970, the Republicans proposed that authority for setting and enforcing standards be vested in a new National Occupational Safety and Health Board, whose members were to be appointed by the president. According to Democratic bills introduced in January 1969 and March 1970, the secretary of labor should set and enforce standards. In December 1970, a joint Senate and House conference committee worked out a final version of the conflicting bills. Since unions traditionally considered the Labor Department their natural ally in Washington, the jurisdictional issue was of the utmost importance to them. According to the Nader report on occupational health, "the pressure from the unions bore down on the issue of who should set the standards. Before the conference had begun, the union representatives . . . had decided that what they wanted above all else was that the Department of Labor, and not a board, set the standards. In order to reach this goal, the unions were willing to make certain concessions . . ." (Page and O'Brien, 1973). In the resulting compromise, the secretary of labor was given standard-setting and enforcement authority, while a quasi-judicial Occupational Safety and Health Review Commission received authority to exercise final administrative review of enforcement cases. According to Section 12(a) and (b) of the Act, the Commission is composed of three members appointed by the president for terms of six years.

The second issue, concerning the substantive criteria to be used in setting standards, received much less attention in the phase preceding passage of the Act. Under Section 6(b)(5) a standard for a toxic material must be set at the level . . .

> which most adequately assures, to the extent feasible, on the basis of the best available evidence, that no employee will suffer material impairment of health or functional capacity even if such employee has regular exposure to the hazard dealt with by such standard for the period of his working life . . . In addition to the attainment of the highest degree of health and safety protection for the employee, other considerations shall be the latest available scientific data in the field, the feasibility of the standards, and experience gained under this and other health and safety laws.

This is the only place in the statute where the feasibility requirement appears. According to Doniger (1978), the requirement was added to Section 6(b)(5) by the Senate Committee on the suggestion of Senator Javits. In his individual views attached to the report, the senator explained:

> As a result of this amendment, the Secretary, in setting standards, is expressly required to consider feasibility of proposed standards. This is an improvement over (the section in the absence of the

> amendment), which might be interpreted to require absolute health and safety in all cases, regardless of feasibility . . .

The appropriateness of the term feasibility in this context is highly debatable, but the comments of Senator Javits make clear the real purpose of the clause — to induce OSHA to consider costs of regulation in setting health standards.

In view of the precedents (e.g., Section 5(g) of the 1963 Clean Air Act stating the necessity of giving due consideration to the "physical and economic feasibilty of securing abatement of any pollution proved"), it seems unreasonable to argue, as Ashford (1976) does, that the feasibility requirement in the OSH Act probably meant only technological feasibility. Rather, the intentional ambiguity of the language has provided many possibilities for administrative discretion and for legal opposition by vested interests to proposed health standards. In its first ten years of existence, OSHA has promulgated only ten new health standards. No carcinogen standard has been issued after the benzene standard was struck down by the Court of Appeals of the Fifth Circuit on October 5, 1978.

THE MODEL APPLIED

Following the steps suggested by the institutional-choice model, we begin by identifying the major policy actors. In the arena of occupational safety and health these actors are: federal and state bureaucracies, industries and their trade associations, local and national public-interest groups, and local and national labor organizations. On some issues, academic experts as well as governmental and industrial toxicologists have played a significant role.

National labor organizations were probably the most determined opponents of state regulation. The reasons for this opposition have been conveniently summarized by Ashford (1976):

> (1) The national unions will not be able to exercise sufficient influence at the state level, since (a) management organizations are relatively more powerful there, (b) local unions lack the expertise and manpower to be active, and (c) grassroots worker support for occupational health and safety issues is just beginning to be significant, but the effectiveness of local leadership does not yet compare to that of the

> more policy-oriented national union leadership. (2) The poor record of the states prior to the OSH Act gives support to the belief that the states will not do a good job. (3) Whatever the arguments are for state takeover with regard to safety, the states do not have the research capability necessary to tackle the more severe and prevalent occupational health problems.

National union leaders are well aware of the difficulties of achieving safety and health benefits through collective bargaining. Issues concerning working conditions tend to have low priority in the bargaining agenda since financial gains are of more immediate interest to workers and their local representatives. Hence, federal legislation in this area strengthens the position of the union leadership with respect to the rank and file and to the unorganized members of the workforce. The following statement made by one union leader in an interview with John Mendeloff (1979) is revealing:

> The restraints on collective bargaining are very obvious; we don't have the power to get that stuff from management. Collective bargaining could be used more, but people tend to see themselves as impotent. OSHA helps to focus on the problem; how else could you get national attention to the problem of setting a level for some new material like vinyl chloride?

This explains why by 1970 a bill on occupational safety and health had become one of the top legislative priorities of union leadership. Moreover, since regulation in this field was to be done mostly by means of standards, it was important that standard-setting authority be vested in a federal agency that labor viewed as its department, namely the Department of Labor. As already mentioned, organized labor was successful also in this score.

Activist groups such as Ralph Nader's Health Research Group and the Environmental Defense Fund fully shared labor's doubts about the willingness and capability of the states to provide adequate protection in the area of occupational health. The notion of giving priority to the quality of working conditions over the traditional wage goals of collective bargaining was also very much in line with the basic philosophy of the environmental movement. In addition, the shift of regulatory authority from the state to the federal level would produce significant economies of scale in the acquisition of influence by such means as lobbying and negotiations. Since some minimum threshold expenditures (e.g., to hire a professional staff) must be made before effective action becomes possible, national public-interest groups have a clear interest in concentrating their efforts in Washington, rather than diluting them in fifty state capitals.

Finally, both labor and activist groups felt that the expertise available to industry in occupational health and safety could be matched only by a heavy presence of the federal government in this area. On a number of occasions, represenatives of organized labor and activist groups have expressed the need of compensating the limited research capabilities of their organizations by greater reliance on federal research institutions. The OSH Act seemed to offer a number of interesting possibilities in this direction, through the creation of a National Institute for Occupational Safety and Health (NIOSH) and of advisory bodies whose membership includes representatives of labor and of the public.

Traditionally, business groups have vigorously opposed any direct federal role in matters of safety and health in the workplace, arguing that this is a state function. It has already been indicated that prior to the passage of OSH Act in 1970, occupational health standards were mostly developed by unofficial groups like the American Conference of Governmental Industrial Hygienists and the American National Standards Institute, and voluntarily adopted by industry as consensus standards or guidelines for good engineering practice.

OSH Act has changed the concept of occupational health standards in three significant ways. First, the national standards are now legally enforceable. Second, standards promulgated by OSHA are no longer expressed only in terms of exposure limits but include sampling techniques, reference analytical methods, medical examinations, labeling of hazardous containers and areas, work practices for hazard control (including the use of protective equipment and clothing), apprisal of employees of hazards to which they are exposed at the workplace, monitoring and record keeping of environmental sampling, and medical examination results. Finally, recommended standards must be based on publicly available information that may be evaluated by anyone, including union representatives, and other interested parties (Powell and Christensen, 1975).

Clearly, such changes imply heavier costs for industry; stricter regulations amount to a significant redefinition of property rights. Yet, industry's interest in mounting a determined resistance to a federal takeover should not be exaggerated. For one thing, even the old decentralized system of regulation was becoming increasingly stringent. Pressures from ACGIH and other professional groups, and from the states, to reduce to a minimum worker exposure to carcinogens and other substances had been increasing since the early 1960s. Thus, in 1961 beta-naphthylamine was banned by the Commonwealth of Pennsylvania, and in 1967 regulations were issued requiring that a permit be obtained from the Commonwealth's Department of Health for industrial operations involving potential exposures to certain substances (Rose, 1976). Also, interstate variations in the stringency of regulation threatened to introduce unfair competitive advantages for companies located in certain states, while complicating the administrative problems of compliance for firms operating in several states.

Most important, industry must have realized, more clearly than anybody else, the enormous difficulties of setting and implementing defensible occupational health standards. The basic difficulties are of two types. First, the lack of a firm scientific foundation on which such standards could be based. For example, procedures used by toxicologists to determine virtually safe doses (VSD) for exposure to carcinogens involve extrapolations downward from the range of observed effects. A variety of equally plausible mathematical functions may be used in the extrapolation procedure, but the choice of function has a major effect on the determination of the VSD.

The second difficulty concerns the very nature of standards as policy tools. Voluntary standards and guidelines, such as those issued by the ACGIH and by NIOSH, can be determined on the basis of health-only criteria, since they are not meant to be regulatory instruments but rather to supply scientific inputs to subsequent decisions. Mandatory standards, on the other hand, **are** policy tools and as such must include, more or less explicitly, considerations of costs and benefits. Typically, estimates of economic impacts will be at least as uncertain as estimates of safe dose levels and other biological parameters.

To take full advantage of the possibility for dilatory tactics inherent in the scientific and economic uncertainties, industry needed only a few and apparently minor changes in the language of the statute. One such change was the feasibility requirement added to Section 6(b)(5) of OSH Act by the Senate Committee, on the suggestion of Senator Javits. Other procedural requirements, like the publication in the Federal Register of proposed standards and the possiblity of petition for judicial review, can also be effectively used to delay regulatory action. The results have been mentioned already. In ten years, OSHA has promulgated only ten health standards: three between 1970 and 1974 (asbestos, vinyl chloride, and a group of fourteen carcinogens), one in 1976 (coke ovens), and six in 1978 (lead, arsenic, DBCP, cotton dust, acrylonitrile, and benzene).

For example, in the case of the vinyl chloride (VC) standard set in 1974, industry opposed the proposed level of one part per million (1ppm) on the grounds that OSHA lacked sufficient evidence on the harmfulnes of VC at low doses; that it was technologically impossible for plants producing VC to meet the 1ppm ceiling; and that the cost of approaching the ceiling would force the companies out of business. Conceding the industry's claims of infeasibility, OSHA finally promulgated a somewhat weakened permanent standard. Subsequent experience was to show that meeting the 1ppm standard was not as difficult or costly as industry had predicted.

The convenient elasticity of the feasibility requirement has been aptly described by David Doniger (1978) in a detailed case study of the VC standard: "OSHA's statements and actions suggest that it was following an unarticulated principle that a standard is not feasible if it would cause more than slight changes in the number of firms in an industry, or in an industry's profit and growth rates, its output, and competitive position". According to Ashford (1976) even NIOSH, which is supposed to base its recommendatons exclusively on the best scientific judgement, objectively determined, sometimes recommends criteria at variance with what is suggestd by the scientific evidence alone.

A number of trade associations closely watch OSHA's activities: The American Industrial Health Council, an organization expressly created for the OSHA rule making; the Society of Plastic Industries, which has been particularly active in opposing the VC standard; and the American Petroleum Institute, the organization that defeated OSHA on the benzene standard. As already mentioned, the benzene standard has been invalidated by the Court of Appeals for the Fifth Circuit on October 5, 1978. The standard was struck down because the court found that OSHA had failed to make quantitative estimates of the benefits of the standard and weight them against the costs to see if the balance was reasonable.

What about the position of the regulatory bureaucracy? An expanded federal role in the area of occupational safety and health means, of course, an increase of budget, employment levels, and political power for the federal bureaucracy. However, it was not difficult to guess that the financial and political costs of implementing occupational standards were likely to be high. There were precedents. In the case of air pollution control, for example, HEW's Public Health Service had been unwilling, back in the mid-1950s, to become involved with the problems of abatement and control. The health service apparently realized that serious efforts to determine dangerous levels of air pollution would lead to controversy, especially if it would have a role commending air quality or emission standards (Tobin, 1979).

The prospects for the enforcement of occupational health regulation must have been even more alarming. Consequently the possibility given by OSH Act to the states to develop and enforce their own standards, under OSHA's supervision, was compatible with the interest of the federal bureaucracy. According to Ashford (1976), by early 1974 OSHA policy was "to shift to monitoring of state plans rather than continuing Federal enforcement activities upon commencement of enforcement by states with operational approved plans". It is easy to see that from OSHA's point of view this was an optimal strategy, since it minimized the agency's political costs while giving it considerable control over the states.

According to Section 18(c) of the Act, acceptable state plans must meet a number of specifications whose purpose is to ensure that state standards and implementation procedures (including right of entry and inspection without prior notice) be at least as effective as federal standards and procedures. Once a state plan has been approved, the secretary of labor is required to make a continuing evaluation of the state's performance and to withdraw approval for substantial failure to comply; OSHA provides 50 percent of the funds to run the state's program. In this way, all the political and half of the financial costs of implementation could be shifted to the states. At the same time, labor unions and public-interest groups were told that a state's standards and enforcement procedures would go just as far as federal efforts toward reducing accidents and deaths in the workplace.

The vagueness of the statutory language in connection wth the approval of state plans increased OSHA's bargaining position with respect to state bureaucracies. Interpretation of the at-least-as-effective requirement is necessarily subjective, even when applied to such specific items as exposure levels and number of inspectors. In the case of the general-duty clause it becomes practically impossible to determine objectively whether state performance is at least as effective as federal performance. Consequently, the monitoring system gives a great deal of discretionary authority to OSHA and in particular to the assistant regional directors for occupational Safety and health.

Not all states have been eager to grasp the possibility for independent regulation offered to them by Section 18 of OSH Act. Major industrial states like New York, New Jersey, Illinois, and Pennsylvania have chosen to withdraw plans previously submitted. As of 1976, only twenty-three states operated under OSHA-approved plans. Like EPA in the case of air pollution control, OSHA has been forced by the logic of the situation to unwillingly exercise its power and to become the target of sharp criticism coming from management, labor, activist groups, the Office of Management and Budget, and even the Council of Economic Advisers.

CONCLUDING REMARKS

The institutional-choice approach to the analysis of public policy formation and implementation rests on a simple but important insight. Individuals and groups pursue their goals in the policy arena not only by acting within the constraints set by the given institutional framework, but also by attempting to modify those constraints in their favor. The implications of this extension of the traditional model of rational choice, in which institutions are defined exogenously, are far-reaching. Policies that seem superior when judged by criteria relevant to the traditional approach lose much of their attractiveness in the extended model. Conversely, what in the traditional perspective appears to be a paradoxical result, turns out to be a natural (though not necessarily desirable) outcome when the interactions among different institution-changing forces are taken into consideration. Normative recommendations that fail to take such interactions into account are bound to fail.

Despite the generality of the approach, some policy fields are more interesting areas of application of the institutional-choice model than others. Typically, these are relatively new arenas, such as safety legislation and pollution control, where administrative arrangements, jurisdictional responsibilities, even the definition of property rights (e.g., between producers and recipients of pollution) are still in flux and hence particularly open to institution-changing strategies. Also the technical nature of the issues and the uncertainty surrounding the scientific basis of regulation promise large rewards to successful attempts to manipulate the flow of information or to change cognitive and cultural paradigms. Finally, rules facilitating the formation of coalitions and the control of free riders assume great strategic importance where there are large numbers of potential actors with only limited stakes in the policy outcomes. Not surprisingly, many applications of the approach are found in the general area of social regulation. While different authors use somewhat different conceptual models, the similarities in both approaches and conclusions are much more remarkable than the differences. As an example, one may compare the above discussion of occupational safety and health legislation with the analysis by Paul Downing and Gordon Brady (1979) of the Clean Air Act of 1970. Since the two studies have been conducted independently, their similarities are all the more striking.

The model of institutional choice developed in this chapter is at best a first approximation to the complexity of the policy process. Much remains to be done in the way of conceptual refinement and empirical testing. Just as the initial assumption of monolithic interest groups had to be relaxed (at least to the extent of distinguishing between national and local organizations) in order to explain observed behavior, it will also be necessary to view regulatory agencies as coalitions of diverse participants who have somewhat different goals and resources. Serious problems of information processing and the complexity of the scientific issues involved in environmental and health regulation assign a special role to epidemiologists, toxicologists, and other public health professionals operating in the agencies. Therefore, a more explicit treatment of professional behavior in a bureaucratic context should be given priority in any further development of the institutional choice model.

REFERENCES

Ashford, Nicholas A. 1976. Crisis in the Workplace (Cambridge, Mass.: MIT Press).

Calabrese, Edward J. 1978. Methodological Approaches to Deriving Environmental and Occupational Health Standards (New York: John Wiley and Sons).

Dinman, B. D. 1972. "Non-Concept of No-Threshold: Chemicals in the Environment," Science 175, pp. 495-497.

Doniger, David D. 1978. The Law and Policy of Toxic Substances Control (Baltimore: The Johns Hopkins University Press).

Downing, Paul B. and Gordon L. Brady. 1979. "Constrained Self-Interest and the Formation of Public Policy," Public Choice 34, pp. 15-28.

Goldberg, Victor P. 1974. "Institutional Change and the Quasi-Invisible Hand," The Journal of Law and Economics 17 (October), pp. 461-492.

Mendeloff, John. 1979. Regulating Safety (Cambridge, Mass.: MIT Press).

Page, Joseph and Mary-Win O'Brien. 1973. Bitter Wages (New York: Grossman).

Powell, Charles and Herbert E. Christensen. 1975. "Development of Occupational Standards," Archives of Environmental Health, vol. 30, pp. 171-173.

Rose, Vernon E. 1976. "Standards for the Control of Carcinogens in the Workplace," Journal of Occupational Medicine, vol. 18, no. 2 (February), pp. 81-84.

Tobin, Richard J. 1979. The Social Gable (Lexington, Mass.: Lexington Books).

17 MODELING ENVIRONMENTAL REGULATION

Paul B. Downing and Kenneth Hanf

This, the final chapter of this book, deals with how to study systematically what we have observed in bits and pieces in the individual chapters. In the first section of this chapter we will discuss some of the key findings of the preceding chapters in terms of the common features of the implementation process. Taking the set of general characteristics as our point of departure, we will suggest how one might approach modeling environmental implementation behavior in section II.

I. COMMON FEATURES OF THE IMPLEMENTATION PROCESS

When we originated the conference and book idea in 1979, we anticipated a wide variety in the operation and effectiveness of the control programs of the several countries to be studied. We reasoned that institutional structures would vary widely, thus yielding substantial data on the effects of institutional structure on program output. We also expected that significant cultural differences among countries would generate different reactions to the same institutional structure thereby making institutional structure comparisons less certain. Now that we have completed this effort we find much more commonality among programs than was anticipated. This similarity among programs and outcomes may result from the copying of one program by agencies and law makers in other countries, but we believe that this is an unsatisfactory explanation. In particular, we observe that some of these structural characteristics of pollution control institutions were set in the last century. They cannot be the result of the copying of institutional structures over the past few years. Instead, we believe that common institutional structure and functioning are the result of an evolutionary process of meeting an essentially identical problem in each country. We develop these common problems and reactions below.

We note the following common features of the regulatory implementation and enforcement process in the several countries studied:

- they are multi-actor interactive processes;

- these interactions involve elements of strategic behavior, a central component of which is bargaining among key actors;

- these patterns of interactions are formed by the behavior of interest-motivated actors, pursuing multi-argument utility functions under constraints set by the fact of mutual dependence and limited resources; and

- the result of these interactions is incomplete enforcement insofar as the standard for adequate implementation is the realization of the objectives stated in environmental laws and policies and in subsequent programmatic specifications.

There appears to be a general consensus that interaction, bargaining, and "implementation deficits" are the inevitable and unavoidable result of government action to control pollution.

A. Institutional Structure and Functioning

Quarles (1976) has pointed out that a government environmental program must be judged on what is done, not what is said. The same is true when judging that program's institutional structure. A program may place responsibility for setting emission standards with an expert national agency but that exercise may prove fruitless if enforcement officers responsible to local governments routinely modify (ignore) those standards in the process of bargaining for compliance. Universally, we find that the ultimate control decisions are made through interactions between the emitting source and a local or regional official. National officials are almost never directly involved. There are two exceptions worthy of note because they represent two of the more successful control programs: automotive emission control in the United States and sulfur content of fuels in Germany and Italy.

In order to understand variations in institutional structure and what differences these variations make we will build on the Knoepfel and Weidner discussion of these issues which is summarized in their figure 10-1. As they note, in most countries ambient air quality standards may be set at the national level, as in Germany, Italy, and the United States, or they may be set locally, as in France and England (or the United States prior to 1970). There is little evidence to suggest that air quality standards play a significant role in implementation in either case. They are often treated as goals rather than as legally binding constraints.

Monitoring of air quality is a function typically carried out by or at least coordinated by the national level. Again it is not clear how monitoring affects control decisions, but information on environmental quality does seem to play some role in determining actual control levels. A dirty environment gives local/regional control officials more ammunition with which to bargain in their dealings with a source. Unfortunately, monitor placement and monitoring techniques as well as simple operation can substantially alter the results of a monitoring effort. Control monitoring allows an agency (national, regional, local) to adjust findings to its advantage, but since agencies at various levels may favor more or less control it is impossbile to develop a consistent relationship. While there is evidence to suggest that this does occur, there is no systematic relationship between control over monitoring and environmental quality.

The setting of emission and/or product standards is done at several levels simultaneously. Standards serve as little more than general guides and more often as the agency's opening offer in the bargaining process. Yet considerable attention has been paid to the setting of these emission standards as Krupnick, Magat, and Harrington have demonstrated (chap. 4). This is because the announced standards do, indeed, condition the bargain by setting the upper bound. We have no evidence, however, that indicates that the setting of higher effluent standards leads to more control or to a cleaner environment. We do have evidence that the setting of product standards, at least for low sulfur fuels, does, when enforced, lead to some improvement in environmental quality.

Organizational structure and finance was not as variable as we expected. All countries have a national program with central authority for environmental control. In some cases regulatory authority and technical expertise resided in the same national agency, and in other cases it was separated within the national government or between jurisdictions. Again, this distinction appeared to make little difference in terms of actual outcomes. If a policy maker found it advantageous to use this technical expertise, it was available in all countries. But it need not be used.

Finally, administrative instruments and processes were amazingly similar across countries. A cooperative approach with a succession of informal steps prior to formal action was found to be universal. Formal action was employed as a last resort and court action was highly infrequent. This was true in the secretive environment of the Alkali Inspectorate as well as the more open environment of Italy. The only case where courts were used extensively was in coastal zone management. Here it is those denied permits who initiated the action. In this case, the courts typically supported the agency. In all other cases the courts seem quite reluctant to penalize emitters and create substantial information burdens for the control agency to overcome. Agencies, facing the prospect of high costs and low return, avoid the courts.

The final message on institutional form is not that it is totally irrelevant. Rather, it is that other aspects of the problem dominate and variations in institutional form exert only a small influence on environmental quality and control outcomes. Instead of focusing on institutions, it is desirable to focus on the interactions between the control official who has immediate contact with the emitter and the emitter himself. Institutions and their policy outputs provide the context for the bargaining process, but they do not dictate the terms.

B. Interacting Parties

The various chapter authors have characterized the implementation process as complex bargaining. The term "bargaining" is not to be interpreted literally as a formal process of sitting down at a table and hammering out an agreement as a labor union and a firm would bargain over a contract. Rather it is a shorthand for the notion of a complex interactive process among various parties that results over time in control decisions. We shall discuss five different types of individuals and groups who are involved in the implementation process.

The most obvious group involved are the firms and their representatives. Employees of the firm deal directly with control agency personnel. The most frequent contact is between the plant engineering staff and agency control engineers or inspectors. However, plant engineers can do little on their own. They must clear agreements and expenditures with higher management. This clearance process can involve financial personnel and lawyers. Questions that these people are likely to ask include how much the proposed action would cost and whether the expense can be avoided. This involves a review of the legal and political position of the firm. Firm personnel will check with other firms in the area and in their industry (Ullmann, chap. 14). The industry association becomes active as a representative of the firms in higher level agency decisions such as the setting of national emission standards (Krupnick, Magat, and Harrington). These and other interactions are often quite informal and sometimes indirect. A firm official talks to someone who knows a politician. The politician asks polite questions of the control agency inspector's superior who, feeling some pressure, asks the inspector what is going on. Often these subtle indirect pressures generate an impression in the mind of the control agency personnel that it might be prudent to go slow. While firm personnel may concentrate on local issues and control of individual plants, their industry associations and corporate headquarters can devote attention to national level activity, including environmental legislation. Efforts to change the rules of the game are part of the overall interactive process in which the firm engages (Majone, chap. 16, and Downing and Kimball, chap. 13).

A second important group of actors is citizens. Citizens become involved in individual plant control decisions primarily through complaints to local pollution control authorities. Direct interaction with the firm is very rare. A citizen has other means of affecting control decisions. The avenue of subtle political pressure is open to them as it is to the firm official. The lack of political power can be overcome by joining with others in a citizen interest group (CIG) (Downing and Brady, 1981). However, CIGs are typically underfunded. Thus, they concentrate their funds on legislative efforts to change the game and on legal efforts to set precedents. A legal precedent puts pressure on all local control authorities simultaneously. Consequently, it is a potentially high payoff option for the CIG. There is an old adage that you cannot fight city hall (or in this case the local control agency). This does not appear to be true. Direct citizen action does affect agency behavior and indirect action can place effective pressure on it as well.

Agency personnel are the third major group involved in control decisions. Indeed we argue that local or regional personnel engaged in direct contact with emitters ought to be the focal point of an analysis of implementation policy, for it is they who reach the agreements, issue the orders, and sign the consent decrees. This is not to argue that other agency personnel are not important, for they do have a significant impact on what the inspector knows, the constraints he faces from above in reaching decisions, and the support he can produce to convince the source to control. The activities of agency personnel are not always directed at emitters. Often agencies attempt to change the rules of the game through modifications of laws and through favorable judicial interpretations. They interact formally and informally with firms and industry groups, citizens and citizen groups, politicians, and the courts at the national, regional, and local levels. The agencies at each level never act with complete autonomy. They lack authority that rests in another level or another agency, or they are constrained by possible takeover by another level, or they lack resources to act independently. Thus, interactions among pollution control agency personnel are part of the overall bargaining process.

Politicians become involved at various stages in the implementation process. The immediate and most obvious involvement is through the passage of enabling legislation. But this is perhaps not as important as the provision of the budgetary resources needed to pursue efectively the requirements of those laws. Politicians deal directly with agencies in their formal oversight capacity and in numerous informal ways. A competent bureaucrat knows which politicians are important to the agency and how any particular action is going to square with that politician's preferences. And the politician's preferences are influenced by his/her constituency.

C. Characteristics of Decision Making

The general observation in all the preceding chapters is that pollution control implementation can be characterized by the complex interactive process that we have discussed above as formal and informal bargaining. We now wish to discuss the characteristics of the outcome of this process.

The first common characteristic we find is a preference for "voluntary compliance," by which we mean control by a source without the imposition of penalties or fines. The strategies employed under voluntary compliance, as revealed in several chapters, are as follows:

1. Extension of deadline for meeting emission standards;

2. Reduction of the stringency of standard;

3. Elimination of fines or legal action for past violations;

4. Reference to courts only in the most serious cases of non-cooperation.

In the bargaining process three elements, which are obviously interrelated, play an important role in determining the outcome. Perhaps most powerfully demonstrated by Krupnick, Magat, and Harrington but discussed by most authors is the political power of the contenders in the bargain. If a firm is powerful, it can expect greater time to install equipment and less stringent standards. If there is strong proenvironmental sentiment in an area, control will be more stringent. The second element is stated in terms of equity or efforts to reduce the adverse economic and social impacts of control. High control costs, transitory unemployment, and the possibility of economic dislocation usually lead to more time and less stringent standards. A third element that becomes highly relevant if the source is emitting something that can be observed by the public is citizen complaint. Active citizen complaints generate efforts to control.

Another universal characteristic of control policy and its implementation is the use of the concept of "best available technology." The concept did not originate in the 1970s. But although it has been around for the last century at least, its long history has not diminished the difficulties agencies face in using it. It is still a matter of interpretation and, consequently, a source for the administrative discretion necessary to carry out a voluntary compliance strategy.

Secrecy in the agency, particularly with regard to the control requirements of the sources, is also a common characteristic. Downing and Kimball, among others, found that control agencies typically have two files for each source. One, containing the permit, self-monitoring reports, and other relevant information, is open to the public. Another, containing detailed technical information on process and control technology, is confidential and not available to the public or to other control agencies. This confidential file contains the information necessary to determine if the source is being required to meet the emission standards set by this or another level of control agency. Without public access, it is not possible to establish the link between standards set by the U.S. EPA and actual control at the source. This reduces the ability of procontrol groups and other agencies to monitor local agency performance. Agency secrecy reaches the extreme in the British Alkali Inspectorate. In spite of its effect on monitoring of agency performance, it has been argued that the effect of secrecy may be positive in that it allows voluntary compliance and without it firms would be even more reluctant to control.

The level of agency that deals directly with a source depends upon the size and complexity of the source's pollution control problem. Small sources and easy cases are handled by local nontechnical agencies. More complex cases are handled by regional authorities and involve technical agencies that may or may not be a part of the regional agency responsible. Finally, national agencies become involved in a few very large cases that are politically important.

A final basic characteristic of environmental control is the distribution of payments. The regulatory approach seems to imply that sources must pay for control. However, in every country there are mechanisms for subvention of some of these control costs. Downing and Kimball (chap. 9) discuss both direct and indirect subsidies in the United States while Ziegler discusses much the same process in Russia.

D. Technical Reasons for Implementation Deficit

There are a number of technical reasons for the shortfall of actual experience. Control of emissions in modern industry is a highly complex technical issue. Krupnick, Magat, and Harrington have shown that high quality technical support studies increase the stringency of standards. Poor studies lead to a shortfall. Brady and Bower (chap. 2) list agency inadequacies that contribute to the shortfall. Among the problems they found were inadequate permit review, infrequent and cursory inspections, poorly trained inspectors, high turnover of inspectors, and inadequate monitoring techniques and equipment (inadequate being defined as less than possible in practice). They also list a series of source problems including design deficiencies, inadequate operation and maintenance, changes in production processes, changes in inputs, and unavailability of specified fuels. Other chapters have similar lists of technical deficiencies. In fact these so-called technical difficulties are in reality a symptom of the general problem of enforcing regulations under constraints. By adopting inadequate technical procedures an agency can reduce stringency without overt and politically damaging action.

The issue of relevance for the future is why these "technical" reasons are allowed to exist and what can be done to reduce them. We do not pretend to have the answer to this question but we hope that the suggestions we make for modeling the implementation process will move us in the right direction.

E. Does Regulation Work?

In spite of all the discussion about implementation deficits, the chapters are in agreement that the regulatory process, for all its faults, has made a difference. Sources have controlled. Dente and Lewanski suggest that at least one major source of emission reductions has been the fact that control through the use of low sulfur fuels is a less expensive method of producing in Italy (chap. 6). In a test of this hypothesis in another context, White shows that underlying economic choices cannot explain emission reductions for automobiles, at least in the United States (chap. 3). In other words, regulation has been effective in reducing emissions from new cars, yet these cars do not meet the standards set for them.

While there is widespread agreement that regulation has generated efforts to reduce emissions, there is mixed evidence of an improvement in environmental quality as a result. A relationship between the SO_2 control effort and ambient air quality could not be established in the European studies reported here. But there was one important exception. The requirement of low sulfur fuels did have a positive effect on air quality. In the United States air quality has improved in some places and for some pollutants, but it has deteriorated at other places. Water quality has shown more consistent improvement but even here the results are mixed.

II. MODELING IMPLEMENTATION

Having discussed the common features of pollution control regulation, we are now prepared to explore the modeling of the implementation process.

A. Self-Interest as a Behavioral Assumption

Economic modeling traditionally assumes that an individual will make choices so as to maximize his/her self-interest. However, self-interest is often too narrowly defined. The model does not necessarily imply that an individual will have no regard for the well being of others or that an individual will have no interest in the preservation of the environment. The statement that an individual maximizes his/her self-interest is perfectly consistent with desires to improve the social or economic conditions of others and with desires to improve the environment. Therefore, let us assume that each individual has a desire (or utility) for improvements in environmental quality as well as a desire for other goods and services.

Each individual, in attempting to maximize his/her utility will be faced with possible alternative expenditures. They can expend resources on environmental improvements and on other things. The decision of how much to spend on environmental improvements and how much to spend on other things depends upon two considerations. One is the value the individual places on environmental quality vs. the value he/she places on other things. These values depend upon how much the individual already has. If he/she has a great deal of environmental quality, the value of a little more is likely to be small while if he/she has very little, the additional value is likely to be large. The same is true for other things. The second consideration is how much it costs to acquire a little more environmental quality or a little more of other things. The more expensive it is to acquire something, the less of it will be acquired by the individual. The more the individual has to spend, the more he/she will acquire of both environmental quality and other goods.

These simple facts can be used to analyze the behavior of any actor in the implementation process. All that is necessary is to place that individual actor in the implementation process and analyze the costs of alternative actions. This is what we will do in the next section.

B. Classes of Individuals and Their Cost Constrained Behavior

Let us define three types of individuals involved in the implementation process. One is the government employee. This employee could be a member of the control agency, or of some other agency involved in the control process or, he/she could be a politician. We will call this individual the control agency manager. Another type of individual is a representative of the emitting source. It is convenient to think of this individual as being an employee of a private firm that generates pollution but it is not necessarily the case since publicly owned facilities are also emitters. We will call this individual the emitter. A third type of individual is a person who is adversely affected by pollution. While this individual may be thought of as being independent from economic ties to government or business,this is obviously not the case. We will call this individual the citizen. We will examine the behavior of these three types of actors in some detail.

Control Agency Manager

We have assumed that the control agency manager has a desire for improvements in or preservation of environmental quality and other goods. In the literature on bureaucracy it is traditional to assume that the agency manager is attempting to maximize discretionary budget (Niskanen, 1971 and 1975). This discretionary budget represents all the other goods and services the manager might acquire. Not that there are many ways a control agency manager (bureaucrat) may use discretionary budget. Discretionary resources can be allowed to further other goals of the bureaucrat. In a multi-period model, discretionary resources can be allocated for this period to affect the bureaucrat's input parameters in future periods. This feedback can be very important. The second goal we attribute to the bureaucrat is improvements in environmental quality. It is certainly true that at least some of the people who have been assigned to top positions in federal pollution control agencies have previous records and substantial national reputations as being "proenvironment." Many others within the control agency also will favor improvements in environmental quality.

The implications of these two goals can now be explored. Under the usual utility maximizing assumptions, the bureaucrat will be willing to trade-off some of one goal for an amount of the other goal and remain at the same utility level. Such a utility function is shown in figure 17-1 where DA is defined as a vector of discretionary activities and EQ is defined as a vector of environmental quality outcomes. EQ increases to the east (right) and DA increases to the north (upward).

Note that it is not strictly necessary for the agency manager to prefer both vectors of goods in a multi-period model. Suppose that the agency bureaucrat is indifferent to both present and future environmental quality. The bureaucrat is a pure maximizer of the present value of discretionary activity. In the absence of feedbacks in future periods, maximizing DA in each period will maximize its present value. This being the case, the bureaucrat's utility surface in any period would appear as horizontal lines increasing to the north. However, if input parameter values (and therefore the DA attainable) in future periods depend directly upon the EQ he or she provides in this period, the bureaucrat's purely discretionary activity maximizing behavior over the multiple periods would include positive (derived) preferences for EQ in early periods. It is also possible that the bureaucrat will be indifferent to discretionary activity. He is a pure present value of environmental quality maximizer. Again, the affect of discretionary activity during this period on inputs in subsequent periods must be considered. If there is a positive relationship between this period's discretionary activity and next period's input parameters, the bureaucrat will have a (derived) preference for DA in early periods. Thus, the bureaucrat may use some funds this period to influence legislators who provide budget and legal authority. Discretionary expenditures in this period can increase the agency budget and the ability of the bureaucrat to obtain more effective control in subsequent periods.

In seeking to maximize his or her preference function, the bureaucrat faces a budget constraint. This budget constraint is derived from available inputs, cost functions, and prices. The agency manager does not produce his or her consumed environmental quality directly. It is the emitters who control emissions and thus control EQ. The agency manager can influence their choices by using the available inputs to produce intermediate outputs, which in turn affect emitter choices. At any point in time the inputs available to the agency manager include the existing set of laws, general administrative regulations, and court interpretations of those laws; the agency budget, including any constraints on the use of funds, such as required grants or research; personnel; and information on the state of the world. Information includes knowledge or estimates of the actual condition of the environment, source emission controls and the expected reactions of the other

Figure 17-1

Tradeoffs Among Goals of the Control Agency Manager

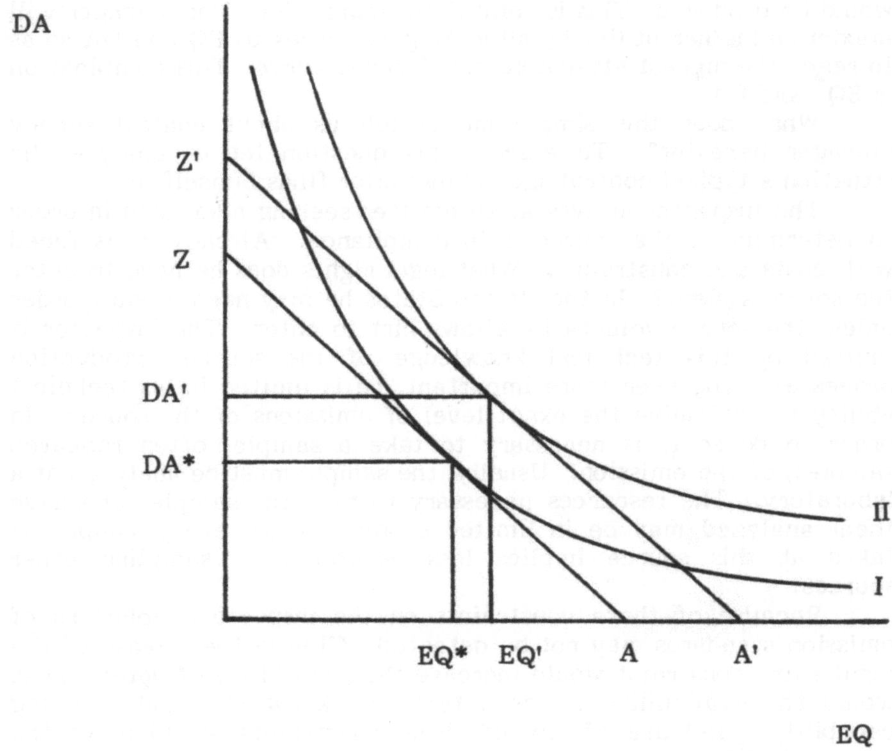

groups to agency policy. The intermediate outputs that these inputs can produce include: regulations on individual source emissions and environmental quality standards; agreements with emitters on the level and timing of control; citations and court action for violations of the regulations; information on the state of the environment and the agency's position on important policy; and spending on discretionary activities of various sorts. These intermediate outputs combine with activities and preferences of the other groups to produce the final outputs received by the agency manager.

There is a cost of each input, and its affect on EQ will vary. There is some combination of expenditures on intermediate inputs that will maximize EQ given the agency budget. This combination is represented by point A in figure 17-1. As the control agency manager employs fewer resources on EQ and uses them for discretionary activities, the attainable EQ in this budget period will decline while the level of discretionary activity will increase. If all the manager's resources are spent on DA, no improvement in EQ would be produced. This is point Z on figure 17-1. The manager will maximize his/her utility by allocating resources to EQ and DA so as to reach the highest attainable indifference curve. This combination is EQ^* and DA^*.

What does this simple model tell us about control agency manager behavior? To answer this question let us analyze the situation a typical control agency inspector finds himself in.

The inspector arrives at an emitter seeking admission in order to determine if the source is in compliance. Already he is faced with costs and constraints. What legal rights does he have to enter the source's plant? In the United States he may need a court order unless the source voluntarily allows him to enter. The inspector is limited by this technical knowledge of the source's production processes. And even more important, he is limited in his technical ability to determine the exact level of emissions of the source. In order to do so it is necessary to take a sample, often repeated samples, of the emission. Usually, the sample must be analyzed at a laboratory. The resources necessary to take the samples and have them analyzed may be in limited supply. Thus, every sample he takes at this source implies less capability of sampling other sources.

Because of these constraints on the inspector, violations of emission standards may not be detected. Clearly the release of the legal entry constraint would increase the probability of detection as would the availability of more technical knowledge and sampling capability. Release of any of these constraints would move the attainable EQ to some higher level. If the constraint were released by an increase in budget, AZ would shift out (to A'Z' in figure 17-1, for example). This would produce both higher DA and EQ. However, if the legal constraint were relaxed, attainable EQ would be increased without affecting attainable DA. The result is again an increase in both DA and EQ actually reached.

Once the inspector completes his visit and has detected a violation, he is faced with other costs. Pursuing this violation implies using resources (time) that could be used to detect other perhaps more serious emissions or to pursue and generate control of other previously detected violations. What are the costs of pursuing this issue? Effort must be spent convincing the source to take corrective action. The more resistant the source, the more effort it will require. Hence costs are increased. A source becomes more resistant when it has political power to influence agency decisions or when the cost to it of increases in control is high. Based on these cost elements we would expect the agency inspector to concentrate on less controlled sources (i.e., it is less costly for them to increase control) and less powerful sources. These are typically smaller sources. There is a countervailing incentive however. The more serious the emission, the more environmental damage is done. Thus, given the desire to improve environmental quality, the inspector would gain more utility from controlling high damage sources (Hill, chap. 5). Often, these are larger sources. The result of these two factors may generate a situation where the inspector allocates more resources to intermediate size than to large or small sources. Some sources may be ignored completely either because they are too small to bother with or too powerful to make it worth while expending limited resources on them (Downing and Kimball, Brady and Bower).

The position the inspector finds himself in relation to regional and national agencies also affects his choices. A stringent emission standard set at the national level increases the effectiveness of this enforcement effort, as do high quality technical advice and research. Pressure to pursue violations actively, such as the threat of takeover of the inspection and enforcement process by a higher authority, increases the cost of discretionary activity. This shifts the budget line AZ by lowering the Z intercept. The result is greater EQ.

This discussion is not intended as a comprehensive analysis of inspector behavior. Rather, it is intended to be indicative of how a self-interest analysis of implementation might proceed. We will now turn to a brief discussion of the other actors.

Emitter

The emitter is faced with a choice between improved

environmental quality, which we presume has positive value to him, and other things (Ullmann, Hucke, Downing and Kimball). For simplicity let us collapse all these other things into one and call it the profit of the firm. The emiter is then facing a situation analogous to figure 17-1 except that DA is replaced by profit.

In controlling emissions the emitter uses resources that could directly or indirectly increase profit. Here we can see that if the firm receives a subsidy for pollution control costs, the attainable EQ is increased and more EQ **and** more profit are possible. An emission standard can bring various responses. If the standard is less stringent than the environmental quality outcome that would have been chosen by emitter in its absence, the standard has no effect on behavior. This is the case argued for by Dente and Lewanski. If it is more stringent, it can potentially constrain behavior and reduce profit. The emitter will seek methods of reducing this constraint, such as lobbying, negotiation, delay, court action, etc. We need not labor the details as they are obvious at this point.

Citizen

The citizen is also faced with a tradeoff between EQ and other things. On a personal basis, he/she could spend money on a catalytic converter to reduce emissions from his/her car instead of on a coat. The question is which gives them greater utility (remembering that there can be an altruistic component to their utility). The incentive facing the individual will lead him/her to take some action to control environmental quality. That action will be biased away from control because of the public good nature of improvements in environmental quality. I might find that the gain in environmental quality yields me 10 units of utility but the coat yields 12. I will buy the coat. But others gain from my pollution control efforts. If my neighbors value the control it may be that the total value of control to myself and others is greater than the total value of the coat. Neglecting the value to others, I make the wrong choice for society (although the right choice for me under the circumstances). The problem becomes a little more complex if the citizen sees a direct relationship between the level of control required of a source and their employment and income. Then the amount of income available is inversely related to the level of EQ reached. This does not imply that the citizen will seek zero control of emissions, but it does suggest that he/she will seek less than they might otherwise have sought.

The citizen's efforts to improve EQ can take several avenues. Direct citizen action such as complaints to local control authorities is one possibility. Indirect action through a political organization such as the Sierra Club is another (see Downing and Brady, 1981). The combination of efforts chosen will depend upon the relative costs and effectiveness of the alternatives. Tax deductability of contributions to certain lobbying efforts reduces the cost of this option increasing its use.

C. The Outcome: Constrained Bargaining

Each of these groups, acting in its own interest will develop a strategy designed to obtain its utility maximizing EQ. The likelihood that all three groups would agree on the same EQ is small indeed. This generates conflict. Bargaining is a method of resolving conflict. We are not suggesting that the three groups sit down and bargain until an agreement is reached, although this sometimes happens. Usually the mechanism is more complex and indirect. Each group will seek out individuals and situations that offer to yield high returns for resources spent. For citizens it may be the courts; for emitters, the agency; and for the agency, the legislature. As one group is successful in pursuing a policy it becomes more advantageous for another group harmed by it to increase its effort to resist and for another group helped by it to reduce its own effort along this line. The result of this reactive process can eventually be an equilibrium where all three groups seem to agree that the achieved EQ is about right even though, in the absence of costs and constraints, each would prefer a different outcome. Or it could result in efforts to return to the legislative process so as to redefine the set of viable bargains (Majone).

CONCLUSION

In this chapter we have reviewed some of the significant findings of this book and have suggested a modeling approach for developing a more systematic understanding of the implementation process. The paradigm employed is that of constrained self-interest. Incomplete enforcement is the natural (and inevitable) result of the conflict generated and the compromise required by this conflict.

Perhaps we should not think of enforcement deficits as an indicator of bad public policy. Rather, as we have argued in the introductory chapter, we could view the initial legislative goal setting process as a first attempt at a bargain designed to resolve the conflicts. The interactive process by which the law is implemented can then be viewed as a way of refining that bargain by adapting to local conditions, constraints, and pressures. The implementation process makes options and the costs associated with them more clear. We cannot expect legislative bodies to explore all these options in detail. It is probably not efficient to do so.

We are not suggesting that the existing system is optimal. We are suggesting that proposals for other forms of institutions should be compared on the same basis. Legislation will not anticipate all costs and constraints. Policy will be adjusted to recognize the realities of the basic problems.

This brings us back to our initial question. Do institutions matter? We have argued that as institutions are changed they alter costs and thus prefered choices for one or more groups. Changes have the potential of substantially affecting public policy. However, given the interactive nature of the implementation process, any advantage gained by one group as a result of institutional change will be at least partially offset by the reactions of others who now find that policy is moving away from their prefered position. It is advantageous to such groups to increase their efforts to fight such a change both before it happens, at the legislative stage, and after legislation has been adopted.

All this suggests that public policy evolves over time and that it is shaped by the underlying costs and constraints. It is not so surprising, then, that we found less variation among countries in institutions and effective policy at the implementation level than we expected. To a large degree, underlying parameters appear to be about the same, and incomplete legislative knowledge is universal. Institutions designed to deal with the same basic problem tend to look alike.

REFERENCE

Downing, P.B. and G.L. Brady. 1981. "The Role of Citizen Interest Groups in Environmental Policy Formation," in M. White, ed., Nonprofit Firms in a Three Sector Economy, COUPE Papers on Public Economics 6:61-93.

Niskanen, W.A., Jr. 1975. "Bureaucrats and Politics," Journal of Law and Economics (December).

Niskanen, W.A., Jr. 1971. Bureaucraccy and Representative Government (Chicago: Aldine).

Quarles, J. 1976. Cleaning Up America (Boston: Houghton Mifflin).

ABOUT THE AUTHORS

Dr. Blair T. Bower
Resources for the Future
1755 Massachusetts Ave., NW
Washington, DC 20036

Blair T. Bower is a private consultant, a registered civil engineer in the state of California, and consultant-in-residence at Resources for the Future (RfF). From 1965 to 1973 he was the associate director and research engineer of RfF's Quality of the Environment Program. He is co-author with Allen Kneese of "Environmental Quality and Residuals Management".

Dr. Gordon L. Brady
Department of Economics
Yale University
New Haven, CT 06520

Gordon L. Brady is now Senior Economic Policy Advisor to the President's Council on Environmental Quality. He received a Ph.D. in Economics from Virginia Polytechnic Institute and State University in 1976. In 1981, he received a Master's in Legal Studies from Yale Law School. Much of the material for this paper was developed while he was Brookings Economic Policy Fellow at the President's Council on Environmental Quality 1978 to 1979.

Dr. Hans Bressers
Department of Public Administration
Twente Univeristy of Technology
PO Box 217
Enchede, Holland

Hans. Th.A. Bressers received his Ph.D. from Twente University of Technology in 1983. There he specializes in public administration and methodology. He has been a lecturer at the Department of public administration of Twente University of Technology since 1977. He has written several articles and congress papers in the field of policy analysis and evaluation with applications to Dutch environmental policy.

Dr. Bruno Dente
Instituto politico-amministrativo
Facolta di Scienze Politiche
Universita de Bologna
Via Giusseppe Petroni 33
Bologna, Italy

Bruno Dente is Associate Professor of Administrative Science, Faculty of Political Science, University of Bologna, Italy. His main research interests concern local government and policy analysis. His main publications are about staff relationships in the national civil service, the birth of neighborhood councils, the institutional performance of the new agencies for the development of mountain areas.

Dr. Paul B. Downing
Policy Sciences Program
Florida State University
Tallahassee, FL 32306

Paul B. Downing is Director of the Policy Sciences Program and Profesor of Economics at Florida State University. He received his Ph.D. from the University of Wisconsin and has taught at the University of California-Riverside and Virginia Polytechnic Institute. A year at the U.S. EPA initiated a research program on the implementation of pollution laws which has lead to several publications in this field.

Dr. Kenneth Hanf
Faculteit der Sociale Wetenschappen
Erasmus Universiteit Rotterdam
Postbus 1738
3000 Dr. Rotterdam, Netherlands

Kenneth Hanf is Senior Lecturer in Comparative Politics in the Department of Politics and Pulbic Policy at the Erasmus University in Rotterdam, The Netherlands. He holds a Ph.D. in Political Science from the University of California-Berkeley and was previously Research Fellow at the International Institute for Environment and Society in the Science Center, Berlin. His research and publications are focused on problems of implementation of public policy, with an emphasis on environmental policy.

Mr. Winston Harrington
Resources for the Future
1755 Massachusetts Ave., NW
Washington, DC 20036

Winston Harrington has been on the staff at Resources for the Future since 1976. His research interests include the behavior of regulatory agencies, air quality enforcement, and environmental benefit estimation.

Dr. Michael Hill
School for Advanced Urban Studies
University of Bristol
Rodney Lodge
Grange Road
Bristol BS8 4EA, England

Michael Hill is a Senior Lecturer at the School for Advanced Urban Studies in the University of Bristol, England. He has held previous appointments at the Universities of Oxford and Reading. His publications include The Sociology of Public Administration, The State, Administration and the Individual, and Understanding Social Policy. He is particularly interested in the implementation of policy by government agencies.

Dr. Jochen Hucke
Droysenstr. 3
D1000 Berlin 12 Germany

Jochen Hucke studied economics, sociology, and public administration at the University of Cologne. From 1975 to 1980 he conducted research at the Institut fur Angewandte Sozialforschung, University of Cologne; since 1980 at the Institute fur Stadtforschung, Berlin. His research focuses on empirical projects on environmental policy formation and implementation and on methodological problems of public administration research.

Dr. James N. Kimball
Senior Economist
Virginia Electric and Power Co.
Richmond, VA 23261

James N. Kimball received his Ph.D. from Virginia Polytechnic Institute. He is currently Director of Cost Research at Virginia Electric Power Company. He has published several papers on pollution enforcement and cost of service estimation.

Dr. Peter Knoepfel
Institute for Advanced Studies in Public Administration
University of Lausanne
Lausanne, Switzerland CH 1015

Peter Knoepfel is Professor for Administrative Science at the University of Lausanne (Institut de Hautes Etudes en Administration Publique). He studied law at the University of Berne (Switzerland) and public administration at the Free University of Berlin (West). Research assistant at the Institute for Public Law at Berne University (1974-1975). 1978-1982 Research Fellow at the International Institute for Environment and Society at Science Center, Berlin, working as coordinator of a long range project comparing program formulation and implementation processs in air quality control policies of seven European countries.

Mr. Alan J. Krupnick
Resources for the Future
1755 Massachusetts Ave., NW
Washington, DC 20036

Alan J. Krupnick received his doctorate in economics from the University of Maryland. For the last three years he has worked at Resources for the Future in the areas of cost-benefit analysis of environmental regulations, the design of environmental policy, and bureaucratic decision making. He has also consulted with the States of Maryland and Missouri on developing their air pollution control strategies.

Dr. Rudy Lewanski
Instituto politico-amministrativo
Facolta di Scienze Politiche
Universita de Bologna
Via Giusseppe Petroni 33
Bologna, Italy

Rodolfo Lewanski is an Assistant Professor of Public Law at the Faculty of Political Science, University of Bologna, Italy. His main research interests are in the field of environmental policies and politics, local government and policy analysis; his main publications deal with environmental legislation and policies, ecological movements, regional government, and cooperatives.

Professor Wesley A. Magat
Fuqua School of Business
Duke University
Durham, NC 27706

Wesley A. Magat is an Associate Professor of Business and Policy Science at Duke University and received his Ph.D. from Northwestern University. He spent the last several years working as a conslultant to Resources for the Future on a series of projects concerned with rulemaking in federal agencies and the effects of environmental regulation on innovation.

Professor Giandomenico Majone
IIASA
Schossplatz 1
A 2361 Laxenburg
Austria

Giandomenico Majone (Ph.D. in statistics, University of California-Berkeley) is Professor of Statistics, Faculty of Economics and Social Sciences, University of Calabria, Italy, and Research Scholar at the International Institute for Applied Systems Analysis, Laxenburg, Austria. He has done work on different problems in regulatory decision making and is currently writing a book on policy analysis.

Dr. Genevra Richardson
Department of Law
University of East Anglia
Norwich, England

Genevra Richardson was a research officer at the Centre for Socio-Legal Studies at Wolfson College, Oxford. Since 1979 she has been a lecturer in law at the University of East Anglia.

Professor Paul Sabatier
Division of Environmental Studies
University of California
Davis, CA 85616

Paul Sabatier is Associate Professor of Administration and of Environmental Studies at the University of California-Davis. He has co-authored several recent books and articles on policy implementation in the U.S. and Europe, chiefly in the areas of coastal land use regulation, air pollution control, and education.

Dr. Arieh A. Ullmann
School of Management
State University of New York
Binghamton, NY 13901

Arieh A. Ullmann is Assistant Professor of Business Policy and International Management at the School of Management, State University of New York at Binghamton. He received his doctorate from the St. Gall Graduate School for Economics, Business and Public Administration in Switzerland and has worked as a research fellow at the Science Center in Berlin, Germany. His research interests are in the areas of business strategies toward government and public policy.

Dr. Helmut Weidner
International Institute for Environment and Society
Potsdamer Strasse 58
D-1000 Berlin 30, West Germany

Helmut Weidner has been a Research Fellow at the Department of Political Sciences, Free University, Berlin, and is now a Research Fellow at the International Institute for Environment and Society of the Science Center, Berlin. Presently he is co-directing a cross-national comparative study of environmental policies and politics in advanced industrialized countries.

Professor Lawrence J. White
Department of Economics
New York University
90 Trinity Place
New York, NY 10006

Lawrence J. White is Director of the Economic Policy Office, Antitrust Division, U.S. Department of Justice on leave from his position as Professor of Economics at the New York University Graduate School of Business Administration. He received his Ph.D. from Harvard University. He has published several books and numerous articles with major emphasis on regulation and pollution control in the automobile industry.

Professor Charles E. Ziegler
Department of Political Science
University of Louisville
Louisville, KY 40292

Charles E. Ziegler is Assistant Professor of Political Science at the University of Louisville, Kentucky. He received the Ph.D. in Political Science at the University of Illinois at Urbana-Champaign. His articles on Soviet environmental policy, political socialization and worker participation have appeared in various journals. He is curently working on a book on Soviet enviromental policy.

MIX
Papier aus verantwortungsvollen Quellen
Paper from responsible sources
FSC® C105338

If you have any concerns about our products,
you can contact us on
ProductSafety@springernature.com

In case Publisher is established outside the EU,
the EU authorized representative is:
Springer Nature Customer Service Center GmbH
Europaplatz 3, 69115 Heidelberg, Germany

Printed by Libri Plureos GmbH
in Hamburg, Germany